Global-National Networks in Education Policy

New Directions in Comparative and International Education

Series Editors:
Stephen Carney, Irving Epstein and Daniel Friedrich

This series aims to extend the traditional discourse within the field of Comparative and International Education by providing a forum for creative experimentation and exploration of alternative perspectives. As such, the series welcomes scholarly work focusing on themes that have been under-researched and under-theorized in the field but whose importance is easily discernible.

It supports works in which theoretical grounding is centered in knowledge traditions that come from the Global South, encouraging those who work from intellectual horizons alternative to the dominant discourse. The series takes an innovative approach to challenging the dominant traditions and orientations of the field, encouraging interdisciplinarity, methodological experimentation, and engagement with relevant leading theorists.

Also available in the series

Affect Theory and Comparative Education Discourse: Essays on Fear and Loathing in Response to Global Educational Policy and Practice, Irving Epstein

Education in Radical Uncertainty: Transgression in Theory and Method, Stephen Carney and Ulla Ambrosius Madsen

Internationalization of Higher Education for Development: Blackness and Postcolonial Solidarity in Africa-Brazil Relations, Susanne Ress

Resonances of El Chavo del Ocho in Latin American Childhood, Schooling, and Societies, edited by Daniel Friedrich and Erica Colmenares

Understanding PISA's Attractiveness: Critical Analyses in Comparative Policy Studies, edited by Florian Waldow and Gita Steiner-Khamsi

Global-National Networks in Education Policy

Primary Education, Social Enterprises and 'Teach for Bangladesh'

Rino Wiseman Adhikary, Bob Lingard and Ian Hardy

BLOOMSBURY ACADEMIC
LONDON • NEW YORK • OXFORD • NEW DELHI • SYDNEY

BLOOMSBURY ACADEMIC
Bloomsbury Publishing Plc
50 Bedford Square, London, WC1B 3DP, UK
1385 Broadway, New York, NY 10018, USA
29 Earlsfort Terrace, Dublin 2, Ireland

BLOOMSBURY, BLOOMSBURY ACADEMIC and the Diana logo are
trademarks of Bloomsbury Publishing Plc

First published in Great Britain, 2022
This paperback edition published in 2023

Copyright © Rino Wiseman Adhikary, Bob Lingard and Ian Hardy, 2022

Rino Wiseman Adhikary, Bob Lingard and Ian Hardy have asserted their right under the Copyright, Designs and Patents Act, 1988, to be identified as Author of this work.

All rights reserved. No part of this publication may be reproduced or transmitted in any form or by any means, electronic or mechanical, including photocopying, recording, or any information storage or retrieval system, without prior permission in writing from the publishers.

Bloomsbury Publishing Plc does not have any control over, or responsibility for, any third-party websites referred to or in this book. All internet addresses given in this book were correct at the time of going to press. The author and publisher regret any inconvenience caused if addresses have changed or sites have ceased to exist, but can accept no responsibility for any such changes.

A catalogue record for this book is available from the British Library.

Library of Congress Cataloging-in-Publication Data

Names: Adhikary, Rino Wiseman, author. | Lingard, Bob, author. |
  Hardy, Ian (Associate professor of education), author.
Title: Global-national networks in education policy: primary education,
  social enterprises, and "Teach for Bangladesh" / Rino Wiseman Adhikary,
  Bob Lingard and Ian Hardy.
Description: London; New York: Bloomsbury Academic, 2022. |
  Series: New directions in comparative and international education |
  Includes bibliographical references and index.
Identifiers: LCCN 2021017225 (print) | LCCN 2021017226 (ebook) |
  ISBN 9781350169180 (hardback) | ISBN 9781350169197 (ebook) |
  ISBN 9781350169203 (epub)
Subjects: LCSH: Education and globalization–Social aspects. | Teach for
  Bangladesh (Project) | Philanthropy–Social aspects.
Classification: LCC LC191.A275 2022 (print) |
  LCC LC191 (ebook) | DDC 370.116–dc23
LC record available at https://lccn.loc.gov/2021017225
LC ebook record available at https://lccn.loc.gov/2021017226

ISBN: HB: 978-1-3501-6918-0
PB: 978-1-3502-2509-1
ePDF: 978-1-3501-6919-7
eBook: 978-1-3501-6920-3

Series: New Directions in Comparative and International Education

Typeset by Newgen KnowledgeWorks Pvt. Ltd., Chennai, India

To find out more about our authors and books visit www.bloomsbury.com
and sign up for our newsletters.

Contents

Series Editors' Foreword		vi
Acknowledgements		viii
List of Abbreviations		xi
1	Teach For Bangladesh: Rethinking Comparative Policy Research in Education	1
2	Theorizing Policy Mobilities in Education	33
3	Changing Governance of Primary Education in Bangladesh	59
4	Social-Enterprising the Public Sector in Bangladesh	85
5	Governing Teacher Education as Social Enterprise through Teach For Bangladesh	121
6	Learning from Researching Teach For Bangladesh as Social Enterprise	153
Notes		175
References		181
Index		209

Series Editors' Foreword

The field of comparative and international education requires its researchers, teachers and students to examine educational issues, policies and practices in ways that extend beyond the immediate contexts with which they are most accustomed. To do so means that one must constantly embrace engagement with the unfamiliar, a task that can be daunting because authority within academic disciplines and fields of study is often constructed according to convention at the expense of creativity and imagination. Comparative and international education as an academic field is rich and eclectic, with a long tradition of theoretical and methodological diversity as well as an openness to innovation and experimentation. However, as it is not immune to the conformist – especially disciplinary – pressures that give academic scholarship much of its legitimacy, we believe it important to highlight the importance of research and writing that is creative, thought-provoking and where necessary, transgressive. This series offers comparative and international educators and scholars the space to extend the boundaries of the field, encouraging them to investigate the ways in which underappreciated social thought and theorists may be applied to comparative work and educational concerns in new and exciting ways. It especially welcomes scholarly work that focuses upon themes that have been under-researched and under-theorized but whose importance is easily discernible. It further supports work whose theoretical grounding is centred in knowledge traditions that come from the Global South and welcomes perspectives including those that are associated with post-foundational theorizing, non-Western epistemologies and performative approaches to working with educational problems and challenges. In these ways, the series provides a space for alternative thinking about the role of comparative research in reimagining the social.

Global-National Networks in Education Policy: Primary Education, Social Enterprises and 'Teach for Bangladesh' is the sixth volume in the New Directions in Comparative and International Education series. The work is an invitation to continue thinking about the emerging phenomena of organizations affiliated to Teach For All, the global network of social enterprises that coordinates programmes that follow the model pioneered by Teach For America in the United States, now present in fifty-nine countries spread across all continents.

Adhikary, Lingard and Hardy avoid both a deterministic top-down approach on the consequences of globalization in education policy and practice and a naive bottom-up reading that romanticizes the local as the sole locus of agency. Instead, the book proposes a complex study of the ways in which the discourse of social entrepreneurship is currently shifting our perceptions of the borders and attributes of education. The authors take Bangladesh not so much as a case study but as a site in which the tensions between public and private, social responsibility and accountability, and public good and private interests produce a unique, historically and geographically informed phenomenon that is neither a cut-and-paste Teach For All copy nor a fully independent project. The result is an important monograph that provides powerful insights to scholars and practitioners interested in understanding some of the ways in which education policies and all the intertwined discourses that inform them flow unevenly around the globe.

Stephen Carney, Irving Epstein and Daniel Friedrich

Acknowledgements

We would like to acknowledge the support of Mark Richardson and Evangeline Stanford at Bloomsbury Academic for their support of this book project, from the contract signing through to production. We would also most sincerely like to thank Stephen Carney, Irving Epstein and Daniel Friedrich, the series editors of the New Directions in Comparative and International Education series, for commissioning our book in their series. Specifically, we would like to thank Stephen Carney for his enthusiasm about the book when Bob held initial conversations about it with him, and Daniel Friedrich, whose work on Teach For Argentina and Teacher For All has been particularly useful and insightful for the research reported in this book.

Heartfelt thanks are also offered to all those in Bangladesh who participated in the research reported in this book. In particular, we offer many thanks to the founder of Teach For Bangladesh, who was interviewed for this research and who assisted in conducting it. We also thank those governmental and non-governmental actors who willingly participated in and assisted the research. Without this cooperation, the research would not have been possible.

Rino

This book has its roots in the doctoral research I carried out in the School of Education, the University of Queensland, Australia, under the supervision of Bob and Ian. I cannot thank them enough for their enabling guidance and empowering contributions, without which the book would not have seen the light of day. The Australian government and the University of Queensland conjointly funded the PhD research, and I gratefully acknowledge this support. I am deeply thankful again to Bob and Ian for their continued support during the post-PhD co-authoring of this book. The theoretical, methodological and empirical outcomes presented in this book would not stand the way they do without Bob and Ian being there. I consider myself fortunate as well as privileged to have been able to work with them on this book project. My heartfelt thanks to the School of Education at the University of Queensland for the post-thesis fellowship that allowed me access to library and digital resources. I extend my sincere gratitude to Archi for supporting me during the writing of this book. Thanks, Mr Albert and Mrs Rosemary, for always being there as caring and encouraging parents.

Bob

I sincerely thank Rino and Ian for their collegial and collaborative approach to the research that is the basis of this book and also in writing this book together. I also acknowledge Rino's outstanding PhD thesis, which constitutes the significant empirical basis for this book.

Many academic colleagues have contributed to my thinking about changing imbrications between global, national and local relationships in respect of education policy influences and effects. I thank especially Katja Brogger and John Benedicto Krejsler of Aarhus University, Denmark, for great discussions during my time there as visiting professor in 2019, which have contributed substantially to my thinking and understandings about these matters. I would also like to thank Riyad Shahjahan and Diego Santori for their very helpful, insightful and supportive comments on Rino's PhD thesis.

As always, I acknowledge the contribution of Carolynn Lingard to all of my academic work and also our son, Nicholas Lingard.

Ian

Principally, I would like to acknowledge and thank my co-authors, Rino and Bob, for the opportunity to be part of this project. It has been a privilege to work with them to develop the ideas presented in this volume, both in relation to Rino's doctoral research that informed earlier theorizing in relation to education provision in Bangladesh and Bob's long-standing commitment to better understand the interplay of the multiple global, national and local scalar relations that characterize educational policy production and enactment. While there is considerable attention to practice-based theory development 'about' the Global South, there is much less robust, considered engagement, reflection and consideration of the nature of educational policy practices 'with' those with first-hand knowledge and lived experience, in dialogue with long-standing traditions of educational policy sociology and with comparative educational studies. This book would not have been possible without Rino's passion for and interest in understanding how new forms of social-entrepreneurial activity have sought to influence Bangladesh's public education or Bob's reflections on the nature of the interweaving of the local and the global in educational policy production.

I thank my family and friends for their continued support and encouragement of the work of a sometime peripatetic academic seeking to better understand the broader sociopolitical circumstances that constitute our work and lives.

Abbreviations

AVPN	Asian Venture Philanthropy Network
BCB	British Council Bangladesh
BCG	British Council Global
BRAC	Building Resources Across Communities (currently named); Bangladesh Rehabilitation Assistance Committee (first name); Bangladesh Rural Advancement Committee (second name)
CAMPE	Campaign for Popular Education
CEO	Chief Executive Officer
CS	Civil Society
DC	Donor Consortium
DD	Deputy Director
DfID	Department for International Development
DG	Director General
DLI	Disbursement Linked to Indicators
DNA	Deoxyribonucleic Acid
DPE	Directorate of Primary Education
EFA	Education For All
ELCG	Education Local Consultative Group
ERD	Economic Relations Divisions, Planning Ministry
EU	European Union
FTI	Fast Track Initiative
GDP	Gross Domestic Product
GIZ	German Federal Enterprise for International Cooperation
GPE	Global Partnership for Education
ICT	Information and Communication Technology
IRR	Internal Rate of Return
IRS	Internal Revenue Service
JARM	Joint Annual Review Mission
JCM	Joint Consultative Meeting
LLB	*Legum Baccalaureus*; Bachelor of Laws (LL meaning plural of law, laws)
LLC	Limited Liabilities Company

MBA	Master of Business Administration
MDGs	Millennium Development Goals
MoPME	Ministry of Primary and Mass Education
NAO	Network Administrative Organization
NBR	National Board of Revenue
NGO	Non-governmental Organization
NGOAB	NGO Affairs Bureau of Bangladesh
NP	New Philanthropy
ODI	Overseas Development Institute
PAL	Porticus Asia Limited
PEDP	Primary Education Development Programme (I–IV)
SDGs	Sustainable Development Goals
SE	Social Enterprise/Social Entrepreneurialism
SENScot	Social Enterprise Network Scotland
SEUK	Social Enterprise UK
SWAP	Sector Wide Approach to Programming
TFA	Teach For America
TFAll	Teach For All
TFB	Teach For Bangladesh
UCL	University College London
UN	United Nations
UNESCO	United Nations Educational, Scientific and Cultural Organization

Interviewees/Participants

The following 'interviewee/participant' abbreviations are used in the text to identify research interview extracts:

SGO	Senior Government Official
I/NGO-SO	International Non-governmental Organization or Social Organization
DCM	Donor Consortium Member

1

Teach For Bangladesh: Rethinking Comparative Policy Research in Education

Introduction

The specific empirical focus of this book is the Bangladesh manifestation of a globally circulating, social entrepreneurial teacher education reform movement which originated in the United States under the broad rubric of Teach For [organizations].[1] Teach For America (United States), Teach For China, Teach For Australia, Teach For Norway, Teach First (UK) and Teach For India are all specific national iterations of the broader Teach For phenomenon. These are constituted as non-profit organizations, which aspire to reform teaching and fast track teacher education reform with a long-term goal of producing education system leaders and reformers. Today, there are fifty-nine such organizations networked globally. These individual entities are supported by a broader 'global organization', Teach For All (TFAll), that seeks to 'accelerate the network's progress' (Teach For All, 2020). Founded in 2012, Teach For Bangladesh (TFB), a central consideration of this book, is one such individual organization.

The focus of the Teach For organizations is to 'train' top-quality university graduates as schoolteachers but with the long-term goal of these graduates becoming system leaders and reformers with social entrepreneurial mindsets, working both within and beyond education. The putative goal of these organizations is to address and eliminate educational inequality. In the words of Teach For All (2020):

> To tackle the complex challenges facing children in disadvantaged communities, we need a coalition of leaders addressing the problem in all of its complexity. Each network partner recruits and develops promising future leaders to teach in their nations' under-resourced schools and communities and, with this

foundation, to work with others, inside and outside of education, to ensure all children are able to fulfill their potential.

What is perhaps less emphasized is the overt leadership capacity building goal of the organization (see Adhikary & Lingard, 2020; Ellis et al., 2016; Friedrich, 2014). More specifically, the goal is to develop the leadership capacities of the individual Teach For corps members (called 'teaching fellows'), most of whom would be expected to then engage in careers beyond education. This is a short-term approach to teacher education and teaching reform spearheaded by the Teach For corp. Ellis and his colleagues (2016) have nicely captured this modus operandi in relation to the high-quality graduates, mainly from well-off families, who constitute the Teach For workforce in the title of their paper on the Teach For phenomenon, 'Teaching other people's children, elsewhere, for a while'. Furthermore, they observe that 'the principal motive underlying *Teach For All*'s rhetoric is the cultivation of a cadre of leaders and a form of neoliberal social entrepreneurship that it claims will solve the problem of 'broken' societies, public services and, specifically, schools' (Ellis et al., 2016, p. 60).

Thus, TFAll is the network umbrella to which TFB is a partner. TFAll was created by the founders of Teach For America and Teach First in 2007. It is a 'network of independent organizations', including TFB, with a mission of expanding educational opportunities and addressing inequality at a 'global scale'. A key feature of TFAll is its reliance on and usage of social entrepreneurs (SEs). Individual SEs from respective countries conforming to TFAll philosophy, world view and programme model are supported to initiate TFAll satellites in their home countries. In Chapters 4 and 5, we elaborate on the character of social enterprises and the ways in which education non-governmental organizations (NGOs) such as TFB are transmogrifying into social enterprises with significant future implications for the governance of the primary education sector in Bangladesh. We note though that governance does not replace entirely the more traditional practices of government and bureaucratic structures and practices but rather works with these in inflected and hybridized ways.

As a 'global organisation' TFAll strives to increase the 'individual and collective impact' of its network partners (Teach For All, FAQ, 2015). As such, it works towards 'educational equity and excellence for all of the[ir] nations' children' (Teach For All, FAQ, 2015). However, TFAll partners are not franchises but share the 'unifying principles' and 'aims and objectives' to 'accelerat[e] global impact' to reform national schooling systems by creating young educational leaders (Teach For All, FAQ, 2015). TFAll facilitates 'the interest of social entrepreneurs' wanting to 'adapt *TFAll*'s approach in their own countries' (Teach For All, FAQ, 2015). TFAll staff provides extensive induction support to 'immerse them in understanding the *Teach For All* mission' and its 'unifying programmatic and organisational principles' (Teach For All, FAQ, 2015).

TFAll's funding comes from five sources, namely: (a) major gifts from individuals and foundations, (b) regional support, (c) corporate partnerships, (d) government and multilateral partnerships and (e) friends of TFAll. Money raised by TFAll supports network partners and SEs, enabling the transfer of practice knowledge, and provides operational guidance for national partners. So as to develop necessary information technology, administrative systems and global/local fundraising structures aligned to its mission, TFAll's money is mainly expended on 'staff, specialists, technology, travel and conferences' (Teach For All, FAQ, 2015).

The Teach For phenomenon is part of the changes in education governance in systems around the globe and also globally (Lingard et al., 2016). These changes see the involvement in educational reform of agents other than state actors, including philanthropists, philanthrocapitalists, SEs, impact investors and edu-businesses as well as individuals from NGOs and international organizations (e.g. aid agencies, the UN, UNESCO). We might see this as partial outsourcing of statecraft. This involvement of non-state actors in the work of the state is evidence of a move to network governance, which today has been stretched globally (Ball & Junemann, 2012). These non-state actors are involved in all aspects of the policy cycle, stretching from agenda setting for policy and policy text production through to implementation and evaluation. Koppenjan and Klijn (2004, p. 25) have captured well the character of this new mode of network governance: 'In the world of network governance, government is understood to be located alongside business and civil society actors in a complex game of public policy formation, decision-making and implementation.' Of course, the specific manifestation of network governance plays out in path-dependent ways in all nations; its manifestation in a nation such as Bangladesh is different from that in Australia, for example. We have noted that governance does not replace more traditional modes of political and bureaucratic practices. The new network governance thus is interwoven with more hierarchical practices, combining what Appadurai (2001) calls cellular and vertebrate relationships, resulting in what has been referred to as heterarchical governance (Ball & Junemann, 2012).

Until the end of the Cold War, schooling policy in most nations, especially those in the Global North, appeared to be under the sole jurisdiction of national and subnational governments, reflecting the Westphalian reality of a clearly demarcated distinction between national and international policies. While this observation clearly applies to the nations of the Global North, the extent to which it is applicable to the nations of the Global South is perhaps open to question. This is because of the ongoing impact of colonization, what we might see as the 'colonial present' (Gregory, 2004), and the long-term impact of aid on these nations, including in relation to their schooling provision. However, in the context of globalization, all nations have been affected today by the mobility of policy ideas that circulate globally. Ball (1998) and Carney (2011) have spoken in this respect of 'policyscapes', one aspect of what Appadurai (1996) has described as the flows of globalization. Appadurai refers to the cultural flows of ideas, people, images, finance and technologies. TFAll and TFB can be thought of as policyscapes. The processes of globalization have seen schooling policy affected now by policies and discourses emanating from beyond the nation, an aspect of the new post-Westphalian political reality.

In the context referenced earlier, we have seen the emergence of: rescaling of policy (Brenner, 2004), a global education policy field (Lingard & Rawolle, 2011) and the impact in education policy of the new spatialities that have accompanied globalization processes, including topological relations (Amin, 2002). In respect of these, there has also been talk of fast policymaking and acknowledgement that policymaking imaginaries have been de-bordered, yet their implementation remains a stubbornly localized set of practices (Peck & Theodore, 2015). It has also been persuasively argued that the global mobility of policy models, for example, Teach For, has compressed, elided in some cases, the research and development phase in the policy cycle (Peck & Theodore, 2015, p. 224). We have today in education policy terms the mobility-fixity binary when analysing such policy, a binary we need to go beyond in analytical terms. Related, we have ever-changing relations and directionalities among global, national and local effects in both policy discourses and policy enactment (Larsen & Beech, 2014; Piattoeva, 2019; Lingard, 2021).

While the central empirical focus of the book is TFB, our attention to this reform is stimulated by a desire to better understand network governance and policy mobilities in the context of the changing and complex imbrications of global, national and local effects. Furthermore, we are interested in making a contribution to comparative education and comparative education policy analysis. In respect of the latter, we take what has been referred to as a policy sociology approach to understanding and analysing education policy (Ozga, 1987, 2019). We thus seek in this book to make a contribution to comparative education policy analysis by gesturing towards necessary methodological and theoretical innovations. These are addressed throughout but also briefly considered here.

Situating TFB in Bangladesh

Before providing a succinct descriptive account of the nature of TFB, we feel it important to describe the country. The history of Bangladesh has been affected by colonization and post-colonization, initially being a part of the larger Indian subcontinent, then part of Pakistan following partition from India in 1947, through to independence as a separate nation in 1971. From its inauguration, Bangladesh has constitutionally aligned with social-democratic and welfarist ways of sociopolitical thinking and economic arrangements. However, after the assassination of its first president in 1975, successive governments, including the current regime headed by the first president's daughter (Kabir, 2010, 2013), have made substantive constitutional amendments and embraced market liberalism, a manifestation of neoliberal capitalism (Islam, 2016; Quadir, 2000). Beginning in the 1980s and throughout the 1990s and subsequently, the Washington Consensus has had considerable impact on politics and policymaking in Bangladesh, mainly through the deliberations of the World Bank and the IMF and their structural adjustment programmes (see Bhattacharya, 2002; Bhattacharya & Chowdhury, 2003; Nguyen & Ali, 2013). These organizations demanded various conditionalities targeting macroeconomic policy reforms based on market liberalization. Substantial reforms in governance and decentralization (Quibria & Ahmad, 2007; Nuruzzaman, 2004) accompanied effects in the education sector.

The impact of these structural adjustments resulted in Bangladesh being the world's 'second most supportive [nation] of a free market economy' – now a 'capitalist heaven' with a global market friendliness score of 80 per cent, second only to that of Vietnam (95 per cent) (Ayres, 2014). This transformation into what is essentially an open market economy profoundly reshaped the policy environment for other non-economic fields (e.g. education) of the country – a phenomena referred to after Bourdieu as a 'cross-field effect' (Lingard & Rawolle, 2004; Rawolle, 2005). Here, discourses of education were framed in economistic terms concerning the production of human capital and aimed at development. These changes can be seen as a path-dependent manifestation of neoliberal globalization (Adhikary, 2014; Chowdhury & Kabir, 2014; Kabir, 2010,

2013) with particular effects on the primary education sector (Ahmed, 2013; Chowdhury et al., 2018; MoPME, 2015).

Bangladesh is a small nation with a land mass of 147,570 square kilometres and a population of 162 million people. The primary education system, consisting of 122,176 primary schools and 527,798 teachers educating 19,067,761 students (BANBEIS, 2017), is one of largest in the world. There is much poverty and inequality in Bangladesh; according to 2018 Asian Development Bank data (ADB, 2019), slightly more than 21 per cent of its population lives below the national poverty line. For a number of interrelated reasons, Bangladesh has increasingly become receptive to substantial exogenous influences, inter alia, in education policy and governance (Adhikary & Lingard, 2017). These factors include the country's geopolitical positioning (Ahmed, 2013; Jacques, 2000), scarcity of resources and funding (Lewis, 2011), willingness and perceived need to learn from the developed world (Ahmed, 2013; Gustavsson, 1991) and external aid dependency (Ahmed, 2016; Alamgir et al., 2014) so as to meet international development goals and commitments (Lewis, 2011).

These critical needs and associated external impacts are reflected in major changes in policy and governance, particularly in primary education, marking the adoption of a sector-wide educational programme approach through a series of Primary Education Development Programmes (PEDP I, II, III and IV; see Chapter 3). The PEDP programme designs, administers and evaluates the primary education sector through a consortium of external donor agencies and a network of NGOs, together with relevant Bangladesh government ministries and departments. The PEDP programme approach and associated exogenous interests now constitute an educational policy environment and governance modality that include transnational actors and participations through public-private partnerships and GO-NGO collaborations (see MoPME, 2015; Prime Minister's Office, 2017). The actor dynamics within the PEDP are also characterized by power asymmetry, wherein the government is required to deliver evidence-based performance to secure subsequent phases of external donor funding. However, NGOs have also become competitive receivers of such external donor funding.

Bangladesh now has 2,554 listed NGOs (NGOAB, 2017), of which more than 936 I/NGOs are working in the primary education subsector (CAMPE, 2016). Some of these I/NGOs, most notably BRAC,[2] Save the Children, SHARE (Supporting the Hardest to Reach through Basic Education) and UNICEF,[3] have displayed considerable strength in successfully addressing issues in primary education such as access and gender parity in primary schooling (Ahmed,

2016). In recent years, in line with development goals and UN agendas (e.g. the MDGs and SDGs), the focus of I/NGO work is increasingly shifting from equity in access and gender parity to 'quality of education'. Apart from these traditional I/NGOs, new philanthropy-backed reform organizations have recently been active in the NGO landscape, particularly in the primary education sector; such entities represent a local manifestation of broader global flows of social entrepreneurial ideas and resources powered by philanthrocapitalism. TFB is one such NGO that prefers to call itself a social enterprise with a long-term vision to change the whole primary education system of Bangladesh (PESoB).

Teach For Bangladesh

A central empirical focus of this book is TFB, which is situated and analysed in the context of the matters considered to this point and against the specific backdrop of Bangladesh presented earlier. We provide here a short descriptive account of TFB.

Launched in 2012, TFB has now been active in the country for nearly a decade as an NGO approved by the NGO Affairs Bureau of Bangladesh (NGOAB). To be able to work in the field of primary education, the organization had to secure permission from the Bangladesh Directorate of Primary Education (DPE). Vernacularizing TFAll's programmatic goals in Bangladesh, TFB recruits, trains and places fresh university graduates as full-time teachers in select primary schools, the majority of which are government run and located in poor communities. In Bangladesh, TFB is generally viewed as a local NGO providing quality teaching to disadvantaged students. In addition to this equity focus are the less articulated social entrepreneurial mandates, values and practices underpinning a desire to change the whole PESoB. Linked to these observations, a central focus of the analysis provided in this book is the macro policy move for NGOs to become social enterprises and the desire to restructure public service provision in this image. These matters are addressed in more detail in Chapters 4 and 5.

In its programme rationale presented to the NGOAB, TFB identified specific education issues within the primary education system and linked them with educational inequity and broader social disparities existing in Bangladesh. In making its case for challenging inequity, TFB highlighted systemic issues such as the socio-economic condition of deprived children, hard-to-reach rural school locations, insufficient numbers of primary schools in urban areas, high student-teacher ratios, lack of facilities in classrooms and inadequate numbers of properly trained and motivated teachers. These problems were articulated as barriers to quality education, particularly for the children of families earning less than $2 per day (NGOAB Document, November 2015).

Viewing such educational issues as forms and causes of social disparity and inequality, TFB identified two stakeholder groups to work with: (a) meritorious educated youth with potential leadership qualities, and (b) deprived or less-supported neighbourhoods, their children, their schools, families and inhabitants. The organization identifies 'extremely meritorious young university graduates with ability to lead the country in future' and then 'recruits them as full time Fellow Teachers' (NGOAB Document, November 2015, p. 3). These fellow teachers[4] work in deprived schools for two years and are then expected to support/lead education throughout their lives drawing on developed professional capacities (NGOAB Document, November 2015, p. 3).

While the fellows get higher salaries than their government counterparts, unlike the latter, the former are not required to sit for the primary teachers' qualification exam. The fellowship begins with a six-week residential 'bootcamp' (the descriptor used by the founder) called the Winter Academy, and then the fellows attend a tailored one-and-a-half-year master's programme offered by the BRAC Institute of Educational Development, BRAC University.[5] This programme is conducted during the weekends, and the fellows attend it synchronously with their teaching work in primary schools during the week (Thomas & Lefebvre, 2020).

These fellow teachers, recruited through an open call and selective telephone interviews, are required to teach English, maths and science to second and third graders of selected underprivileged schools in Dhaka city. According to the TFB proposal to the NGO Bureau, the first-year recruited teachers were expected to teach in twenty-two deprived schools and the second-year intakes in thirty-five more, all located in Dhaka (NGOAB Document, November 2015, p. 14). These schools are generally government primary schools as well as a small number of other NGO schools. TFB's three-year plan of action included the recruitment and training of 75 fellows in the first year, 130 in the second year and another 130 in the third year.

The fellow teachers were also expected to offer 'international standard quality teaching' to 8,250 children from twenty-two schools in the first year and 13,650 children from thirty-five other schools in the second year, following the Bangladesh government curriculum. According to NGOAB documents, the classroom performances of TFB fellow teachers were to be monitored by TFB staff once a month, followed by a final evaluation. In using the performance and evaluation data, opinions from the head teacher, teachers and other related government officers were also to be sought (NGOAB Document, November 2015, p. 15). The future plan of TFB can be summed up in four simple phrases: working with(in) the government; establishing new collaborative modes of activities; setting TFB as an example to be followed and; scaling up TFB nationwide.

Situating the Study in Multiple Ways

In the Literature on the Teach For Network and Organizations

There is a growing body of research literature which deals with the Teach For network and organizations. This literature is diverse in its focus on global, national and local orientations and has different theoretical framings. The now quite extensive literature on Teach For organizations also ranges widely in foci, methodologies and aims. This scholarship has formed a significant backdrop to our book, *Global-National Networks in Education Policy: Primary Education, Social Enterprises and 'Teach For Bangladesh'*. To put the growing extent of this work into perspective, a generic online library search at the University of Queensland identified more than seventy-five research items, of which six were doctoral theses from some of the world's very best research universities, four were commissioned reports evaluating Teach For organizations, five were journalistic reports and the remaining sixty publications were journal articles, mostly from high-status US-based outlets.

We were also excited to have discovered eight book titles directly contributing to Teach For topics. These included *Examining Teach For All: International Perspectives on a Growing Global Network* (Thomas et al., 2020), *Lessons to Learn: Voices from the Front Lines of Teach For America* (Ness, 2013), *Teach For America and the Struggle for Urban School Reform: Searching for Agency in an Era of Standardization (Educational Psychology)* (Crawford-Garrett, 2013), *Learning from Counternarratives in Teach For America: Moving from Idealism towards Hope* (Matsui, 2015) and *From 'Teach For America' to 'Teach For China': Global Teacher Education Reform and Equity in Education* (Lam, 2020).[6] These books are generally comprehensive in their approach to various aspects either of the TFAll network as a movement or of a specific Teach For organization and related issues and dynamics. Other books included voices of those who had worked for Teach For organizations, as evident in their titles, such as *Teach For America Counter-narratives: Alumni Speak Up and Speak Out* (Brewer & DeMarrais,

2015), *Teach For All Counter-narratives: International Perspectives on a Global Reform* (Brewer et al., 2020) and *Teaching in the Terrordome: Two Years in West Baltimore with Teach For America* (Lanier, 2012).

The literature on TF networks and organizations deals with interesting topics motivated, inter alia, by promotional, reactionary, critical, number-centric, investigative and explanatory impulses. We have identified eight broad categories of work that overlap methodologically, theoretically and in terms of topics. First of all, a large body of quantitative research was readily discernible. Alongside a meta review that located TFAll within the larger body of teacher education research (Anderson, 2020), we identified a diverse array of statistical research that mostly addressed relationship or impact questions. This body of statistical research on TF phenomenon can be divided into different categories, with the effect of TF on achievement and improvements of various kinds outnumbering other studies (see, e.g. Antecol et al., 2013; Backes et al., 2018; Glazerman et al., 2006; Penner, 2014, 2016, 2019; Turner et al., 2018; Xu et al., 2011). Other interesting topics included the link between racial tolerance and teacher-student optimism about the future (Dobbie & Fryer, Jr., 2015), TF and teacher attrition (Heineke et al., 2014), TF clustering strategy and teacher attrition and mobility (Hansen et al., 2016), teacher stress and well-being (Stoneburner, 2018) and age of entry and teacher continuation (Donaldson, 2012). While studies have compared the effectiveness of TF and non-TF graduates (Darling-Hammond et al., 2005), factors influencing TF teacher retention (Donaldson & Johnson, 2010) or TF's impact on teacher labour market outcomes (Curran, 2017) have suggested valid concerns. Other topics also included corps members' evaluation of their 'trainers'[7] (Carter et al., 2017), analyses of loans and grants' links to motivation to join TF (Coffman et al., 2019) and TF's influence on beliefs about education (Conn et al., 2020).

Secondly, and more at a discourse analytic level, we found works on personal narratives of corps members (Ahmann, 2016), comparative cultural appraisal (Blumenreich & Gupta, 2015) and dialogues between corps members and their mentors (Gabriel, 2017). A discursive approach was also taken in works that focused on individual corps member's learning experiences (Covert, 2014), heroic narratives and dilettantism in relation to TF teachers (Clement, 2018) or certain discourses that promote symbolic violence in the TF practice. Such discursive analytics focused more on the teaching dimension of TF programmes rather than the broader politics of their establishment and enactment. A third trend in the literature paid attention to critical race analysis, critical theory and social justice in regards to the practices of TF networks and organizations.

Specific topics included race and culture conscious counternarratives of students and teachers (Irizarry & Donaldson, 2012), links between white teacher saviour movies and TF narratives (Cann, 2015), TF corps' negotiation and navigation of larger fields of power (Kretchmar, 2014) and TF-university partnerships facing differences in perceptions of social justice (McNew-Birren et al., 2018). Critical approaches were further applied in examining TF's symbolic violence and the perpetuation of structural inequity (Anderson, 2013), corps' reaction to scripted curricula (Carl, 2014) and TF's apparent link with black and Latinx communities in the United States (Muñoz et al., 2019).

Although comparatively smaller in number, organizational analysis categorized a fourth set of research work. For example, researchers studied the evolution of TF's Summer Training Institution (Schneider, 2014), the relationship between charter schools and Teach For America (Lefebvre & Thomas, 2017) and the nature of foundational and organizational challenges for TF organizations in India, China and the UK (Hennessy & Krishman, 2016). Interestingly, relatively few articles on TF in leading academic journals explained the need for reconceptualization of TF for further improvement (Hopkins, 2008), why the 'superhero/transformer' view of the corps needed deeper intellectual engagement (Trujillo & Scott, 2014) or why TF teachers continued to teach or leave teaching (Donaldson & Johnson, 2011).

The largest cluster of qualitative research on TF was based on perceptions of participants and associated personnel. Such research indicated two broad trends in relation to experiential reflection and the nature of external dynamics. For example, self-reflective and experiential-based research included topics about site-based experiences of TF corps members, mentors and administrators (Veltri, 2008), as well as accounts of personal attributes, characteristics and career aspirations of new teachers (Straubhaar & Gottfried, 2016) and experiences of corps members in special education classrooms (Thomas, 2018b). One rather comprehensive research project delved into corps members' lives viewed from (a) temporal, (b) physical, (c) cultural, (d) economic, (e) organizational, (f) political-legal and (g) personal angles (Veltri & Brewer, 2019). Other such topics broadly included experiences of 'synchronous' service teachers (Thomas & Lefebvre, 2020), civic engagement of TF corps (Keen, 2010) or perceived role of TF in teachers' long-term career aspirations (Gottfried & Straubhaar, 2015). These studies targeted the individuals in question, with some studies eliciting perspectives in relation to educational inequity (Trujillo et al., 2017), rationales for TF model's expansion to cities without teacher shortages (DiCamillo, 2018), corps' perceptions of classroom self-efficacy (Zappetti, 2019) or how

TF experience influences school leadership (Taylor, 2017). Studies addressing a broader political perspective included comparing the ideological appeal of Teach For organizations (Straubhaar, 2019) or corps members' view of citizens facing market-based reforms (Sondel, 2015).

More relevant to the field of education policy, another thread of qualitative research on TF organizations corresponded to policy analysis, including critical policy analysis, as well as economic analysis. For instance, researchers studied how teachers were positioned as the embodiment of alternative teacher education policy (Thomas, 2018a), or how TF enjoys a marketing advantage over other teacher education programmes (Labaree, 2010), or how TF's financial support for election campaigns is used as a policy strategy (Hoff, 2008). Linked to such studies was investigative sociological research on venture philanthropy's link to TF (Zeichner & Peña-Sandoval, 2015) or on TF's supplementing impact on teacher labour policies (Dwinal, 2012). Cochran-Smith and Zeichner (2009) have criticized Teach For America as an example of the residualization and deprofessionalization of teaching and teacher education, as part of the broader moves to privatize and involve non-educators in the 'reform' of US schooling (see Hursh, 2016, 2017). A few researchers have looked into the financial dynamics of TF; such topics included how foundation donations are central to enabling the continuation of TF (Sawchuk, 2013), or how TF has increased its credential's exchange value (Maier, 2012), or even how TF is related to the deregulation of university-based teacher education (Kretchmar et al., 2018).

Focusing on the discursive formation of TFAll as a global policy and the differences in its web-based articulations in various national contexts, Ellis and colleagues (2016) provide a comparative analysis of the rhetoric used in the official websites of Teach For America, Teach First UK and Teach For China, all constituent members of TFAll. They also provide an analysis of the rhetoric of the website of Teach For Norway, which is not formally affiliated with TFAll. (The Norwegian entity is actually 'owned' by the Oslo public school system and functions almost as a quasi-public-private partnership with the state-owned Norwegian oil company Statoil and the University of Oslo and focuses, unlike the others, on science teaching in primary schools, with its teachers working in urban schools in poor communities in England during their training.) Ellis and colleagues (2016) chose these sites for analysis as they provided a good opportunity to understand how a globally travelling policy 'touches down' in different national contexts: how the policy became translated in these contexts.

While identifying the various ways the policy is vernacularized in these very different contexts, Ellis and colleagues (2016, p. 64) specify four 'recurring tropes' on all the websites. These are: teaching as a 'short-term mission' rather than established career-long profession; the 'mission is essentially one of leadership' (Ellis et al., 2016, p. 64); teachers are conceptualized as leaders, while 'teacher education becomes reconfigured as "leadership development"' (Ellis et al., 2016, p. 65); and 'philanthropically endowed social entrepreneurship' is deemed to be the solution to issues of inequality and educational disadvantage and 'to problems of "broken" or underdeveloped public services such as schooling' (Ellis et al., 2016, p. 65). On the last, for example, they show that more than 90 per cent of students taught by Teach For America teachers are black or Latino and most live in poverty. With Teach For China, the focus is on rural communities as the sites of poverty, where mostly graduates from US universities teach (also see Lam, 2020). Ellis and colleagues are interested in the interweaving of global and national effects in relation to the Teach For movement – what we depict as the imbrications of global, national and local relations in policy.

Our review of the literature suggests some gaps, particularly in relation to TF as embryonic social enterprises (see Ellis et al., 2016; Friedrich, 2014 for the significance of such orientation). While TF organizations are visible today as NGOs (as in Bangladesh) or as foundations (as in China), the significance of these organizations in understanding global policy mobility and network governance, which are important foci of this book and its analysis, has not been extensively researched to date (nonetheless, see Friedrich (2014) on Teach For Argentina and Lam (2020) for Teach For China). Friedrich (2004) has examined Teach For Argentina's formation of social entrepreneurial subjectivities as the driver for change (also see Chapter 5 in relation to the TFB founder), analysed TFAll as a 'multilateral agency' advancing cross-national policy borrowing (Straubhaar & Friedrich, 2015), scrutinized TFAll as a mode of public-private partnership signalling the erosion of the public in education (Friedrich, 2016) and proposed reformative prescriptions for TFAll so that the organization dialogues better with its satellites (Friedrich et al., 2015). Furthermore, we situate our analysis of TFB in the comparative education literature, which we turn to in the next section. Specifically, we conjoin policy sociology in education (Ozga, 1987, 2019) with comparative education, proffering a comparative education policy study of TFB.

The study reported in this book is in dialogue with Ellis and colleagues' (2016) 'findings' in relation to the four underpinning tropes of TFAll and also with the need to understand and theorize global, national and local relations in respect of a travelling policy. Our findings also resonate with Friedrich's (2014) focus on this movement as a social enterprise, and the rhetoric around this organizational form as a (putative) way of addressing poverty and educational disadvantage. Our study differs in its empirical basis utilizing on-the-ground evidence, especially research interviews, and in the way TFB is seen as part of a broader realignment of NGOs as social enterprises for the possible future reform of the entire public sector in Bangladesh.

In Comparative Education

Shaped by the effects of successive and ever-changing world orders (Manzon, 2018, p. 94), comparative education as a field changes as the world changes (Cowen, 2014, p. 4). While the history of this field cannot be writ large (but see Phillips & Schweisfurth's (2014) attempt to do so nonetheless), conjunctural phases observed by No'Voa and Yariv-Mashal (2003, p. 424) reveal clear links between a changing world and a developing field. During the late nineteenth century (1880s), comparative education as a field was born alongside the emergence of mass schooling systems and the curious desire for 'knowing' (phase 1) other schooling systems so as to learn from them. In the 1920s, in the broader context of the post–First World War period, a need to 'understand' (phase 2) other schooling systems became pressing, as European nations became increasingly competitive economically and as political tensions escalated.

The ethos of knowing and understanding others as central rationales for comparative education gave way to another phase, the 'constructing' (phase 3) in the 1960s. This was the period when postcolonial nations, following independence from colonial masters, needed guidance in their economic development journey and in respect of their schooling systems. Comparative education in this period revealed the rise of the technocratic influence of international agencies and the associated impact of the so-called scientific approach; the exportation of educational 'solutions' became standard practice. These developments might be seen as working to encourage the epistemological exclusion of local knowledges and also witnessed some of these postcolonial and decolonial aspirations functioning more as a 'colonial present' (Gregory, 2004). Takayama has written most insightfully about the colonizing aspects of the history of comparative education (see Takayama, 2018, 2019, 2020a,b; Takayama et al., 2017).

As the world stepped into the 2000s, comparative education emphasized 'measuring' (phase 4), situated against the rise of a post-Westphalian system of governance and the post–Cold War dominance of neoliberal globalization. In this context and in relation to education, the OECD and IEA's international testing regimes (e.g. PISA, TIMSS, PIRLS) saw the emergence of a global education policy field and global policy, as these International Large Scale Assessments (ILSAs) constituted the globe as a commensurate space of measurement. We also witnessed some convergence of education policy discourses and also new spatialities affecting education policy, which will be dealt with throughout the book. For nations of the Global South, various UN agendas had similar impact, including EFA, MDGs and the current SDGs and related outcome indicators of success or otherwise (see Chapter 3). A cottage industry of research around these tests has precipitated the danger that No'Voa and Yariv-Mashal (2003) document, namely, that comparative education is in danger of becoming a mode of governance as comparison has become central to the new mode of educational governance both globally and within nations (see Hardy, 2021; Lingard et al., 2016; Ozga, 2009). We support No'Voa and Yariv-Mashal's argument that comparative education must be focused on producing understanding of education, which requires the application of multiple social science theories and methodologies. This might be seen as research *of* education, including *of* education policy, as opposed to instrumental construals of research *for* education and *for* education policy. We would argue, though, that the understandings so produced can, and should, inform policymaking in education.

Zooming into its more recent history, primarily since the 1970s, comparative education shifted its sociological gaze on education systems to problems and solutions (Hurst, 1987, pp. 9–10). The framing of comparative issues in problem-solution terms necessitated theories to align with the practices of policymaking (Epstein, 1995, p. 8). In the 1980s, comparative education became more applied and began to emphasize the borrowing of effective models or their key features for improvement-oriented reforms (Morris, 2015, p. 470). From the 1980s into the 1990s, the concept of reference societies became important again in comparative education (Schriewer, 1990; Schriewer & Martinez, 2004), whereby nations looked to other nations' schooling systems, now in relation to performance on ILSAs, to borrow and learn (see Steiner-Khamsi, 2004). We see here processes of 'externalization' at play. Waldow (2012, p. 418) defines 'externalization' 'as a discursive formation that can become relevant in the context of borrowing and lends itself easily to the purpose of producing legitimacy for national schooling reforms'. This is the period when comparisons could be seen as situated within an emergent global education policy field, but also in path-dependent nation-based ways. It is in this period that methodological globalism challenged methodological nationalism, even as the national continued to exert influence (Lingard, 2021; Piattoeva, 2019). However, and as we argue in the next section, with the recent rise of new nationalisms and ethnonationalisms in many nations across the globe, we now need to move beyond this global-national binary.

Thus central research questions within this field relate to the potential for improving systems by understanding practices and policies that function better, garner acceptance, often become mobile and are variously imported and implemented within different national settings, always in path-dependent ways (Powell, 2020, p. 4). However, the assessment of how effective policies and practices within a certain national setting are is increasingly evaluated within a global perspective, often from the perspective of ILSAs (Cook et al., 2004, p. 130).

With policymaking now intertwined with and affected by new technologies, new authorities and interests keep challenging research priorities, with output measurements augmenting 'an extensive system of knowledge' (Fenwick et al., 2014). As a result, the scope for comparison in the legitimization of specific reforms (programmes, practices, policies, etc.) becomes globalized (Powell, 2020, p. 15). Today, one mainstream conception of comparative education is that which is expected to be pragmatic and non-ideologically scientific by valuing 'best-practice' and 'evidence-based' analysis. Prefigurative of reforms, such research and associated data are largely desk based and involve large networks of consultants, think tanks and researchers deployed by transnational and international organizations (Morris, 2015, p. 471).

Linked to such developments are new methodologies that promote comparative studies as tools for educational policymaking (Broadfoot, 2000, p. 357). Constitutive in practice of what Rizvi and Lingard (2010) refer to as research *for* policy, such nomothetic policy research demands sociological attention both in formulative and manifest forms – research *of* policy. Certainly, the latter approach is not representative of the mainstream comparative research we have so far described. Yet it is, arguably, central to understanding policy and reforms in the field of comparative education today. Indeed, in many ways, the domain of education policy can be seen as located within the broader field of comparative education, so much so that the making of education policy and associated politics have often been argued to be the central focus of comparative education (see No'Voa & Yariv-Mashal, 2003, p. 423). While research *of* policy often tends to be sociological in nature, and aims to understand the political as well as psychosocial dynamics that speak to various origins, causalities, processes and effects, such policy research must also account for the rising impact of global phenomenon (Broadfoot, 2000; Cook et al., 2004; Powell, 2020).

Comparative education's enabling of reforms (see earlier) – in fact a global education reform movement (GERM) (Sahlberg, 2016) – is the positivist-nomothetic (Lenhart, 2018) epistemological context that this book seeks to understand sociologically through a focus on networks and mobilities in educational reforms. A focus on fast policy mobilities around the globe also demands some methodological innovations. Chapter 2 in Peck and Theodore's Fast Policy (2015) provides very useful thinking about and exploration of methodological considerations in the context of policy mobilities. Gulson and his colleagues (2017) have also considered such matters in respect of global policy mobilities in education. Gorur et al. (2019) provide an insightful consideration of methodological issues for comparative research today and also argue that our methodological choices make the world legible in particular ways for our research and understanding.

So, what sort of an understanding of comparative education do we frame and apply in this book as researchers? What kind of comparison is even remotely related to the way we approach policy mobilities and networks methodologically and conceptually? Can policy networks be compared? If so, how do we account for the nation-state or its cultural and administrative residuals? How do we even frame a unit of analysis in relation to the alternative path of comparative education that we have taken in this book?

It is not always necessary that comparative education research exhibit a 'surface' form of comparison (i.e. India versus Iran) to assume 'comparative' status (Cowen, 2014, p. 5). Comparative insights can be generated via units of comparison other than at the country level; rather, they can relate across communities within countries, multiple times, networked cultures, emerging values and ways of learning (Little, 2010, p. 846). In this book we have deployed all of these sites of comparison. In fact, comparison can be framed laterally across multiple cultural narratives without necessarily being confined to categories embedded within Western metaphysics of classical modernity (Rappleye, 2019, p. 13).

In order for this to happen, adds Rappleye (2019), practitioners of comparative education need to widen their 'imaginative cosmos' and allow for a 'historical consciousness of the field' as ever changing – all to neutralize the impact of a long-enduring Hegelian dialectic world view of an epistemic rigidity. Comparative education today can be practised as a form of cultural critique, one grounded in the experience of self-loss leading to epistemic migration (reflexivity; and more than mobility) (Kim, 2014) that supports immigrants of being (Rappleye, 2019).

In fact, it has long been argued that neo-comparative education research should emphasize learning and its relationship with culture (Broadfoot, 2000).

In a time of rapid globalization in conflict with deeply problematic forms of ethnonationalism, comparative education must permit a simultaneous understanding of historical forces, social structures and individual biographies written in a coherent version of political and cultural codings of processes related to education (Cowen, 2014, p. 10). For buried beneath the unitary label of comparative education is the empirically diverse field of multiple comparative 'educations' (Rappleye, 2012). Silova views such multiplicity in terms of a Wonder(land), rather than of an exclusive science of comparative education. She argues in favour of opening spaces for 'multiple ways of making sense of the world, and multiple ways of being' (Silova 2019, p. 444). Ethnography has long been one powerful way of making sense of worlds and ways of being. Yet, as our book illustrates, globalization has had significance for ethnography (now global ethnography), and the growth of network governance in education globally has also carried significance (network ethnography).

Ethnography can help nuance comparative understandings of processes. In this regard, globalization has meant that the labelling of groups and actors as being 'inside' or 'outside' of a system or professional or research community is becoming increasingly difficult. Given how powerful group identities are in continuous flux and with boundaries becoming permeable, less stable and difficult to draw, McNess and colleagues (2015, p. 395) have advanced the concept of a 'third liminal space' from where an ethnographic imagination can becomes more relevant to the global condition and conditioning of policy. They suggest, further, that it is in such ethnographic spaces that the 'boundary between worlds, where historical, social, cultural, political, ethical and individual understandings, meet' (McNess et al., 2015, p. 395). No'Voa and Yariv-Mashal (2003, p. 434) rightly argue that our understanding of space/spatialities needs to be imbricative of multiple temporalities located in imaginary and virtual flows through which communities are created (also see Anderson, 1983; Appadurai, 1996). We argue that when it comes to studying a phenomenon that involves both global and national/local dimensions, neither a national nor an entirely global ontology holds, and that a much more culturally grounded, ethnographic approach is necessary. While the generic unit of comparative analysis is mostly framed in nation-state centric ways, we now need to consider global-local imbrications (Lingard, 2021), an approach inclusive of multiple and competing spatio-temporalities. Such an onto-epistemological rethinking through spatio-temporalities can account for 'virtual, imaginary and geographical' dimensions at once 'moving away from sensorial perspectives' of fixity (No'Voa & Yariv-Mashal, 2003, p. 434).

Comparative education has long functioned as a space in which the coloniality of power was enacted (Sobe, 2017, p. 340). While comparative education's epistemic challenge to progress, modernity, dominance and subordination remains rooted in postmodern, poststructural and postcolonial thinking (Ninnes & Burnett, 2003, p. 279), Takayama (2011) proposes the need for serious engagement with different intellectual traditions besides the dominant mainstream (epistemological plurality) to address any potential regression to academic neocoloniality in the present. Comparative education today stands as an invitation to crossing and bridging boundaries (Kim, 2020, p. 5). In this space we need both windows and mirrors; while windows invite newness and help imagine a future standing on the present, mirrors help reflect back at the past that has brought us to where we are today (Evans & Robinson-Pant, 2007, p. 1).

For reasons outlined earlier, we must be critical about the national identifiers we use to explain phenomena that can no longer be fully captured in nation-state terms (Takayama, 2011, p. 460). Going beyond methodological nationalism requires the study of 'trans-cultural mixing' in which boundaries between cultural forms and identities are fluid rather than fixed (Takayama, 2011, p. 463). Transcultural mixing occurs through spatio-cultural topologies wherein multiple and sometimes competing temporalities can coexist. Regarding education policy analysis, Ball (2012, p. 93) has observed:

> Education policy analysis can no longer sensibly be limited to within the nation-state – the fallacy of methodological territorialism. Policy analysis must also extend its purview beyond the state and the role of multinational agencies and NGOs to include transnational business practices.

We would add that the role of global philanthropies also needs to be considered (Junemann & Olmedo, 2019; Tompkins-Stange, 2016).

How we research the ways the multiple spatialities of globalization play out in contemporary education policy production (Larsen & Beech, 2014) is central to both theory and methodologies in contemporary comparative education. This requires moving beyond the methodological nationalism/methodological globalism binary, which we consider in the next section of the chapter.

One additional matter needs to be commented on in relation to comparative education in the era of the Anthropocene and climate emergency. Rappleye and Komatsu (2020) have argued persuasively for the necessity of rethinking comparative research in response to the clear reality of objective limits to natural resources of all kinds and the impact of the climate crisis. Silova (2019) and Silova and colleagues (2020) have also written instructively about the need for such rethinking.

Beyond the Binary of Methodological Nationalism and Methodological Globalism

Until the end of the Cold War, schooling and schooling policy were seen to sit almost solely within the jurisdiction and remit of the nation. This was the period of Westphalian politics with a clear demarcation between national and international policies. Mass literacy (and we would suggest mass numeracy), which was an outcome from the introduction of mass elementary schooling, helped constitute the 'imagined community' of the nation (Anderson, 1983). Unacknowledged in social science research during that time was an implicit assumption that the social and the nation were homologous. Methodologically, in social science research on education, the approach was what has been called 'methodological nationalism'.

The end of the Cold War and the globalization of the economy with cuts in tariff barriers and the ushering in of a more neoliberal free trade regime challenged further Westphalian politics and the assumption that education policy was simply the remit of the nation-state. The new post-Westphalian politics saw complex overlapping and interweaving in multiple directions of global, national and local relations. The demarcation between national and international politics was increasingly blurred. International organizations such as the OECD, IMF, WTO, UN and the like ushered in multiple global policy fields and global policies with some global policy convergence at the level of the discourses framing policy. Policy imaginations were de-bordered (Peck & Theodore, 2015), but policy enactment was still very much a localized and vernacularized matter. Appadurai's (1996) talk of 'context generative' and 'context productive' relations between globalization and the local is another way of thinking about the complexity of global-national-local imbrications. This new geopolitics spawned challenges to methodological nationalism, or methodological territorialism in Ball's (2012) words earlier, within the social sciences and in educational research, specifically in policy sociology and comparative education. There was an ushering in, in methodological terms, of a 'methodological globalism' (Clarke, 2019, p. v).

More sophisticated understandings of the complex relationships among global, national and local actors and effects have more recently challenged the either/or binary of methodological nationalism or methodological globalism. Larsen and Beech (2014), for example, suggested that with methodological globalism, 'much globalisation research has focused on how the national has mediated the global'. Within such renderings, they add that the emphasis has been on how the global has affected the national and the local. They suggest that we need to go beyond these binaries and a one-way top-down set of effects and instead acknowledge what are complex imbrications that work in multiple directions and ways among the global, the national and the local. Sassen (2001, p. 260) has argued that these latter are not exclusive entities, but today 'they significantly overlap and interact in ways that distinguish our contemporary moment'. We might say that the local, the national and the global have become projects of each other. We could add that authoritarian populist backlashes against globalization have also seen the emergence of new nationalisms and ethnonationalisms, evidenced, for example, in former president Trump's America First and in the UK's Brexit. This has seen ever-changing global-national and local imbrications in politics and policymaking, matters we will reflect upon throughout the book. It is in this context of developments in theory and contemporary realpolitik that we are arguing there is a pressing need to go beyond the binary of methodological nationalism/methodological globalism. There is one final related point to make here, that is, that the new spaces, places, scales and so on of education policy today are also constituted by policy as well as being contexts of policy work (Papanastasiou, 2019).

Positionality of the Researchers

Following Bourdieu et al. (1999), we accept that in social science research, indeed in any research, there is no such position of epistemological innocence available to researchers. We agree as well with Bourdieu who suggests that articulation of researchers' positionality in relation to the objects of research means the production of more plausible and ethical insights and understandings. We are also wary of social science research that unreflexively applies Western-developed theories in non-Western contexts, which in our view functions as epistemological exclusion and as a contemporary form of colonization. Appadurai's (2001) observation that non-Western sites must be more than empirical mines for the application of Western theory is particularly salient. We agree with his argument that the full internationalization and a properly inclusive epistemology of research practices must acknowledge the right and indeed necessity of non-Western non-global North researchers to develop theory and speak back to theories produced in the high-status universities of the metropoles. We also acknowledge the danger in comparative education of research being conducted on the education systems of developing nations in a way that functions as a bird's eye logocentric, top-down account of global effects in these systems. We have sympathy here with Carney's (2019) argument that on-the-ground, bottom-up accounts of the ways in which local and national actions affect the global in messy and contested ways are also necessary. These are matters we have also considered earlier, where we have argued the imperative of moving beyond both methodological nationalism and globalism, and the need to acknowledge the multiple and interwoven relationships and directionalities of the global, the national and the local (Larsen & Beech, 2014; Piattoeva, 2019).

This book has been a collaborative production among the three authors. Only one of the three authors, Rino Adhikary, has life experience in Bangladesh and has actually spent time in the field in Bangladesh, visiting and collecting data reported in this book, and which is the basis of the analysis provided. The fieldwork included in-depth immersion in the cultural, political, historical and social/sociological fabrics of the research sites and substantive interaction with those with whom Rino was engaged during this process, including thirty-two semi-structured interviews. These accounts were deeply and interactively discussed by the three authors in ongoing and substantive ways, both during data collection and subsequent to it. This reflected our acceptance that data analysis begins from the first moment of conceptualization of the study, through to the initial stages of data collection, and later consideration of the data corpus as a whole. We also worked within an assumption that theory and data collection are intimately imbricated in each other. Here we are at one with Bourdieu's description of social science research in the field as 'fieldwork in philosophy' (Bourdieu, 1990; Lingard, 2015).

We recognize the necessity of challenging the epistemological violence performed by non-reflective applications of Western knowledges, theories and epistemological traditions. As such, we have endeavoured to engage in epistemological reflexivity. We recognize that in terms of theory, multiple traditions are always at play, and always hybridized, even as some may be at greater risk of being subsumed or colonized by more 'dominant' knowledge traditions. Recognizing these ongoing tensions is at least a beginning to trying to challenge the sorts of epistemological innocence that characterizes so much social science research.

In our collaboration, there was space for dialogue and for the empirical to challenge dominant theoretical approaches and foci. For example, even though the research began its empirical attention methodologically as network ethnography, realizations from the actual field transformed the theoretical approach towards what we have called ethnographic networks; this extended the initial attention to network ethnography. We soon recognized that the initial network ethnography had to be complemented by much deeper ethnographic fieldwork – in situ, on the ground. This, perhaps, also allows the overcoming of what appears to be the implicit flat ontology in network ethnography, often related to Western epistemologies and researcher positionalities when focusing on Global South nations/contexts.

If we are to be true to our convictions as researchers of substance, our positionality matters; we cannot go beyond our circumstances; one cannot have a view of our work beyond the point from which our gaze has originated and reached. Nonetheless, we have been very mindful in our research collaboration of the constructedness of our various ways of seeing. Our collective efforts to develop understandings of these ethnographic networks constituted a key finding of the research, which we elaborate further in Chapter 4, focusing upon the work of social entrepreneurship in network governance processes. This collaboration can be better understood through our individual experiences in relation to one another. The data collection that provides the backdrop to this book was carried out by Rino, while the analysis worked reflexively across our three-way collaboration. Rino's experiences also confirm Edward Said's point that for some and in some circumstances, displacement can be productive for thinking theoretically and against the grain, as it were.

We note as well that postcolonial theory has been created and developed by members of the Global South diaspora who have been educated and now theorize in the elite universities of the Global North. They have sought to constitute more epistemologically inclusive research, theories and epistemologies. In rejecting epistemological innocence, we have also tried to research and theorize in epistemologically inclusive ways and continue to struggle towards such ends.

In what follows, we document the researcher positionality of each of us. Where we are positioned geographically, historically, economically, and in relation to career trajectories, gender, all matter. We are thus working with a concept of positionality here in relation to comparative education policy research that acknowledges, inter alia, our geographical and geopolitical locations, theoretical standpoints, career positionings, life experiences and location in a temporal sense (see Kabir & Chowdhury, 2021; Lingard, 2006; Rizvi & Lingard, 2010, pp. 46–9).

Rino

For me, the research reported in this book has as its backdrop a path-dependent and oftentimes contingent history of biographic complexities, intellectual confusions and unpredictable inner developments. My co-authorship of this work is an outcome of a relatively long academic journey that became ever refined. My birth and upbringing in a semi-urban 'city' of an overpopulated, less-developed country (Bangladesh) at a time of embryonic globalization left no room for me to realize the existence of another world, 'big, bright and beautiful', that needed to be accounted for. I was 'happy' with my limited life, not knowing that happiness could nuance degrees of comparison elsewhere.

It is during the time my teacher-father, after much agitation, managed to buy a Japanese black-and-white TV that my imagination expanded beyond my 'happy' town. For the first time, I was excited to see life in the capital city of Bangladesh, Dhaka. But something magical and enthralling settled in once Bangladesh Television started broadcasting American serials such as *MacGyver*, *The Fall Guy*, *Miami Vice*, *Thunder in Paradise* and so many irresistible others. Listening to Michael Jackson, Backstreet Boys, Richard Marx or Bryan Adams was one thing, but *seeing* them performing on stage was simply hypnotic within a world of my own – another world! Imagination, and a curiously agitating one, took hold of me, and I could not resist its presence within my inner engagements as it expanded later through the internet days continuing through to today! Some call it 'globalization'.

Running alongside this unsettling imagination was something deeply situated, something very 'local'. I recall those days of St Joseph's High School in Khulna city, an Italian-led Catholic school in Bangladesh from which my parents retired after more than thirty years of 'service in Christ' and where I was schooled. I have long forgotten the curricular learnings, most of them obsolete today; but I certainly remember the lasting marks that the schooling left on me. Only one thing in the school was constant for the ten years I was there: I was to sing the national anthem every day in the assembly with recurrent goosebumps. Deeply emotional, we were trained to love Bangladesh – as deeply as one's own mother. The idea that education was meant only for the benefit of others and of the nation our 'great leaders' so bravely freed for us was instilled in us. My imagination of life's movement never crossed such boundaries, even when I felt deeply indulged with my *MacGyver* imaginations, but again, until something else occurred.

In 2009, an academic from a US institution visited BRAC University (my then workplace), and I was to accompany her during her research trips to remote villages in Bangladesh. She asked if I had ever seen 'the other side of the world', to which I replied, 'Only on TV and the web.' But her very presence 'in person' and our 'trusted' conversations helped me imagine myself walking the streets of the other side of the world; if it were not a possibility, why would she ask? Imagination for the first time wanted to become action. Once it rose to a manifest level, I started searching for scholarship opportunities. Success in this enterprise took me to Denmark, Spain and, for the past five years, Australia. Experiences resulting from the active persuasion of a deep and powerful imagination have brought me to this book through paths of overlapping ideologies, patches of calibrated academic relationships, solitary tunnels of sometimes debilitating circumstances and life lessons that imagination can only operationalize when actively followed. The book is inspired by imagination (Anderson, 1983) at large and its world-making capacity (Appadurai, 1996). Ethnic, cultural, intellectual, aesthetic and artistic bases of my research and positionality are no longer rooted either in the East or in the West but grounded in some of the senses, sensibilities, rationalities and aspirations that I derive from my life to this point. It is complex and uncertain; but I am thankful for the journey and for the impetus to continue on.

Bob

I come to this research and the writing of this book very much aware of my own researcher positionality in relation to each. I accept Bourdieu et al.'s (1999) stance noted earlier that, in social science research, there is no such thing as epistemological innocence. That is, I agree strongly with Bourdieu's position that we need to articulate our positions in relation to the research object, both empirically and theoretically, so that we can get closer to good-quality social scientific analysis. I also acknowledge very much my position as a privileged white male, an emeritus professor at one of Australia's elite universities. However, I did come from a working-class family, and my parents only had primary education; I was very much a beneficiary of the post-war economic boom in Australia and the related expansion of secondary school and university provision. I was the privileged beneficiary of Commonwealth scholarships in both upper secondary education and at university. In a sense, my trajectory matched the claims of schooling and the construction of meritocracy and weakening of ascribed social characteristics on opportunities. I acknowledge that this was more likely to be the experience of working-class boys than working-class girls.

I understand the call from postcolonial theorists of the necessity of deparochializing our research (see Appadurai, 2001; Connell, 2007), that is, regarding the Global South as much more in research terms than simply sites where Northern theory can be applied, as simple sites of empirical data collection, rather than of academic theorizing. As an undergraduate at an Australian university I always wondered when we might study some Australian sociology and pondered whether there was, or indeed even could be, such a thing as an Australian sociological theorist and related theory. I was also located in a Northern elite university (Durham University) for a time during my MA studies. However, both the University of Queensland (where I did my undergraduate and PhD studies) and Durham University were located on the periphery, to some extent, of the large and influential, theory-producing elite universities in powerful Global North nations (e.g. the United States, UK, France, Germany), which have deep historical provenance on their side. This sense of a peripheral academic/intellectual location still remains, given so much of my career in Australia, even though with globalization, the mobility of contemporary academics has seen the periphery speaking back to the centre as it were. Today, some Australian academics have become leading world figures in various domains of the social sciences, including in education. Yet, I understand how Bangladesh, the focus of this book, is very differently positioned in the globalscape in global geopolitics than is Australia. It is also positioned differently in respect of globally flowing policyscapes.

I moved as an academic for a time to the UK and held professorships at both the University of Sheffield and the University of Edinburgh. At the latter, I held the prestigious Andrew Bell Chair of Education. Yet, I felt like an outsider, while acknowledging that what postcolonial theorists such as Edward Said would call 'displacement' (and I am not equating my privileged displacement with that of refugees of various kinds) was also an experience that provoked much learning for me. I had to question many of my taken-for-granted assumptions. I had much earlier (1975–76) completed an MA as an international student at Durham University and had a similar experience. Now, while Australia was colonized by the British, it was also a colonizer, having a devastating and unconscionable impact on Indigenous Australians and, at the same time, colonizing Papua New Guinea. Thus, Australia is positioned somewhat ambivalently as part of the Global North; so, for example, Australian academics are urged to publish in international high-status journals (read as non-Australian) with impact on academic writing and publishing and on the social sciences in Australia. I have visited much of Asia, taught in Singapore on a doctoral programme, advised and consulted in Hong Kong, visited India and many other nations in Asia and researched in Japan. However, I have not visited Bangladesh. What I know about Bangladesh has come for my working with doctoral students across time, including our co-author Rino Wiseman Adhikary. I have also read extensively about Bangladesh. Thus I need to say that this book has in part derived from the educative conversations the three co-authors of this book have had about empirical matters, research methodology issues and theory in the course of Rino completing a top-quality PhD at the University of Queensland on TFB. These conversations are manifest evidence of Said's point that he always learnt from teaching, and, for me, doctoral supervision has always been a deep and educative pedagogical experience. The three of us brought different experiences, knowledges and understandings to the PhD journey, and this book is one result of that collaborative learning. The writing of the book has been a truly collaborative learning experience and works from a stance which rejects epistemological innocence.

Ian

As a white, middle-class male working at a research-intensive university in a Western, albeit 'peripheral' Northern, context for a decade, who grew up in rural Australia and has not visited Bangladesh, I cannot claim to have substantive, first-hand knowledge or experience of the educational reform agenda described in this volume or of the Bangla context more broadly. My previous experiences of working at a regional university in New South Wales, Australia, teaching in schools in rural and suburban Queensland and my own experience of growing up in rural Queensland gave me some appreciation of the precarity that characterizes many individuals, families and communities, particularly in rural and regional Australia. However, this is of a different order to that characterizing the experiences of many peoples in many parts of the Global South, including Bangladesh. I cannot claim to have experience of the incredible disparity that seems to characterize the distribution of wealth in major centres in Bangladesh, such as Dhaka, or of the poverty and the struggle for survival that characterizes people's lives in many urban and rural communities throughout Bangladesh, and the subcontinent more broadly. I also have only fleeting experience of the sometimes incredible economic growth and development in some developing contexts (most notably central Java in Indonesia, when I was invited to give a guest lecture at the University of Muhammadiyah Purwokerto). While grounded in an earlier (paternal) generation's experiences of the hardships of establishing a livelihood in a harsh physical landscape, later (maternal) generational ethnic discrimination against 'Ities' (Italians) as 'new Australians', and more recent experiences of relative rural decline, my own background remains one of relative privilege, even as this is a privilege imbued with the sedimented effects of these earlier experiences and alongside more recent challenges that characterize working and living in increasingly performative and neoliberal environments characterized by rising nationalism, challenges to democracy and sociopolitical discord in the Global North.

However, my ongoing discussions and engagements with colleagues and students from many other countries, particularly from the Middle East, east Asia, south-east Asia and southern Asia, including Bangladesh, together with ongoing visits to several countries in Asia, Europe and North America, have engendered something of a more 'global' disposition than would have been the case had I not had the opportunity for such experiences. Working closely at the University of Queensland with an academic colleague originally from Bangladesh, and co-developing a project based on the educational experiences of school students in Bangladesh, has further helped to develop insights into the nature of educational practices in that context. Spending time with his family and engaging with other people from Bangladesh through his engagement with the Bangla community in Brisbane (and beyond) have been productive of a habitus inquisitive and interested in learning more about this country and its peoples. Working with Rino during the four years of his doctoral studies, and other Bangla students over the past ten years, and with Bob and other academic colleagues as a co-advisor with many international students over the years has helped enhance at least some preliminary understandings about the nature of educational provision in many countries, including Bangladesh. More recent, ongoing conversations between the three of us as authors of this volume, in conjunction with four years of engagement in prior roles as advisors and doctoral student, have enabled understandings that would not have been possible otherwise and at least some confidence that the second and third authors might presume to be involved in the production of a volume such as this. These discussions and associations continue and are generative and iterative as well as being productive and ongoing.

Chapter Structure

Logic of the Book Structure

While the original study (Rino's PhD; see Adhikary, 2019) informing this book focused empirically on TFB as a specific, localized (at a national level) manifestation of the broader 'global' Teach For movement, a localized globalism (Santos, 2002), TFB was revealing of only part of the story of the local constitution of the Teach For movement. Rather more curiously, TFB sat integrated between a history of partnership-based reforms in the governance of public education and a movement for social entrepreneurial reconstruction of public sector provisions in Bangladesh. Clearly, the initial 'network ethnography' undertaken to map out and understand the make and movement of TFB revealed the influence of a large network specific to the TF phenomenon in Bangladesh. However, while interviewing 'on the ground', this network multiplied and involved a range of state but mostly extra-state actors clustering into two other networks revealing to the transformations within which TFB sat. Like the one specific to TFB, such networks included a variety of social entrepreneurial individuals and groups who were seeking to influence both the provisions of primary education and broader public sector in Bangladesh.

However, while the original research 'began' with network ethnographic efforts to understand TFB, one methodological outcome of our theoretical-empirical analysis has been the approaching of policy networks in terms of what Peck and Theodore (2015) have referred to as 'policy making worlds'. We view networks as aspirational assemblages constitutive of and active within such worlds of policy and governance within which spatio-cultural formulations and spatio-temporal dynamics underpin various dimensions of powerful flows that networked actors leverage in their efforts to influence policy or steer an agenda. In the empirical chapters of this book, that is, in Chapters 3, 4 and 5, we have analysed and presented three such worlds and the singular or multiple networks that such worlds of policy overlappingly demonstrated. Thus, broadly speaking, we have presented in this book multiple networks of both policy and governance. Chapter 3 is about the history of governance networks within the Bangladesh DPE; Chapter 4 is about a movement-like network that influenced the NGOAB; and Chapter 5 is about TFB and its organizational networks.

However, related to the 'network' theme highlighted in the title of this book, this research revealed the influence of several crucial networks, including a key donor consortium (led by the World Bank), a broader NGO network (representing civil society within DPE), an epistemic network (led by the British Council Bangladesh) and, not least, a policy network led by TFB. As will be highlighted in every chapter in relevant methodological sections, our ethnographic approach to networks has been informed by topological analytics (see Chapter 2), whereby the spatio-cultural formulation of influence within policymaking worlds will be our analytical foci. Seeking to complement network ethnographic methodologies, understanding these networks, through a more ethnographic network approach, became crucial. It is here we provide a network of ethnographies, including our initial network ethnography.

In this book, we build upon these initial learnings and insights, eventually focusing not so much on TFB in and of itself but foregrounding the nature of networks that were instrumental in promoting TFB as a key part of an infrastructure of social enterprises that sought to influence and reconstitute the very nature of public education provision in Bangladesh. It is these networked efforts at rearticulating what educational provision should look like that is our primary focus in this volume. Our emphasis is on TFB as a social enterprise, and our approach is that of a comparative policy sociology in education study. Complementing their situatedness within a country site, we compared multiple (three) sets of networks on the basis of the homogeneity of their cultural essence – social enterprise. In so doing, spatialities and cultural dimensions were our ethnographic categories that would embrace any unit of analysis having some form of cultural enclosure, while network is the dominant form today. Indeed, culture today in no longer gate-kept exclusively by the nation-state, and all the ways in which cultural dimensions can have impact must be taken into account. This is one benefit of a policy sociology of networks approach.

Chapter Overview

Chapter 2 outlines the theoretical resources that helped inform the research reported in this book. Beginning with a theory-driven appraisal of globalization, this chapter, in one sense, views globalization as a respatialization of governance at large. This rationale helps approach education policy 'topologically', that is, in renewed consideration of changing spatialities, culture and power associated with globalization (Amin, 2002). We explain how the topological refers to the enhanced significance of relations over locations, facilitated by new communication technologies. We explore each of these fundamental concepts – spatialities, culture and power – and how they inform our understanding of policy mobility in the context of educational reform in Bangladesh. We argue that even as globalization processes are evident at the level of the local, failing to consider the imbrications (Lingard, 2021) between mobility (global forces) and fixity (older territorial structures of authority) (Peck & Theodore, 2015) means that any attempt to understand education policy is at best partial.

In Chapter 3, we apply for the first time the conceptual resources outlined in Chapter 2 to understand the nature of the network-centric transformations that have occurred in the past few decades within the PESoB. Additionally, we seek to explicate such processes in relation to the governance of primary education in Bangladesh. We focus particular attention on the PEDP as the principal entity responsible for enhancing primary education provision in Bangladesh through various partnerships, and how this programme came to be heavily influenced by a range of influential policy actors working together in networks. In broad terms, network-centric transformations in policy and governance of PESoB are historicized in this chapter. We reveal the history of global-local actors and organizations, whose aspirations and determination have sought to institutionalize networks within PESoB as a model of governance for system management and partnerships. Such an historical approach to system-level governance underscores the 'context of context' (Peck & Theodore, 2015) to help make sense of the rise and role of networks in educational policy and governance in the country. PESoB is now a 'world of policy' governed for and by networks that imbricate (Lingard, 2021) the global and the local/national in spatio-cultural ways signifying new waves of modernity (Escobar, 1995), indeed, modernity at large, as it were (Appadurai, 1996).

In Chapters 4 and 5, we elaborate on the character of social enterprises and the ways in which education NGOs such as TFB are transmogrifying into social enterprises (SEs) with significant future implications for the governance of the primary education sector in Bangladesh. We note that governance does not replace the more traditional practices of government and bureaucratic structures and practices but rather works with these in inflected and hybridized ways. Unlike the focus of Chapter 3, which emphasized the historical making of a 'governance network' that acted more like a heterarchy (Ball, 2012), Chapter 4's attention is primarily focused on a loosely coupled, comparatively fast-paced 'policy network' (Ball & Junemann, 2012). Orchestrated by the British Council of Bangladesh (BCB) this network functioned much like an advocacy movement. We demonstrate how the BCB was a globally networked yet locally active organization, which sought to influence the NGOAB, the national authority overseeing NGO activities and foreign charitable funding in Bangladesh, and to which TFB was accountable. Chapter 4 shows how the BCB as an SE model is being imagined as a broad policy panacea for all public service sectors in Bangladesh. Analysis revealed that SE policy was being actively pursued by an 'epistemic [policy] community' (Ball & Junemann, 2012) comprising glocal actors (Lingard, 2014a; Robertson, 1994) who leveraged a grounded footing within the larger policy landscape of the country. Nuancing such dynamics, we have captured the unique and fast policy sociology (Peck & Theodore, 2015) that empirically illustrated an emerging drive from NGOs to social enterprises or their hybridization in Bangladesh. TFB itself exemplified one such hybrid entity currently active within the primary education subsector of Bangladesh.

While Chapter 3 observed the rise and remit of 'governance networks' in the form of a System Wide Approach to Programming within the Bangladesh DPE, and Chapter 4 revealed a quango leading a movement-like policy network seeking to influence the NGOAB in favour of a social enterprise sector and complementary policies, Chapter 5 revisits TFB's social entrepreneurial imagination and the way such an imagination imbricated the global and the local. TFB manifested 'officially' in the form of an NGO that sought to have substantive, 'large scale' impact on public education provision. The chapter reveals how those involved, including the founder of TFB, sought to govern teacher education as a social enterprise, with TFB as the primary vehicle through which these governance processes were to be undertaken.

Chapter 6 concludes the book. We summarize our insights and contributions, including the need to conduct on-the-ground ethnographies to complement network ethnography; TFB functioning as a de facto social enterprise; TFB as part of the broader transformation of NGOs as social enterprises; the potential future impact of this social enterprise approach on restructuring public schooling and more broadly the public sector in Bangladesh; the de- and re-territorialization of the concept of social enterprise; the significance of the imagination to the reforms documented; and the implications of our research for both comparative education and policy sociology in education.

2

Theorizing Policy Mobilities in Education

Introduction

This chapter outlines the wider theoretical resources which framed the research on Teach For Bangladesh (TFB) reported in this book. We begin by appraising globalization theoretically and emphasizing that globalization in one sense is a respatialization of governance at large. This rationale provides a useful direction to approach education policy 'topologically', that is, in renewed consideration of changing spatialities, culture and power associated with globalization (Amin, 2002). 'Topological' refers to the enhanced significance of relations over locations facilitated by new communication technologies. We explore each of these fundamental concepts, spatialities, culture and power to inform our take on policy mobility in the context of education and reform in Bangladesh. Even in relation to this less-developed setting, and for reasons outlined in Chapter 1, globalization dictates that without considering the imbrications (Lingard, 2021) between mobility (global forces) and fixity (older territorial structures of authority) (Peck & Theodore, 2015) any attempt to understand education policy risks missing the mark. Peck and Theodore (2015) have explicated this fixity-mobility binary, arguing that there is a tension between them in both the policymaking imagination and making policies work in local contexts. On the latter point, they observe that *'making policies work* very often remains a hands-on, messy and very much "local" affair' (Peck & Theodore, 2015, p. xvii; emphasis original). These matters are also considered in the conclusion of the book, Chapter 6.

'Imbrication' is a concept worth paying close attention to from the outset. Recent sociological research on spatialities suggests a useful definition of imbrication as the 'blending' or 'layering' of 'components', which manifests as 'an interweaving of the existing and the created', 'the natural and the built' (Loughran, 2016, p. 312). What is notable in Loughran's (2016, p. 311) argument is that imbrications are meant as and for 'transformations ... into culturally valued spaces'. Thus, culture and cultural formulations are central to any form of imbrication of the intended global and the apparently local/national, which are often expressed in terms of mobility and fixity, respectively. Viewed as such, Loughran contends that imbricated spaces are socio-spatial intersections and related agentic representations of hybrid cultural value.

Returning to the topological: in our view, intellectual reflections on how spatialities, culture and power overlap and constitute globalization as respatialization of governance promises specific benefits. It helps approach policy sociology without having to entertain an a priori ontology and allows for a wider angled theoretical lens to discover networks as a part of spatialities. Moreover, within this broader framing, we can engage with a more curious account of *why* networks are empirically and theoretically central to our study, and thus, methodologically important as well. We are thus able to locate concepts such as networks and heterarchies within the grand spatio-cultural mechanisms of globalization by conceptually framing the overarching firmament within which education policy occurs today – the topological environment.

The topological environment of globalization basically facilitates conditions necessary for 'efficient impact' through spatio-cultural formulations, in the main. Such an efficiency logic proliferates in the form of a 'topological rationality' – empirically, theoretically and methodologically. This is understandable in terms of three overlapping axes: spatialities, culture and power. In relation to globalization, spatialities invite conceptual clarity on place, space and time to reappraise the argument that space and place can no longer be understood in separation, as ontologically distinct and more so with implications for policy mobilities. *Spaces* are networked and immanent forces in relation to *time*, while *places* are moments of encounter (and therefore ethnographic) wherein networked forces (heterarchies and things; global, national and local) negotiate and establish meanings of an intended practice (e.g. a reform). This is the topological sense of *spatiality* of culture and power on the basis of which we performed our conceptual, empirical and methodological work.

Our second heuristic axis – *culture*, in the topological sense – means the emerging prioritization of connectivities, relationship, interest and affect (nationally and internationally) over considerations of locational situatedness in cultural formation, expression and influence. Here, think of the online drive in relation to the ongoing pandemic. We finalized this volume at the end of 2020, when the 2019 coronavirus had reasserted itself throughout much of the world, particularly Europe and the United States. Interestingly, the pandemic has seen some strengthening of national borders, while at the same time demanding a global response.

Culture is increasingly becoming a globally relational field of co-emergence, whereby continuous change is manifest through the creation and utilization of various (re)ordering practices (spatial) that activate continuity of a specific practice (e.g. a reform policy). In respect of governance and regarding the third axis, the topological manifestation of 'power' can be traced through the prioritization of power-relationships, reach and presence, although in differing degrees in different contexts, in the ways both governments and heterarchies operate today. Insofar as our empirical analyses reveal, 'power' lies in the ability to constitute and control reach, proximity and presence, which are what heterarchies and their interlocutors (Ball, 2012) muster in terms of relational, material and cultural influences.

Methodologically, the deployment of such topological analytics to understand how education policy mobility and mutation (Peck & Theodore, 2015) now occur in a less-developed context has become theoretically essential and empirically insightful. It is within this topological environment and particularly through various cultural formulations mediated by coercive authorities (Castells, 2016, p. 2) that policies move, reach a fixity, mutate with/in (Peck & Theodore, 2015) and become imbricated gradually (Lingard, 2021). Vis-à-vis less-developed contexts, albeit in potentially differing ways, education policy itself has experienced a topological turn in relation to spatialities, power and culture. As the topological manifests itself, what ties the globally mobile forces and mutating national/local fixities to each other are imbricative processes of culture (see, e.g. Adhikary & Lingard, 2019; Lingard, 2021) that demonstrate asymmetric power dynamics and unequal flows/scapes of resources (Appadurai, 1996).

From this broader theoretical postulation on the topological environment for/of policy and the central role that cultural formulations play, we will engage in developing a methodological stem adapted from Appadurai's anthropological thinking on dimensions of cultural flows of globalization. That is, we move from the topological environment to agentic mechanisms of cultural flows that carry resourceful cultural content (be it cricket or a reform) and then vernacularize the same in various national/local sites through what Appadurai (1996) refers to as 'imagined worlds' in the plural.

We argue that it is this world-making capacity and force that have become 'globalizable' and constitute the performative soul of the topological environment. With shared aspirations and formative images (thus cultural), such imagined worlds are the creations of imagined communities (networks). Powerful aspiring actors (not all) from such networked communities co-constitute and participate in moments of encounter (place as placement of practice) wherein the global and the local are incrementally imbricated and then institutionally stabilized. Finally, we will conclude the chapter by discussing practical decisions we had to consider regarding our approach to the empirical work reported in this book.

Topological Policy Environment of Globalization: Spatialities, Culture and Power

Globalization theories revolve around some key themes. For instance, while Appadurai (1996) presents the cultural dimensions of disjunctive flows or scapes (people, money, media, technology and ideas/ideologies), de Sousa Santos's (2002) emphasis is on local rootedness of influence in globalizing and further localizing any cultural phenomena (e.g. policy). As Bourdieu's (1993) field analytics continue to ontologize the global, the politics of scale and associated power reconfigurations (Brenner, 2004; Jessop, 1998, 2000; Robertson & Dale, 2008) within states enable influences of multiple kinds. As time, space and distance compression, facilitated by new technologies, imbue our existential and spatial senses (Amin, 2002; Thrift, 1999), the rise of networked global cities and their influences on national policy arenas become even stronger (Sassen, 2002, 2007, 2013).

When Bourdieu (2003) critiques globalization in dominant discourses as equivalent to neoliberal economic globalization, de Sousa Santos (2002) views it as the mobilization of a concrete meta-policy. Insofar as the performative neoliberal, network modalities and spatial reorganizations of sociopolitical action (Amin, 2002; Castells, 2000; Massey, 1994a; Thrift, 1999) represent global forces, the functioning and structure of the state continue to mediate globally oriented change (Rhodes, 1997; Rosenau, 1997; Ball, 2013, 2012). While heterarchical governance and globalization demonstrably evoke a respatialized environment of hyper-speed, mobility and connectivity (topology[1]), the older territorial and scalar formulations do not fully disappear from any comprehensive appreciation of power (Allen, 2009, 2011). As Raymond Williams (1977, pp. 121–8; 2005, pp. 40–2) argues, cultural phenomena, for example, power, influence or governance, currently are and have always been an admixture of the residual, the dominant and the emergent. This is the present haunted by the past and the future immanent in the present.

These intellectual resources nuance the power 'to govern'. Albeit differences in perspectives and positionalities, these theories mark the deeper sociopolitical and cultural respatializations that have introduced new modes of emergent power. Such new spatial and cultural forms of power supplement and compete with older residual ones, all captured within the dominant forces of neoliberal aspirations. For one thing, the context of these transformations is characterized by complex dynamics of flows, fields, scales, spaces and relationships, which can be understood as spatialities or spatializations. These spatialities and relationships are affecting the nature and functioning of power in politics, policy and governance.

For certain, these two observations can be reciprocal, and they conceptually invoke a new configuration in the complex imbrication between global/transnational power and the functioning of government/bureaucratic authority within a nation. While the nation-state still remains the imagined (Anderson, 1983) yet constitutionally demarcated territory of political deliberation and cultural reasoning, globalization turbo-charges transnational speed, connective intensity and spatial extensions (Allen, 2009). It is in this transformative context that the imbricative role of heterarchies is to be understood, for they work through networked relationships, extended and anchored spatialities and sustained connectedness. They are the navigators of porous borders.

Globalization is thus a process of, a reason for and an outcome of transformations that need to be understood in relation to the new spatialities that seek to exercise imbricative impact on enduring relationships that govern nation-states and societies. When no single definition would suffice, Held and his colleagues' (1999) take on globalization seems to capture the essential transformative details relevant to policy mobilities. These authors view globalization as

> a process (or set of processes) which embodies a *transformation* in the *spatial organization of social relations and transactions* – assessed in terms of their extensity, intensity, velocity and impact – generating *transcontinental or interregional flows* and *networks of activity, interaction*, and the *exercise of power*. (Held et al., 1999, p. 16; emphasis added)

Evidently, globalization is a transformation of power geometry through spatial reorganization of governance of societies. If 'spatial organization' is the 'outcome' of 'attempts to use *space efficiently*' (Adams, 2016, p. 54, emphasis added; Morrill, 1974), spatial organization of society must reorder 'population, spatial distribution of movements, space usage, distance, distribution of economic activities and wealth, cultural and political conditions and historical development' of a society (Klapka et al., 2010, p. 54; Morrill, 1974). An attempt to efficiently organize such socio-spatial factors is practically an act of governing social life by setting new fields and rules of the game. These spatial de-formations and re-formations are the result of powerful global imaginations (Appadurai, 1996). To put it simply, governance as a game (not in the literal sense) is to be played within a global field of plurality, within a global firmament of multiplicity and with a global/izing local mindset.

Thus, the transformation referred to earlier in Held and colleagues' definition means activating a global form/scale of governance as an outcome of spatial (re)organization rationalizing efficiency. When it comes to globalization in the active/verb sense, efficiency is the dominant logic and denominator for acceptance and acknowledgement of power. Accordingly, globalization is to be seen as reconfiguration of the power of governance through spatial reorganization of the social and its economic and political properties on efficiency grounds. Globalization is indeed governance through spatial reorganization of movements, space, distance, economy, culture and politics in ways where capabilities associated with networks, flows and interactions translate into an ability to exercise power assessed in efficiency terms. This needs to be acknowledged, insofar as global-local imbrications matter in relation to the ways nation-states function in the face of globalization.

In Held and colleagues' (1999) definition, the presence of 'transcontinental or interregional' stands as the flipside of the absence of the 'national/state', again marking the new spatialities and possibilities of power. In this sense, transcontinental and interregional can nonetheless be viewed as a proxy for the transnational, for transcontinental is a territorial and geographic demarcation containing nation-states with political, social or cultural specificities, while regional structures are often powerfully supranational and can lead to regional transnationality (think of the EU, and the Schengen visa). Therefore, the resulting 'flows and networks of activity, interaction' and 'the exercise of power' are clearly trans*national* or supra*national*, while the national as suffix still denotes sites of negotiation and sharing of power. Visibly, the scope and nature of the exercise of power have been respatialized; so have been the coordinates of activities, exchanges and relations that new global powers influence or intend to govern.

This respatialized and globally imagined (Appadurai, 1996) governance environment empowers actors that have the ability to exert influence in terms of breadth, depth, speed and acceleration, particularly because changes are assessed in terms of 'extensity, intensity, velocity and impact'. That is, 'change' itself has become the target of efficiency, while spread, depth, speed and acceleration become rubrics for assessing change (impact). Therefore, globalization itself is a process of governance that enables and governs transnational flows, and networks of activities and interactions, where power predominantly lies in speed, acceleration, relationships and connectivities associated with an intended continuum of impact (power to change). Globalization is about spatially activating and enabling the creation of networked systems of efficiency (heterarchies), wherein different forms of power come together and are imbricated to localize 'change' as a normalized continuum (Lury et al., 2012, p. 5). As a transformative process of respatialization, globalization opens up new horizons of possibilities and continuities, particularly for those (including state actors) who can go with the flow, connect and network, and thereby exercise power.

Nevertheless, this changing scenario of governance through spatialities of culture (networks and flows) unfolds in the context of, but also as a result of, the global rescaling of contemporary politics. Such rescaling involves a set of processes, arrangements and mechanisms that enable new relations and agencies inside, beyond and beside the nation-state to practise power and influence, often involving substantial state restructuring (see Brenner, 2004, p. 105; Lingard, 2009, p. 226; Robertson & Dale, 2008, p. 204). The empowerment of heterarchies through the activation of speed, acceleration, networking and connectivities underscores a need to review and reconstruct fundamental concepts of spatialities that facilitate and restrict human action.

Spatialities

'Space' has generally been imagined as 'out there', 'heterogeneous', 'outside of the nation' and more recently 'global', whereas 'place' is understood as 'in here', 'local', 'homogenous' and 'inside the nation' (see Amin, 2002; Massey, 1994a, 2006). Although the foundational signifiers ascribed to spatialities have remained largely unchanged (space, place and time), their meanings have been reconstituted in the face of emerging power properties of globalization. The Euclidian place-space dichotomy has given way to post-Euclidian spatialities understood in terms of 'relationality' and 'reach', basically the topological (Allen, 2009).

When it comes to influence and impact, relationships and reach now matter more than spatial distance and temporal situatedness. Globalization has enabled and placed alternative forms of spatial manifestations at the heart of the intended efficiency in governance. Think of heterarchies, global networks, cyber spaces, social networks, free trade zones. These manifestations, acting as various forms of forces, cut across multiple times, spaces and places coalescing into powerful effects of agency for influence and impact. This shift has recently been explained using vocabulary from political geography: 'topological spatialities', 'topological power', 'topological culture' and 'topological rationality' (see Allen, 2009, 2011; Amin, 2002; Lewis et al., 2016; Lewis & Hardy, 2017); topological denotes relationality, connectedness and reach. For the topological, relations are more important than location.

The ontology of globalization articulated earlier reflects a globalizing situation where 'stretching and deepening of *social relations* and *institutions* across space and time' have become of such enormity and power that both our ordinary life and systems of governance are being profoundly impacted by events 'happening on the other side of the globe' (Held, 1995, p. 20; emphases added). In this context, space-place-time relationships must be rethought as in sync with this rise of 'routinised action at a distance' and 'global connectivities and flows' (Amin, 2002, p. 386). Indeed, the global pandemic is a good illustrative example, yet it also demonstrates the ongoing significance of the national. Although the scalar understanding of the state (Brenner, 2004; Jessop, 2000; Robertson & Dale, 2008) still remains as one thread of spatial reasoning that speaks partially to the power dynamics of globalization, Amin (2002, p. 386) maintains that a 'topological appreciation' of spatiality is essential to understanding the nature and dynamics of other forms of relational and cultural spatializations of power that are 'not reducible to scalar spaces' but have become increasingly pervasive. Even states themselves have started to demonstrate topological spatialities and functions inside their territories (Allen & Cochrane, 2010, p. 1072).

This emphasis on flows, relationships and connectivities (topology), both in practice and in theory, constitutes the topological or relational 'logic' that, according to Amin (2002, p. 386), offers 'a heterotopic[2] understanding of place'. 'Places', Amin contends, need to be conceptualized as 'sites *in* networked or virtual *spaces* of organisation'. While place here is viewed as a site of/for '*placements* of *practices* of might be better varied geographical stretch', 'space' is understood as 'immanent forces' of various kinds: discursive, emotional, affiliational, physical, organizational, virtual, technological and institutional (Amin, 2002, p. 386; emphases added).

Spaces are also carriers of 'organisation, stability, continuity, and change'. Therefore, network has a *net* dimension, which is the immanent space of force that seeks to organize and govern. It also has a performative side, *work* that represents the placement/ anchoring of practice. If put into an equation, Allen's (2009, 2011) argument rightly stands as: 'network = net + work'; highlighting that both space and place, that is, spatialities, are involved here: 'net' in the sense of webbed space/s of relations and connections with collective aspirations (Appadurai, 1996), and 'work' as the negotiated placement of practice in the form of place. In both 'net'ing and 'work'ing, there is an element of topology in the relational sense, for even the latter may involve practical onsite work with underlying primacy of relationalities and connectivities (Allen, 2009, 2011).

This heterotopic understanding of space and place fits well with Massey's (1994a, 2006) articulation of postmodern spatialities. She argues that space and place need to be viewed as interconnected, as an interwoven context of temporal continuum and of course relationally:

> If, however, the spatial is thought of in the context of space-time and as formed out of *social interrelations* at all scales [i.e. immensity of the global], then one view of a place is as *a particular articulation of those relations, a particular moment in those networks of social relations and understandings*. But the particular mix of social relations which are thus part of what defines the uniqueness of *any* place is by no means all included within that place itself. *Importantly, it includes relations which stretch beyond the global as part of what constitutes the local* [-imbrication-], *the outside as part of the inside*. (Massey, 1994a, p. 5; emphases added)

The outside as a part of the inside, but increasingly vice versa, is what we mean by imbrication. In the aforementioned iteration, 'space' has to deal with 'time', whereas 'place' has to do with 'moment'. The continuous 'time' of a 'space' contains one/few moment/s that create/s 'places', when place is the placement of practices. Think of meetings, panel discussions, policy dialogues, seminars and so on. This means we can have spaces both globally and locally but through continuous interactions and relationships over time. We can have networks of global spread, of local span and of a 'glocal' hybrid nature. These are spaces created through networked relationships that can have global, local and glocal actors and with temporal continuity. These are spaces of policy. But when a specific articulation of those relationships is generated (placement of practices, by an active network) at a particular moment, a space for that moment becomes a meaningful place.[3] That is, the relationships within a space of continuity constitute a place when those relationships are given a purposive and eventful meaning in the form of a placed practice. The point to note here is that not all but only the relations which stretch beyond (local but also global) are included in the creation of a place.

Thrift (1999, p. 317) rightly views places as 'hybrids, but a contextual one' where 'copresence has become less important to successful associations'.

In this sense, policy events (such as policy dialogue) are places of meaningful moments through which spaces of networks anchor within nation-states. Thus, to Massey, place is the momentary but effective construction of a particular 'here' through a meaningfully occurring 'now'. As she argues:

> Then 'here' is no more (and no less) than our *encounter*, and what is made of it [in the/is moment or encounter]. It is, irretrievably, here *and* now. It won't be the same 'here' when it is no longer now ... [and] something which might be called there and then is implicated in the here and now... 'Here' [as place] is an intertwining of histories in which the spatiality of those [others'] histories (their then as well as their here) is *inescapably entangled*. (Massey, 2006, p. 139; emphases added)

Thus, 'places' are moments of encounter, wherein forces are embattled not to fight – not anymore – but to negotiate, win and establish meaning of an intended practice (e.g. an education reform). In these moments of encounter, multiple senses and sensitivities of past history and current trajectories of possibilities come together to negotiate the placement of a practice. However, Amin's (2002) focus on practice and Massey's (1994a, 2006) attention to time (history) in defining spatialities of globalization shed light on how heterarchies speed through and create history by soliciting authority through the placement of practices. The networks, which are the constructed vehicles of heterarchies, have their own space; but the impact of those spaces is achieved and extended through the creation of places, indeed heterotopic ones wherein imbrication happens through un/successful encounters.

In this view, places are micro-sites for interactive negotiation of history and meaning underlying the placement of a practice – a trajectory, a continuity, a reform policy. People with the right kind of knowledge, abilities and resources for negotiation become the focus of networking. This renewed understanding of spatialities is inherently topological. Here what matters is networking with the right kinds of relationships (ordering of resources) that can form the appropriate space of influence to later negotiate a practice. Indeed, the central role of imagination is marked here in such ordering of resources (Appadurai, 1996). Nonetheless, the negotiation of history and meaning brings to attention the notion of culture, for culture is key to influence (soft power), and it is constructed and governed spatially.

Culture

The cultural condition portrayed in Held and colleagues' (1999) definition of 'globalization' plays out in the main at a spatial level, which is further reflected and nuanced in Lury and colleagues' (2012) work. The latter group of scholars argues that culture in the context of globalization is increasingly being organized in terms of its capacity for change. On one hand, powerful 'relationships' (here heterarchies, but also other forms of networks) are becoming culturally impactful via global/local networks as they multiply and speed up; on the other hand, 'change' (reform) is reformulated and disseminated primarily as 'culture'. Change is also proselytized as 'constant, normal and immanent', challenging the traditional view of culture as 'exceptional or externally produced'[4] (Lury et al., 2012, p. 4). The result is, contend Lury and colleagues (2012), the rise of a new cultural rationality, where culture itself has become relational (as opposed to individual and subjective) and therefore ephemeral and 'topological'. These authors explain this topological turn in culture emphasizing that

> culture is increasingly organised in terms of its capacities for change: tendencies for innovation, for inclusion and exclusion, for expression, emerge in culture *as a field of connectedness*, that is, of *ordering by means of continuity*, and not as a structure based on essential properties, such as archetype, values or norms, or regional location. (Lury et al., 2012, p. 4; emphases added)

This spatial reordering of culture as in terms of its ability for change, and as a field of immersive connectedness, clearly means that culture is increasingly meant to become relational, open ended, connection based and continually experimental. This connectedness is no longer definable solely in terms of territorial embeddedness or associated frames of references. It is/has to be defined in terms of relationality. This is the a posteriori configuration of the cultural framing of globalization as a 'mode of ordering based on continuity'. This is the topological rationality, the connectivity logic of culture, where cultural 'topology' is

> the setting up of spaces of different kinds of order and continuity in such a way as to enable deformation or change, what Massumi (2002) calls the continuity of transformation. Alternatively, we can describe a topological *surface* as 'a relational field of emergence' (Manning, 2009; Parisi, 2012). (Lury et al., 2012, p. 8)

Therefore, the becoming topological of culture enables practising relationships as culture to be receptive to influence or to influence others. For networked heterarchies, it would be a spatial condition of flexibility and continuity where the impact of a space of deliberation and influence (a network of actors, organizations, resources, ideas and power) can be organized in different permutations and combinations of the connected properties, regardless of their temporal situatedness within distant and diverse settings. In this process, distance, time and territorial location become variables to and contingent upon the relative power of relationships and connectivities that seek to affect (the topological surface). Culture in this sense is no longer a preserved constant or a romanticized sensibility; rather it becomes a negotiated and continuous state of becoming with others, both relational and reflexive.

Topological cultural rationality is, therefore, the combination or arrangement of relationships at whatever point in time, the intended effect (one moment's placement of practice) of the 'relationships' between the entities and things within a space. As Parisi (2012, p. 166) rightly argues, 'Topology has introduced relations to the programming of culture.' We accept, then, that topology has introduced 'change' as a culture to the programming of relationships. Topologies (think of heterarchies) relate to impact and activate continuity as change and through change. Depending on the area and scope of change, heterarchies can flexibly 'net' and 'work', resulting in continuous change, where continuous change is culture.

Such a culture of change is possible only through topological construction and mobilization of spaces. It is topological in the sense that without the ability to modify and recombine relationships, continuous change is impossible. Topological surfaces are not meant to emerge and perish; they can rejuvenate or reproduce through alternative reorderings of existing properties or adding new ones in relation to encounter moments that underscore continuous change. This is the underlying topological rationality of change as culture – the becoming topological of culture. From this perspective, culture utilizes the power and logic of topology, while itself becoming a topological power.

Power

Globalization is a process of reorganized governance through respatialization of contemporary sociopolitical interactions, and economic transactions, accompanied by new modes and arrangements of power. Such power works alongside, across and increasingly within already existing institutional and territorial forms of authority. The rising prominence of relationships and connectivities in the formulation of power, or relationalities as a form of power itself, is coming to the fore (Allen, 2009, 2011; Allen & Cochrane, 2010).

Within the resulting new scheme of policy and governance, national political/administrative authorities now engage with and respond to influences and deliberations that emanate from a global configuration of 'placeless[5] power' (Castells, 2016). Such power operates topologically across but also within older territorialities associated with the nation-state. According to Manuel Castells (2016, p. 2), 'placeless power' is

> the *relational capacity* that *enables* certain *social actors* to *asymmetrically influence* the *decisions* of other actors *in ways* that *favour* the *empowered actors'* will, interests, and values. *Power* is exercised by means of *coercion* (the monopoly of violence, legitimate or not, by the state) and/or by the *construction of meaning* in *people's minds* through *mechanisms of cultural production and distribution*. (Emphases added)

Clearly, the power of relationships lies within relationships of power (Allen, 2009). This power of relationships increasingly overrides other forms and means of power. Such topological or relational articulation of power visibly highlights that nation-states still hold and exercise their power of authority and sovereignty; in Foucauldian terms, these are forms of disciplinary power (Foucault, 1975) and biopower (Foucault, 1978). But what we also see emerge, as Castells emphasizes, is 'cultural production' as a form of power – governmentality (Foucault, 1991b) manifested in the form of soft power (Nye, 1990). Related, Belcher and colleagues (2008, p. 499) argue that topological power is 'not a preformed category' exercised inflexibly upon a flat demarcated territory; rather it is a 'dynamic set of *techniques* of power' (emphasis added).

Important to note in this quotation, topological power can operate through both territorially defined spaces (e.g. nation-states, national media, etc.) and non-territorial spaces (e.g. social media) of control and influence (see Allen, 2009, 2011). Although a topological view of globalization, culture and power prioritizes matters of relationship over considerations of location and distance, it is not incompatible with Sassen's (2007, 2013) argument about the centralization of capitalist power within what she calls 'networks of global cities'. Sassen (2007, p. 23) argues that globalization, inter alia, needs to be viewed through deep reflection on the capital-power-circuitry of what she calls 'networked global cities'. She has identified the rise of a truly global economy comprising a network of approximately forty global cities (see also Castells, 2016). A global circuit of capital, investment and trade now flows through these cities, alongside their respective national economic processes and organization of wealth (Sassen, 2007, p. 23). This network of global cities, according to Sassen (2007, p. 24), represents a 'space of power' that holds the resources and capabilities necessary for global markets to enter and operate within national sites globally.

These global cities, and the powerful business 'tycoons' (Bishop & Green, 2008, p. 9) that inhabit them, today have strong entrepreneurial collaborations with the major cities of the Global South and their local governance systems (Sassen, 2007, p. 24). Sassen's view of global power articulated in terms of locations (global cities) hybridizes the topological sense of transnational power. It is in this sense that we see a network of cities – topographical but acting as topologies. The topologies of power may also be understood to have their moorings in territorial spaces, a view that seems to resonate with de Sousa Santos's (2002) argument that anything that is global has local roots. Therefore, rootedness within this circuitry of global cities can be a major source of power of resourcefulness for global elites and their transnational collaborators who localize reforms topologically.

Networks and Power

The remainder of the discussion on power of networks draws from Allen's (2009, 2011) works that seek to bridge the gap between territorial and non-territorial formulations of power,[6] while at the same time providing a topological understanding. Allen's (2009) view on how power is constituted and exercised in this globalizing time appears to bear strong correspondence with Castells's (2016) view. Allen argues that power can be understood as existing in and exercised through three axes of spatialities: bounded territories, networked flows and topological ties (Allen, 2009, p. 197). Of these three and their combinations, whatever the modality, power needs to be understood as 'reach, proximity and presence' vis-à-vis the placement of practice (Amin, 2002). That is, power is not just extensive, as often thought in relation to states' and corporations' expansion of centralized power over territory/ies. Rather, power is fundamentally intensive in the sense of power-actors' ability to make their presence 'felt at a distance', particularly through the practices of everyday life. This ability can be expressed or exerted through a 'topological mix of distanciated and proximate actions' (Allen, 2009, p. 198). Allen describes this ability to achieve 'reach' as the intensive and pervasive construction of power.

Restating the significance of relationships and connections across spatialities, Allen postulates that even territorially or scalarly articulated forms of power can nonetheless be understood as the result of various networked interactions. Besides scalar and territorial forms of power, new networked forms of power have become prominent as the 'organisational *reach* of the *new elites* and their institutional counterparts cut across political and economic borders' in combination with the 'new social movements and civil society organisations' (Allen, 2009, p. 202; emphases added). About these new forms of 'networked power' and 'power relations', Allen (2009, pp. 202–3) writes:

> The *new kinds* of connection and linkage that lie behind power relationships, in that sense, amount to a somewhat *covert form of resource mobilisation*. On this account, there are no pre-formed powers capable of extension, rather power is *generated* through the *mobilisation of resources within and across extensive networks*. (Emphases added)

Indeed, the power of networks lies in the ability to identify, connect, mobilize and utilize resources to foster impact at a global scale (see also Castells, 2016). This is where relationships start to embody a form of rationality. That is, if relationships and the resources that accompany them can become more powerful than other forms of power in achieving a global sense of impact, relationships are what we seek to become efficient at. Networks, thus, represent a fluid and cross-cutting medium – the 'net' space – that purposively connects resourceful individuals (Ball et al., 2017) and places (Sassen, 2007) together over short or long distances to pursue an apparently common goal (Allen, 2009; Appadurai, 1996).

These networks emerge as a response to the 'proliferation of globalised concerns' (efficiency and impact) that need to be efficiently addressed through action, bringing 'broad sweeping alliances' of 'geopolitical institutions and trans-governmental agencies' and 'the association of NGOs and political protest groups' together (Allen, 2009, p. 203). Thus, networks become powerful and are actually 'power networks' in two ways: one, enabled by technology, networks leverage[7] 'greater movement of resources to control outcome' (speed and diversity of resources mobility); and two, this controlling of outcome becomes possible across specialities (depth, breadth and modal variations of impact). Networked spaces are indeed 'carriers of power through their ability to transmit resources mobilized elsewhere' (Allen, 1999, p. 210).

However, the power dimensions of any network also include the 'work' of the network – 'the mediated *forms of interaction* which *effectively* bridge, broker and connect people and things together in some provisionally stable pattern of relationships' (Allen, 2009, p. 204; emphases added). These are practical processes of imbrication. The network itself is constructed by *capable actors*[8] who select other appropriate actors and facilitate connections between them. Thus the work of the network assumes its power in its 'ability to hook up' others to 'the process of circulation, to draw upon organisational resources to negotiate and persuade other actors to pursue certain goals' (Allen, 2009, p. 204). This is where the 'placement of practice' (Amin, 2002) unfolds both through concrete inter/action and through cultural mediation. The power of the 'work' involved in networking lies in the identification and connective utilization of 'power resources', where 'control', irrespective of spatial and temporal distances, 'merely represents the capacity to muster contacts, artefacts and information of one sort or another as a means to exert power' (Allen, 2009, p. 204).

Thus, a topological understanding of power is not only about how specific actors become more powerful through networked resourcefulness. Even more importantly, it is about how this networked power is utilized through specific practices and in specific ways that enable (quasi)-social 'proximity' and embedded 'reach' to make the powerful 'presence' of heterarchies felt among other powerful actors or among those not so powerful (Allen, 2009). Power topologies are therefore both 'power of connection' (resourcefulness), and 'power of reach' (anchoring influence) (Allen, 2011). Utilizing such arguments, we view heterarchies as power topologies. However, the earlier discussion on the nature of heterarchies in terms of spatialities, culture and power brings to the fore the power of topological rationality, which we suggest has now proliferated in the field of education policy (Figure 2.1).

This topological analogy is particularly relevant for examining the processes and practices of globalization as respatialized governance activated (e.g. through

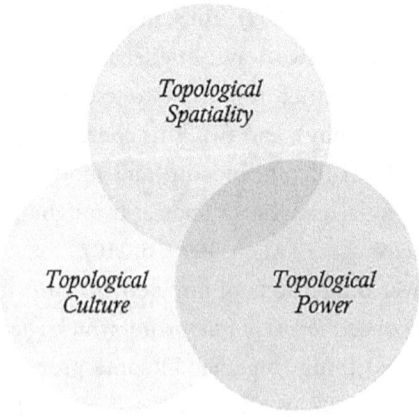

Figure 2.1 The three axes of topological rationality.

policy mobility). Here multisite coverage, long-distance movement and efficiency logics presuppose speed, mobility and reach in cultural, spatial and sociopolitical ordering practices as manifestations of topological formations. Topology refers to the most efficient and effective ordering of mobility, connectedness and reach underpinning imbricative power, while many different orderings are possible. And topological rationality can be understood as a form of reasoning that prioritizes the power of instrumentalizing direct relationships in obtaining optimal efficiency and impact. Heterarchies in education policy operate on such topological rationality that now predefines influence and impact through spatialities, culture and power. We will now turn our attention to the basis of our methodology, drawing from Appadurai.

Topologizing Appadurai: Imagination, Imagined Worlds and Cultural Imbrications

In this section we veer from understanding the topological environment to the topological agencies that imagine, carry and move cultural topologies in relation to policy mobility. We begin with Appadurai's argument that the global primarily occurs at the level of powerful imaginations capable of expansionary insight through what he refers to as 'imagined worlds'. Such imagined worlds act much like spaces wherein relevant portions and properties of authority of the national/local become imbricated. It is in such imagined worlds (here of policy) that the global and the national-local get imbricated by means of spatio-cultural formulations in the main. The broader topological environment of globalization is the firmament necessary for flows that give life to imaginations and imagined worlds.

Here we highlight a fundamental difference between the sui generis Andersonian focus on 'imagination' explanatory to classical modernity and its role in unifying community/nation effect (the largest possible denominator being the nation-state) (see Anderson, 1983), and the 'imagination' in the Appaduraian sense of modernity at large, meaning globalization of imagination in the sense of governmentality. The latter basically differs in its signification of globalization as the environmental facilitation or cultural enabler of the ability to imagine and manifest governable systems of various sizes and shapes as and through what Appadurai (1996, pp. 3, 33, 35 and 45) calls 'imagined worlds'. At the same time, being solid old or late, modernity itself is to be viewed fundamentally as a cultural process but also an historical one (see Escobar, 1995, p. 11).

According to Appadurai, such imagined worlds are results of the new practical roles given to imagination that are capable of large-scale formulations. And understanding this role requires consideration of 'mechanically produced images [think of cultural content], the imagined community [in Anderson's sense; in today's terms, a network] and the French idea of the imaginary (*imaginaire*) as a constructed landscape of collective aspirations [this is futuristic and relates to governance]' (Appadurai, 1996, p. 31). As Appadurai argues, collective aspirations today are 'no more or no less real than the collective representations of Emile Durkheim'[9]; it is undeniable that the strength of such imagined worlds can become no less powerful than ethnonationalism and thus become culturally governable units.

That 'powerful' imaginations – in fact imaginative regimes (Carney, 2009, p. 63) – now can, or are meant to, govern is the thesis here: think of philanthrocapitalism (Edwards, 2008) and managed charity affecting Third World systems at large. Often referred to as the 'n^{th}' generation of capitalism (Olmedo, 2016), this new philanthropic phase dovetails philanthropy with capitalism. Indeed, philanthrocapitalism thrives on

> *the imagination as a social practice* ... the imagination has become an organized field of social practices, a form of work (in the sense of both labour and culturally organized practice), and a form of negotiation between sites of agency (individuals) and globally defined fields of possibility. This unleashing of the imagination links the play of pastiche (in some settings) to the terror and coercion of states and their competitors. The imagination is now central to all forms of agency, is itself a social fact, and is the key component of the new global order. (Appadurai, 1996, p. 31; emphasis original)

Symptomatic of such developments, global corporations and family foundations run by billionaires are increasingly contributing to and participating in international systems (e.g. the UN, UNESCO) in framing globally definable issues and extending their governance solutions particularly into the developing world. In practice, the global unleashing of such 'creative capitalism' (Gates, 2008) governs through 'new philanthropy' (NP) and 'social entrepreneurialism'(SE) (see Ball & Junemann, 2012; Ball et al., 2017; Olmedo, 2016, 2017) nationally (see Chapter 6). The latter two, combined, denote an emerging 'culture' of service-governance that relies on a global system of social investment[10] and venture philanthropy[11] which often coalesce around various forms of funded global movements (Olmedo et al., 2013).

Appadurai further points out that such governance is increasingly becoming mediated by the complex prism of modern media, a process referred to today as deep mediatization of life itself (see Hepp & Hasebrink, 2018; Hepp & Tribe, 2013; Zuboff, 2019). Raising intellectual concerns, mediatized life has become the source of minable life-data (behavioural and thus predictive), so much so that such deeper behavioural data have become the driving currency ('behavioural surplus') of what Zuboff (2019) refers to as Silicon Valley surveillance capitalism. The bottom line is that imagination is no longer a passive psychological unifier of a community sentiment. It has now become powerful enough to create and govern systems of/through culture; imagination has become of utopic value for those who can manipulate its effects.

In this book, we analyse education policy in terms of imagination and cultural formulation, the central arguments of Appadurai's globalization thesis. It is by tapping into the world-making capacity of powerful global aspirations, of particular actors and associated systemic imaginations, that we trace the global-local imbrications in policy processes; we do so by studying locally situated places of action ethnographically. Our ethnographic approach is bottom-up. This is primarily because globalization itself is not definable without concrete practices and recognition of sociologically traceable imbricative impact on the nation-state (and vice versa). Basically, we shed light on what were some of the practical aspects of globalization of policy when it hit the Bangladeshi ground, specifically TFB in this context.

When mobility meets fixity, speed stops. Speed must stop at destinations to perform what it wants to achieve, or else all that remains is impact-less speed and mobility without purpose. Arguably, a key way of identifying impactful mobility today is to try to make sense of culturally situated individuals located within national systems administered to varying degrees by the state. While this does not eliminate the possibility of a truly borderless global future, the more recent resurgence of ethnonationalisms and anti-multilateralism surely has impeded that possibility for some time to come (Lingard, 2021). In fact, every speed is meant to be stopped at some point, at least for a while, for speed/mobility itself cannot constitute a meaningful social life, even as it is exciting. Speed/mobility has the ability to cover, surpass, bypass and discover the already unknown but existing. Speed of light gives omnipresence, that is, the ultimate imbrication of motion and fixity. But what next? Where exploration ends, governance begins, and we are entering another expression of the age of governance globalized. This has deep implications for education policy, governance and practices, as the analyses provided throughout this book will demonstrate.

Methodology and Empirics: From Network Ethnography to Ethnographic Networks

Despite the initiation of our empirical journey with 'network ethnography' (see Ball & Junemann, 2012; Howard, 2002), the nationally/locally moored nature of TFB helped us discover powerful new sets of locally active relationships that were not visible in the network maps we initially generated. Importantly, internet-based network mapping and information mining exercises – the first phase of network ethnography – brought out of the shadows the universe of relationships that broadly animated TFB and its links to a more global power grid alongside its local circuitry of authority. Following that, ethnography in the generic sense took hold as references were made by interviewees of the deeper systemic changes envisioned by a social entrepreneurial future of policy and governance, particularly in the overlapping sectors of education and NGOs. Consequently, it became critically important to catch global-local actors (networks) on occasions and in situations where they were actively performing the act of spatio-cultural formulations facilitative of a social entrepreneurial future – the placement of practice as a spatially framed encounter.

In regard to identifying such 'places' of spatio-cultural formulation, TFB enabled further discovery of 'sibling' empirical sites (policy 'worlds' parented by aspiring social entrepreneurial imaginations). Without the comparative analyses between these sites, TFB's story would be limited within organizational studies (i.e. as an NGO). It would also have been rather monolithic and would lose its representational value to a debilitating degree and at the cost of missing the undercurrents of the interweaving of national/local contexts (Peck & Theodore, 2015). TFB's global policy DNA with its local anchorage and efforts helped us reach a methodological vantage point not too far from or close to the phenomena we were studying: global-local imbrication in social entrepreneurship in education policy in Bangladesh. Such an onto-epistemological foothold helped address an echoing critique that too much policy work today is offered from a global gaze, eliding the local and bottom up (see Carney, 2019). Larsen and Beech (2014) have also critiqued policy analysis in contemporary times that only focuses on global-national, top-down unidirectional effects.

The more we got involved in the 'multiple worlds' (Appadurai, 1996) of policy made available by empirical study, the greater was the realization that there were performative spheres of connectivity active deep within the locally situated pockets of national authorities. It is in such arenas that the global-local imbrications were deeper, more nationally impactful and thus available to ethnographic procedures. We would like to define communities of such nationally performative agents of various kinds as 'ethnographic networks' (see Lingard, 2021, pp. 1–27). As they appeared, ethnographic networks are networks of locally/nationally effective 'action-communities' discovered in situ by participating in spheres of connectivity: meetings, seminars, conferences, policy dialogues, panel discussions, and social media groups besides interviews. Such spheres of activities contained the moments of placed encounters. By 'sphere', we mean an area/zone of activity, interest or expertise.

Interestingly, in all of the three cases ('policy worlds') we studied in relation to social entrepreneurship, we found two sets of overlapping and mutually inclusive networks: one, more globally endowed and oriented, the shadow network (head); and the other, incessantly active with/in the national cores of policy authorities, the active network (hand). These two sets of networks acted together as a form of dyadic spatiality, respectively, of reach (head) and influence (hand). Under these circumstances, the imagination (see Appadurai, 1996) of the head flew as cultural content through the hands extended flexibly from the head to the local or dovetailed into the head from within the local. In either case, we argue, global-local imbrications happened mentally first and at the level of imagination primarily. These imaginations and their cultural properties could be identified in the performances of ethnographic networks.

The shadow network is important here as the source of powerful imagination and associated expansive thinking. Undeniably, ethnography of the head network is extremely unlikely to be capable of being undertaken since it is often inaccessible and may require significant research budget and attention. Moreover, being in situ with the high-flying members of the shadow network is most often as difficult as an impossible dream for some. However, the ethnography of the hand network is possible by tapping into the active efforts of those situated and impactful locally.

We basically studied imagination as traceable in local manifestations (Appadurai, 1996); this was a bottom-up ethnographic journey beginning from the ground. The ethnographic approach adopted was to see what within the apparent fixities told us about the mobilities. We certainly could not be with and catch the mobile, but we could tap into ethnographic moments of apparent fixity, where discourses have local/national impact. It is in those active moments of influence and appraisal that local/national ethnographic networks fire up, produce light and make directions visible, if not acceptable for the time being.

What then is an ethnographic network? In this research, ethnographic networks were identifiably 'disjunctive' communities of locally/nationally 'active' agents of both global and local kinds, who we discovered as impactfully engaged in predesigned and piecemeal-style policy steering activities (Peck & Theodore, 2015) and that were also engaging the actors who mattered most within the national landscape of public policy in relation to social enterprise. We call the networks ethnographic since they were experienced and observed during a point in time within a routinized discursive situation,[12] when the global-local imbrications were being culturally acted upon and felt as in progression by the actors themselves.

Ethnographic networks were populated or were often driven by boundary spanners (Williams, 2005; also see Ball & Junemann, 2012, p. 113) who had interests derived from both the global and the local structures of opportunities created or at their disposal. To reiterate, ethnographic networks are networks of locally/nationally effective 'action-communities' discovered most importantly through participating in spheres of connectivity (with place as a moment of encounter, as a placement of practice). It is during those moments that global-local/national imbrications occur primarily as and through cultural appraisal involving various spatial forms wherein ethnographic networks exercise and rehearse. These events are now increasingly taking place online; however, the 'physical-less' presence does activate a different form of engagement. Insofar as meaningful collective engagements underpinning cultural content are identifiable and can be studied through engaged participation, we can safely call them ethnographic.

The Ontology of Globalization and the Bottom-Up/Top-Down Ethnographic Dilemma

Reflections about ontology demand their own space here. In relation to globalization, if our empirical focus is on the global as a beginning point, the epistemic approach becomes top-down and attention naturally falls to global networks; the onto-epistemological path itself is global. This is also because the global is theoretically predicated upon networks as the fundamental unit of operation. On the other hand, if we focus more on imbrications, the spatial ethnography of the local becomes the entry point. As far as an ethnographic understanding is important for any diasporic researcher in the West from the developing East, with very little global experience in terms of education policy, the local (imbricating/imbricated), indeed, this local site, is the only experientially meaningful gateway to understand the global (see Burawoy, 2000).

Think about the gap in approach and therefore knowledge between a motor mechanic and the manufacturing engineer: the former has in-depth knowledge of the car in relation to its usage, long-term problems and road performance; the latter is more production and design (theory and research) oriented. Much like a motor mechanic, for the developing world researcher, the study of policy mobility is more of a post-production discovery journey through channels and chambers that entertain or resist the touching down of the global. Ethnography appears feasible and doable for such researchers only when the car hits the roads and is accessible. A bird's eye (logocentric) ontology cannot make meaningful sense to such minds due to the very lack of their engagement with what is truly global outside of the nationally performative (Carney, 2019).

Thus, insofar as immersive and engaging first-hand data (data of presence) are concerned, such researchers are left with no choice but to stay close to the ground realities and explore upwards to discover some of the containers of global forces and their presence within the local – all by using, testing and extending theory informed by empirical evidence (Burawoy, 2000). Notably, the local today also reaches out to the global and contains it within various hybrid forms. Thus, this research took a bottom-up approach to policy analysis in the context of globalization and thus differs in onto-epistemological positioning from some of the most influential works of education policy. However, in our approach, we considered neither the global as the raging giant out there performing fast and furious accumulative effects upon the nation-state nor the nation-state as the decisive force dictating what enters, how and to what extent. Rather, we understand that this is a case specific to Bangladesh and similar to other situations; and also that the purpose of this scholarly exercise was to understand what the ground reality had to say about the global-local dovetailing in terms of cultural formulation of education policy.

While network ethnography has been developed further from the way we used it in our original research, we find it important to remain true to the field realities we experienced during the original research reported on in this book. We experienced and explored a methodological need for immersive engagement with compatible data between network ethnography and what we called ethnographic networks. Somewhat compelled by the field realities and dictations of data, what emerged to fill the anxious 'engagement gap' between network ethnography and ethnographic networks was something methodologically similar to 'global ethnography' (Burawoy, 1991) and particularly its 'extended case method' (Burawoy, 2009).

The anxiety seeded in fundamental questions, such as in what practical sense were we performing 'ethnography', to what end or even was it ethnography at all, forced and helped us into methodological innovation (see Adhikary & Lingard, 2019). The answers to such questions were not straightforward; yet they helped us navigate methodological reflections. We realized that although the study began with a network-centric ontology of policy, in actuality, we were seeking to identify the cultural and imaginative core of a mobile policy with its global ingredients.[13] We also had to spot the three connected cases (policy worlds) – TFB, the Primary Education Development Program (PEDP) and a British Council– policy advocacy network – that mediated the same social entrepreneurial cultural content in differing forms and scopes in relation to the education system of Bangladesh. We then aspired to ethnographically understand and compare the sociological processes of construction, dissemination, negotiation, actualization and finally institutionalization of variants of that (social entrepreneurial) policy within those locally connected policy cases.

It is at this stage that we felt we were performing something similar to ethnography of spatialities, a process referred to as ethnography spatialized (see Low, 2017).

This did not involve a homogeneous ethnos with/in a bounded cultural circumference, nor was it an ethnography without ethnos. For this certainly involved ethnography of an identifiable process of cultural formulation with and by a variegated ethnos sufficiently comprised of diaspora. This was an ethnos not in the sense of a nation, but in terms of a broader game of cultural appraisal (engagement) underpinning a social entrepreneurial imagination. The keys here were sociocultural imagination, the spatialities that hosted such eventful spheres and the forms and dynamics of effective engagement.

As a result, 'networks in action' or 'active networks' either newly emerged or were rediscovered through the navigational cues that network ethnographic interviews provided in reaching various spots that mattered most in relation to social enterprise policy. We discovered multiple sites of cultural production, arenas that Arjun Appadurai (2020, p. 5) refers to as 'comparable spheres of connectivity', where moments of encounter occurred. Such spheres of connectivity could certainly be studied ethnographically, for it is in such affiliational, negotiatory but also contested spheres that the global and the local 'engage' in the act of imbrication and become imbricated; and we argue that this imbrication is primarily cultural and imagination driven (Appadurai, 1996).

Thus, our focus on culture and cultural formulation, which is the heart of the matter of ethnography, opened new opportunities for exploring social production – in this case, in the 'context of engagements' with 'bodies, language, affect, translocality and their impact on how we navigate space/place' (Low, 2017, p. iii). Low's view of ethnography provides further scaffolding to what we have done and are proposing in terms of fieldwork for ethnographic networks. Consider the following, which we will elaborate further in relevant sections:

> Ethnographers have an advantage with regard to understanding space and place because *they begin their studies in the field* [resonance with Burawoy]. Regardless of whether it is a long-term study or rapid ethnographic assessment of a place, a *multisited analysis* of a region or a comparison of circuits of mobility and movement, there is an *engagement with the inherent materiality and human subjectivity of fieldwork*. Conceptualisations of space and place that emerge from the sediment of ethnographic research draw on the strengths of studying people *in situ*, producing rich and nuanced socio-spatial understandings. (Low, 2017, p. 4; emphases added)

Conclusion

We began with the hope of applying 'network ethnography' to examine and understand TFB. But we eventually ended up with 'ethnographic networks' of various sizes, shapes and kinds, allowing for ethnographic comparisons of 'spheres of connectivity'. In all of these sociological processes, our target was to understand key mechanisms of global-local imbrications 'performed' within sociological spots that are frequently virtual. It is this ethnographic hunt for performance and action (in situ) underpinning social enterprise – the cultural content – that led us to spheres of performative cultural engagement. Insofar as ethnography is the study of culture, we felt we were methodologically well calibrated in ensuring the fit between means and ends.

In the main, methodological decisions were taken in relation to a policy sociology approach that combined two empirical methods, namely, 'network ethnography' and 'global ethnography'. While global ethnography usefully presents the local as the empirical container of the global, network ethnography offers practical and innovative ways of capturing the relations, resources, spatialities and cultural dimensions that materialize such containment and also give effect to the global and the crossing of national borders. The application of this dual-method strategy invited data sources as varied as official websites, social media pages, posted videos and photos, online news articles, television talk shows and interviews, inaugural speeches, panel discussions, government documents, programme proposals and policy dialogue events. These all informed and oriented the ethnographic semi-structured interviews central to the study that form an important empirical backdrop to this book, and all oriented around particular powerful imaginations. In the next chapter, we turn to a consideration of the primary education system in Bangladesh in relation to heterarchical network governance.

3

Changing Governance of Primary Education in Bangladesh

Introduction

In this chapter we apply the conceptual resources outlined in Chapter 2 to understanding network-centric transformations of the primary education sector/system of Bangladesh (PESoB). Additionally, we seek to explicate such processes in relation to the governance of primary education in Bangladesh. In broad terms, network-centric transformations in policy and governance of the PESoB are historicized in this chapter. Here, we trek along multiple trails of history, excavating footprints of global-local actors and organizations whose aspirations and grit continue to institutionalize networks within PESoB as a model of governance for system management and service partnerships. Such an historical approach to system-level governance underscores the 'context of the context' (Peck & Theodore, 2015) to help make sense of the rise and role of networks in educational policy and governance in the country. The PESoB is now a 'world of policy' governed for and by networks that imbricate (Lingard, 2021) the global and the local/national in spatio-cultural ways signifying new waves of modernity (Escobar, 1995) – indeed, modernity at large, as it were (Appadurai, 1996).

This network turn is demonstrated through our policy mobility case; genealogically (Carney & Bista, 2009), network centrism within the PESoB represents a culture of governance. It is within this historical unfolding of a network-enabling policy environment that the formation and functioning of locally active global organizations (such as Teach For Bangladesh (TFB)) are to be evaluated (see Chapter 5 on TFB). While such evaluations are dealt with in subsequent chapters, this chapter's focus is on the rise of partnership discourses and network practices within the Directorate of Primary Education (DPE) in relation to its overarching systemic apparatus for governance – the Primary

Education Development Programme (PEDP). The PEDP is the principal entity responsible for enhancing primary education provision in Bangladesh. To relate this chapter's epistemology with Foucault's (1982) archaeological approach: if the formal institutionalization of networks within PESoB was a *connaissance* (formal theory of/for practice), we sought to unravel some of the historical junctures of *savoir* (the long-term quotidian context for the theory of/for practice) (see McMahon & Harwood, 2016).

Our research revealed that four subsequent phases of PEDPs have shaped PESoB into a 'governance network' arrangement, revealing the rise of broad-based 'partnerships' (with social enterprises as the principal emerging form) as the culture (practice and discourse) for addressing educational issues predefined globally and committed to locally. In relation to cross-field effects (Lingard & Rawolle, 2004), social enterprises emerged as an all-sector panacea (Adhikary et al., 2020) for the resolution of social problems in sectors from which they did not originate. In the process, the roles and remit of traditional NGOs, including those in education, were redefined (see Chapter 4). To understand this context, we demonstrate how the PEDP programme constituted a 'policy making world' (Peck & Theodore, 2015, p. xvi; also see Appadurai, 1996). PEDP served to both reach and embed/institutionalize multiple and spatially influential entities that connected and leveraged multiple topological elements – power relationships, enabling resources, structural authorities and mediation platforms.

Such spatially influential manifestations blurred substantially the lines between policy and governance. That is, not only were networks practised discursively (Thomson et al., 2013) but they also governed through formalized policies. Put another way: networks were governed for and by policies. Governance networks also acted as policy networks and vice versa. This continues to occur whereby global-local imbrications of various sorts (partnerships, collaborations, dependencies and networks) are becoming central in the making and enactment of education policy in Bangladesh and in educational governance more broadly. Fundamental to such transformations are powerfully de-bordered policy imaginaries (Peck & Theodore, 2015, p. xv) with substantial links to EFA and subsequently MDG and SDG discourses that implicate global-local imbrications in the ritualistic entanglement of power and authority that are increasingly becoming psychosociologically de-bordered, affecting both policymakers and policy.

The history presented in this chapter covers a time span starting from the 1990s EFA to date. We traced multiple co-evolving networks that set out loosely, but gradually became organized, and finally took an institutional form merging into one systemic programme of governance, known as the System Wide Approach to Programming (SWAP). While SWAP now acts as a firmament of policy and governance under PEDP, its historical development is key to understanding its character and influence. This insightful history is illustrative of an initial network effect (drive towards multiple contingent exchange relationships), an intermediary but ongoing network governance effect (meta-governance) and eventually an institutional form of governance network (heterarchic governance) with system-wide impact. In this case, we found that networks were agentic and relational manifestations and yet were fundamentally contingent upon institutional authority and resource variables.

In approaching this historical account of the emergence of heterarchic governance (Ball, 2012) within PESoB, we took a multidisciplinary path by drawing upon relevant political science and public administration literatures, in addition to those from education, comparative education and policy sociology in education in particular. In doing so, we emphasize that any comprehensive and nuanced understanding of network governance requires accounting for its unique character, specificities and evolutionary history, which was particularly important for researching a less-developed system such as that of Bangladesh. Thus, despite our heavy reliance on mainstream theories of network and heterarchic governance (see Ball, 2012; Ball et al., 2017), we nonetheless found wisdom in the view that network governance appears in different empirical forms and is never an exclusive monolith (Kenis et al., 2009, p. 24). We are acknowledging here the path-dependent manifestations of network governance.

We further appreciate that an historical approach to network governance is as important for the less-developed world as it is for the developed world. Typically, the former demonstrates exogenous collaboration, mediated influences and intuitive transformations more than the latter. As a result, such least-developed settings provide fertile test beds (Takayama, 2019; Whitty & Wisby, 2016) for studying 'smart hybridities in governance' (Koppenjan et al., 2019) that leverage and result in policy networks (Ball et al., 2017; Rhodes, 2017c), assemblages (Savage, 2018) and thus policy mobilities (Peck & Theodore, 2015). However, the historical approach we have applied here resonates with Carney and Bista's (2009, p. 194) genealogical approach, which

> attempts to understand the present by tracing back the ways in which certain ideas emerged at particular times; how particular ideas were accepted and found form in terms of the legitimate ways of talking; and how other ideas were excluded, marginalized, or dismissed ... For Foucault [see Foucault & Senellart,

2008], genealogy seeks out the ruptures in history and attempts to expose concepts, ideas, and constructions that, while taken for granted in the present, were actually shaped, contested, and remade in the past.

If such least-developed contexts as Bangladesh are left unexplored or explored ahistorically, the emerging governance practices therein might risk an alienating theoretical and empirical determinism at a time when trust (see Arranz & de Arroyabe, 2013; Srećković & Windsperger, 2013) is increasingly becoming a concern in the global framing and governance (McNeill & Sandberg, 2014) of educational agendas. Most importantly, understanding network governance in less-developed contexts with a historico-sociological approach promises fresh perspectives for contributing to a rights-based approach to research (Appadurai, 2006b), along with a deparochializing approach to education research more broadly (Rappleye, 2019; Appadurai, 2006b). For beyond critiques of coloniality and eco-determinism, there lies an untapped sociological terrain of historical specifics inviting theoretical and empirical attention essential for identifying potentially novel perspectives from grounded realities; such realities help counterbalance theoretical domination by reactivating empirical insights reflexively (Takayama, 2019).

Promoting such reflexivity in network studies, Torfing (2007, p. 10) argues that the many different 'labels, narratives and institutional articulations' of network governance existing today in the West are primarily the results of historical and contextual differences. Therefore, understanding the particular characteristics of governance networks 'should always reflect on how these have been shaped and reshaped by the historical context' (Torfing, 2007, p. 7). In the field of education, and particularly vis-à-vis seminal work on sociology of education-policy networks, the importance of history has only begun to be highlighted (see Peck & Theodore, 2015, p. 238). However, this absence has been identified and argument proffered for the necessity of such empirical work (see Ball et al., 2017, p. 154). Using the topological analytics presented in the previous chapter, we attempt such an historical and empirical approach in this chapter, studying and analysing a whole system programme of governance as a network case in point. Acknowledging that policy itself can be and is governed, and that governance substantially requires policy formulation and enactment, we provide an account of network-centric transformations in governance of an entire education system in a less-developed country.

In this vein, and considering that the developing East largely remains on the recipient side of the 'governance turn' (Börzel & Panke, 2008, p. 153), we ask: how do networks originate, evolve and take an institutional form when it comes to system-level governance of education in a less-developed setting? To address this question, we used interview data collected from Dhaka, Bangladesh, from August to October 2016; this work was begun following ethical approval for the study by the University of Queensland, Australia. All the twenty-two policy elites interviewed gave informed consent. While most of the participants consented to be identified in the research, we deemed anonymity important where this was possible. Despite the wide variety of data sources in the broader study, only interview data collected from policy elites, including high officials from the DPE/Ministry of Primary and Mass Education (MoPME), multi-/bilateral donor representatives, civil society leaders and a few nationally acclaimed academics of education policy and governance, are used in this chapter.

Applying the topological analytics presented in Chapter 2, we demonstrate how PESoB's policy and governance transformed within a 'policy making world' (Peck & Theodore, 2015, p. xvi), wherein the mobility of multiple networks stabilized (touched down), changing roles and altering authorities through the act of governing. The resulting network turn had an initial network effect, a prolonged network governance effect and finally constituted an ongoing governance network modality. Through our analyses, we have sought to try to capture the role of powerful imaginaries at work (particularly via the World Bank[1]), the illustration of the aspiring community and their spatio-cultural work (particularly through various donor consortium and civil society networks) and the cultural flows (various images, discursive and other resources, but mainly commissioned research) (Appadurai, 1996) that gave force to persuasive 'encounters' (Amin, 2002; Massey, 1994b). Along the way we have also sought to specify and illustrate the spatio-cultural dynamics through which cultural flows imbricated the global and the national/local.

The Empirical and the Theoretical: Multiple Networks and Coalescing Effects

According to Bangladesh Education Statistics 2018, the DPE provides education to 18,602 million students through twenty-five types of providers. Among them, the nationalized government primary schools alone educated 13,389 million (72 per cent) students. The total number of teachers was 548,200 of which 60.3 per cent were female. Today, the 2020–21 education sector budget stands at Tk

66,400 crore (664,000 million BDT, $USD7,830 million) for the education sector, of which Tk 24,937 crore (249,370 million BDT, $USD2,940 million) has been allocated for the primary and mass education ministry (i.e. the DPE). Overall, the education budget makes up 11.69 per cent of the total outlay, while its share in the GDP stands at 2.09 per cent (Alamgir, 2020). The MoPME and DPE are responsible for the planning and management of primary and pre-primary education. In 2018 alone, MoPME through DPE prepared and distributed 103,625,480 textbooks to its students. Under the PEDP III programme, 75,257 head teachers were provided leadership training, 67,787 teachers were given ICT in education courses and 68,785 teachers were provided with diploma in education training. All these initiatives and associated investments were made in compliance with the UN's EFA and MDGs.

Bangladesh's endorsement of the 1990s EFA movement resulted in a comprehensive national plan of action[2] that significantly transformed policy and governance of the PESoB. These system-level transformations deepened institutionally through initiatives and developments aligned to the MDGs and subsequently the SDGs (2015–30), for which the country's commitment and performance were internationally celebrated. The impacts of EFA, MDGs and SDGs were manifest through a sequence of donor-supported PEDPs (PEDP I, II, III and IV). Starting in 1997, PEDP continues today in its fourth phase. These EFA-focused PEDP reforms not only introduced new sets of actors, resources and processes within the system but also substantially altered the nature of the government's roles and authority in system design and management (Adhikary, 2019).

These altering effects were particularly mediated by the DPE, which is the nationwide administrative hub/hand reporting to the MoPME. Speaking historically to the deeper transformations within the decision-making architecture of the DPE, the World Bank brought almost all other donor agencies under one networked umbrella (Donor Consortium (DC)), which over the years has become an influential part of DPE's organizational practices. The government was then convinced of the need for a system-wide approach to donor involvement. Additionally, a network of local NGOs (Campaign for Popular Education (CAMPE)) was created through the Fast Track Initiative (FTI; currently Global Partnership for Education) global funding. Its access enabled by the DC network, CAMPE now functions as a network lead of what is described as 'civil society' (CS) representation within PESoB's reformed governance structures. This important history of converging multiple networks is captured in this chapter.

The way in which the PEDP in its current form governs the DPE's nationwide activities is a textbook example of 'heterarchic' governance (Ball, 2012). Understanding the evolutionary stages of developments in its current form needs a wider and multifocal lens (Sørensen & Torfing, 2008). To form such an historically informed perspective, we are adhering to the term 'effect' to emphasize that network-making processes and heterarchic outcomes are historically variable in different places but also at different times within the same setting. Such an inclusive approach to understanding the making of heterarchic governance presented three basic heuristic tropes for reflection: the first is 'network effect' (see Arranz & de Arroyabe, 2013), the second is 'network governance effect' (see Wuyts & Bulte, 2012) and the third is governance network in the sense of heterarchies (Ball, 2012). A few basic questions we thought about were: What do we understand by acting like a network? When can we say that a network is governing (itself and others)? What is the apparently final and phenomenal outcome of networked engagement vis-à-vis governance? Is it a one-off thing? Or is it meant to sustain a broader set of practices, and to what end?

Arranz and de Arroyabe (2013, p. 34) view network effects as comprising 'relations among partners and projects that provide partners with access to information and embedded resources'. A discernible existence of such relational assemblages and dynamics is what we understand as network effects here. While the centrality of exchange relationships is obvious, Wuyts and Bulte (2012, p. 74) argue that a 'network governance effect' emerges as 'sets of two or more connected exchange relationships' that are 'governed' in such ways that 'one relationship is contingent on exchange (or non-exchange) in the other relationships'. This is basically governance of networks – meta-governance – representing 'efforts of ... authorities in steering networks through a different set of rules or other strategies' (Molin & Masella, 2016, p. 494). In research terms, it represents the way in which networks are empirically governed (see Baker & Stoker, 2012; Haveri et al., 2009). Torfing (2007, p. 13) spells it out very clearly:

> Metagovernance includes indirect attempts to influence the processes and outcomes of network governance through network design, network framing and network management. Network design involves attempts to influence the composition, competences, and 'rules of the game' of governance networks. Network framing involves attempts to shape the political, economic and discursive framework of the negotiated interaction within governance networks. Finally, network management involves attempts to keep governance networks on track through selective activation of particular actors, conflict resolution and

provision of relevant inputs in terms of knowledge, support and encouragements. Metagovernance can also take a more direct form in terms of participation in the network-based processes of negotiation.

Kenis et al. (2009) argue that meta-governance involves network structuring (composition), everyday tasks and steering roles within the network itself. Indeed, at the heart of governing through networks – heterarchic governance – is the governance of networks. Such structuring can be of encouragement, mutual action, conflict mitigation, resource distribution and quality assurance. Broadly, these structures often overlap in three forms at any given phase of evolution underpinning specific effects, such as shared governance forms, lead organization forms and network administrative organization (NAO) forms (Kenis et al., 2009, p. 24). Shared governance is the simplest and involves a collective of actors/organizations without a designated, formal and distinct agency to govern network activities. That is, collective activities are completely within the remit of network members themselves. Applied to govern small groups, shared governance network activities are often coordinated by a subset of the full network. Lead organization network members share some common purpose at the minimum yet have individual goals in mind. While there remains some degree of interaction and togetherness, decisions and activities are coordinated through and by one leading member. NAOs are separately established administrative entities that manage and coordinate the network and its everyday activities.

Unlike lead organizations, NAOs are not network members and are established with the exclusive purpose of network governance (Kenis et al., 2009, pp. 24–6). Defined as an 'orchestrator', NAOs can be formal (Jacobson, 2016, p. 44). Jacobson (2016) explains further that the roles of such NAOs include enhancing network legitimacy, solving network-level issues and problems and reducing complexity of shared governance (Provan & Kenis, 2007, p. 236). These roles are orchestrated through important arrangements combining inter-/intra-organizational structures and coordination mechanisms (Jacobson, 2016, p. 44). However, understanding such governance effects requires consideration of the specifics of governance mechanisms, the conditions underpinning the activation of such mechanisms and often the effectiveness and challenges of the mechanisms put to use (see Wuyts & Bulte, 2012, p. 74). In this vein, Molin and Masella (2016, p. 494) invite an understanding of network governance that, among other considerations, places emphases on the contextual factors that underpin any empirically applied form of network governance, the way it is/

was meta-governed and a longitudinal grasp of the developmental stages of such governance.

According to these scholars, such an approach requires attention to: (a) choice dimensions (initial decision-making processes on the appropriateness and relevance of a network form under given conditions); (b) meta-governance dimensions (steering processes and associated tools to ensure achievement of network goals); and (c) evaluation dimensions (relationship between meta tools and outcome of network governance, in terms of effectiveness and democracy) (Molin & Masella, 2016, pp. 502–4). These scholars then propose a broad and customizable analytical framework inviting reflection on starting conditions, form of network governance, meta-governance and the outcome of network governance (Molin & Masella, 2016, pp. 502–4). In effect, this is what we seek to empirically present in this chapter by voyaging historically through the junctural transformations in governance that have occurred since the 1990s to date, marking the institutionalization of networks as PEDP's modus operandi. Within the empirical remit of the DPE-PEDP context, arguably and inclusively, we propose a sociological view of the 'network governance effect' as a historically attuned understanding of the conditions, deliberations, decisions, interactions and processes through which the value and relevance of networked forms of governance are realized and enacted over time through negotiated exchanges, roles, rules and agendas; and institutionally put into a continuum of practice by network actors.

Coming to the topological analytics, the theoretical stem presented in Chapter 2, we view the PEDP programme as a constructed 'policy making world' (Appadurai, 1996; Peck & Theodore, 2015), a world that originated as the manifestation of powerful imaginations of aspirational actors (i.e. the World Bank and others). Parallel to the examination of the inception and growth of networks in terms of 'effects', we also reveal how such effects were created spatio-culturally by an evolving community of aspiring actors. This community of global-local actors initiated network thinking; interacted as a network; constituted other augmentative local networks; and articulated, practised and institutionalized network as a discourse (as practice; see Thomson et al., 2013) within DPE through phases of PEDP. This is the spatio-cultural making of networks as the mode of governance. We also highlight the moments of encounters, where place entails placement of practice and where place is expressed as moments within the temporality of space (immanent forces, here evolving networks) (Massey, 2006, p. 139), which resulted in gradual developments in relation to the unfolding of incremental network effects. Finally, we will also demonstrate some of the network tools through which networks worked empirically as an institutional culture, a professional practice.

PEDP as a Heterarchic Policymaking World: A History of the Network of Networks

System governance of primary education in Bangladesh is now a multi-actor programmatic arrangement in which a heterarchic (Ball, 2012) apparatus comprising of a consortium of donors, civil society network representatives and the government work together. This programmatic arrangement, namely Primary Education Development Programme, is the outcome of network-centric developments broadly linked to Bangladesh's participation in the EFA movement and its relative lack of power in relation to MDGs and SDGs. Over the past two decades, three different networks with their own histories and scope converged locally. We will analyse these histories in terms of choice, meta-governance and evaluation dimensions illustrated earlier (see Molin & Masella, 2016) but also in line with the spatio-cultural analytics targeting global-local imbrications.

Starting Conditions

The initial conditions under which network-centric decisions and transformative moves were made can be captured broadly in three acronyms related to the UN's global development strategies: EFA, MDGs and SDGs. The 'watershed' effect that the 1990s EFA had on the structural and regulatory aspects of PESoB was confirmed and detailed by all the interviewees regardless of their organizational position. With two decades of leadership experience within the DPE, one high official explained the centrality of EFA in activating some of the deeper shifts:

> We *must* start this discussion then from the EFA targets – that Education for All. There, we had an imperative of having a global understanding on ensuring primary education for all … If we talk of globalization, here, we gradually, since then, started experiencing a dependency. Then [1990s] we had the financial crisis. And we had to depend on 45–50% of foreign investment in the form of loan and grant money for development undertakings. We had to depend on donor agencies and developed countries. It is from that dependency that we took the target of achieving EFA goals in our hands and prepared our

programme documents and designs. And we have implemented those. (SGO-2; emphasis added)

This nationally oriented DPE official points out three important conditions, notably, a global imperative, the internal deficiency of resources and resulting dependency on external funding. These were key to understanding the decisions that set in motion a series of transformations in governance through the ongoing phases of PEDP. However, another DPE senior official gave more of a globally oriented perspective on these initial conditions under which the PEDP programme had to be undertaken. He argued that EFA was a programme of/for globalization of education and added:

> Globalization starts with the emergence and acceptance, or the realization of the educational importance among the member countries of the UN. It [education] has been considered as [in terms of] the globe. Hence, the term globalization with the slogan EFA – Education for All. So, the term globalization, whenever it comes, it becomes a *compulsory* issue to implement. It is the obligation of the member countries, to work with and be with the association of UN. So, this is the mandate. And with this mandate there is a timeline – to implement EFA by 2015. Then Bangladesh started working. All governments have a strong commitment to materialize the issue, although there is difference in opinion between the parties holding the power. But regarding the implementation of EFA, government has strong commitment. (SGO-1; emphasis added)

This official, like many others, pointed out how the urge for education for all and the call for a global understanding of education made sense to him in terms of the relationship with the UN. Demonstrative of the interpolative power of a global imagination, he also pointed out an understanding of the nation-state and its government in terms of, and as a part of, a global relational matrix of governments, wherein commitment is competitive and temporally measurable. This is an instance of global-local imbrication at the level of imagination. Such an imagination resonates with the argument we presented in Chapter 2 that globalization is 'governance' globalized. Apart from the realities of internal deficiencies and associated dependencies, this competitively relational and global thinking and acting were some of the important conditions – a 'mental space' (Carney, 2009, p. 65) – that influenced choices underpinning the PEDP programme, which in the following years adhered to networked modes of organizational and educational governance.

Networks Imagined: Evolving Forms and Effects

Donor Consortium

Since the PEDP I, three networks were formulated, longitudinally managed and dovetailed and later formalized to reach to where PESoB stands today. Such network evolutions could not unfold in isolation and in the sweep of a magical moment. Rather, as manifestations of powerful imaginations (Appadurai, 1996), they occurred with and within a systemic assemblage (dispositif) that was gradually morphing towards a SWAP – a System Wide Approach to Programming – for the entire primary education system. Since the beginning of PEDP I and towards the end of PEDP II, all the donor agencies worked separately and bilaterally with the government aiming at educational improvement. It was soon perceived and emphasized that bilateralism required the government to endure redundancies of such unmanageable scale that something needed to be done. One government official explained the pre–PEDP III roles of the government in the following way:

> The situation before [PEDP III] tended to be that the government was running a system. If they wanted to improve teacher training, or someone [donor] had convinced them that they should improve teacher training, there would be a separate project that also had to be approved by ERD [Economic Relations Divisions, Planning Ministry]. In those cases, it was nearly a 100 per cent funding from a donor. And government always had to give in a contribution ... in that way it was different from SWAP: a sector wide approach from just a project. (DCM-2)

Clearly, eleven bi-/multilateral donors at the minimum meant eleven different projects depending on political priorities and in relation to programme variables. Increasingly difficult, both for the government and its global counterparts, bilateralism was being perceived as an efficiency issue over the PEDP I–II years. Enter a powerful imagination (Appadurai, 1996); it was the World Bank who took the issue actively into consideration and started mobilizing advocacy for a networked mode of interaction generative of SWAP. The World Bank official noted:

> World Bank took the initiative [of introducing SWAP]. Because it's ours. SWAP is our terminology. And these are our things, so we presented to everybody [other donors and the government]. Of course, we took the initiative ... Exactly! Exactly! [In] 2011! During the end of PEDP-II, we started selling this idea. (DCM-1)

This is one powerful example of an actor's programmatic 'imagination' imbricating the global and the national. SWAP was important for many reasons, of which the most significant was its ability to compatibly link up networked forms of governance with a system facing the need for efficient donor coordination for all parties involved. Imagination explained in operational but also 'best-practice' terms, SWAP came with the idea of 'harmonisation'[3] of activities, interactions and funding mechanisms between donors and the government. SWAP was considered, particularly by the Bank, as an enabler of much-needed technical and procedural advantage that bilaterally or otherwise was deemed impossible. Such perceived needs for efficiency (see topological rationality in Chapter 2) and technical advantages rationalized – as an instance of the topological rationality of globalization – the World Bank's lead in coordinating efforts towards the creation of a DC network during PEDP III. The interviewee further elaborated the Bank's powerful imagination:

> Exactly! We [donors] became a network, and organized. But these were the first steps. [Until] not as early as 2011, [that] we were very well organized. But still. Now if you look [back] at these programmes [PEDP I and II], though they talk about [referring to these projects as] a programme, these were actually a combination of say twenty projects. Towards the end of PEDP-II, we all [donors] thought that, well we [donors] are now well organized and now we understand what we should do. Now place government in the driving seat, and *we design* something really harmonized – a programme. So, we call it SWAP – Sector Wide Approach Programme. So, it will not deal with specific issues, it will deal with the entire sector at a time. So, whatever you plan, it gets harmonized. And it will be funded by everybody together. We cannot fund separately. (DCM-1; emphasis added)

Evidently, the initial networked assemblage worked as a shared governance form, yet was moving towards a lead organization form (see Kenis et al., 2009, pp. 24–6) with the Bank in the as-yet-informal steering role. While the vehicle and the path were created by the Bank in the main, the government gradually placed its hand on the steering wheel. A powerful figure of speech – the driver's seat – substantially signalled a Third World version of the 'differently organised roles of government' in network governance. What we also note is, gradually, the DC with the Bank's underlying lead took the form of an NAO in the act of governing the system (see next section).

While the DC was the end point of the network-centric path that the Bank laboriously paved and convinced others to follow or drive along, the institutional framing of such a move began in PEDP II. During PEDP II, the donors started collaborating with each other and formed a loosely coupled consultative forum called the Education Local Consultative Group (ELCG). PEDP III transformed ELCG into a DC with a whole system impact (since and hence, SWAP). Even more importantly, it was through ELCG that NGOs' representation was invited and later 'annexed' as 'modernity' within PESoB governance:

> Well, we [donors and government] had lots of different meetings. [During PEDP II, we had] Education Local Consultative Group, which was just, all the donors' work and NGOs (some representative NGOs, mainly donors) working in education. Because that time we did not have PEDP-III as a programme. Ya, so it was basically, many, many, many, many meetings at different levels [of the government], both with our Ministry, and Planning Commission. (DCM-2)

The centrality of meetings is notable vis-à-vis the spatio-cultural formulation of networks and SWAP as the culture of system-level governance. These meetings are heterotopic places (Foucault, 1986; Massey, 1994a, 2006) where encounters are negotiated and placement of practice occurs (see Chapter 2). Importantly, ELCG was not only an evolutionary prerequisite to the eventual DC; it also enabled a local NGO network to take part in consultative meetings that otherwise happened between the government and the DC. With the evolution of ELCG into a formal and institutionalized DC, the NGO network's involvement also became formally dovetailed within the PESoB governance structures. These are practical examples of network management or meta-governance (Baker & Stoker, 2012; Haveri et al., 2009; Torfing, 2007). Such developments also constitute what we have referred to as a network governance effect (Wuyts & Bulte, 2012) in the sense that without the relationship between the DC and the government, the NGO network would not even exist within the governance scene.

During the time of data collection, this NGO network was considered as a civil society representation within PESoB governance. However, the evolution of the ELCG into the DC is an appropriate example of how a loosely coupled issue network – an epistemic as well as aspiring community of mostly global but also local actors – transformed into an active participant in governance with transformative impact; this was further augmented by its inclusion of a civil society network into the act of governance. This is undeniably the story of heterarchic governance of an entire education system. We now turn to the history of the NGO network and its link with the DC network.

The NGO Network

Before SWAP, NGOs in Bangladesh had no 'democratic access' to the decisions and structures of PESoB. Strategic to this democratic motive, SWAP was a move from the ELCG (mostly the World Bank) and later the DC, inter alia, to bring together all the key education NGOs under one networked umbrella, later to be annexed within PESoB structures. Known as CAMPE, this NGO network was funded by what was known in the millennial decade as the FTI fund, which later changed into the Global Partnership for Education, and which is currently active as a partnership-focused fund. Such exogenous funding is a mechanism through which the global and the national-local become imbricated, again around best-practice rationales implicating modernity.

Despite this exogenous funding, CAMPE was, as well, the brain child of a few Bangladeshi NGO leaders who were invited to attend the Jomtien Conference in 1990. These leaders sat together and decided to form CAMPE upon return. One founding member of CAMPE explained:

> By 1990s, the NGO sector of Bangladesh became quite mature. In Jomtien, there were a lot of leading [NGO] organizations [from Bangladesh]. It was during that conference that they decided to create a *coalition* among the NGOs when they come back [to Bangladesh]. That is how CAMPE happened. The discussion happened in Jomtien conference site, and then after the NGOs came back, they decided to have CAMPE formed. (I/NGO-SO-2; emphasis added)

Acting more like an NAO, it was not until 2003–4 that CAMPE developed the shape and character of an organized and managerial network. One DC senior official emphasized the mobilization of EFA's special funding – FTI locally managed by the World Bank – as the key support for CAMPE's origins and development into its current state of affairs, particularly in relation to its research strength:

> Go back to 2003 and 2004, there you will see that, globally, there was an initiative called Fast Track Initiative. Now it is called GPE, meaning Global Partnership for Education. So, through FTI, there was a different fund created, and that fund was targeted for non-government entities so that those entities can collaborate with the government. For example, one of the biggest educational umbrella institutions in Bangladesh is CAMPE, [which] got funding from FTI. And that's how CAMPE came into being. Again, if you look at how CAMPE operates now, what they have been able to do over the course of last ten to twelve or fifteen years, you will see that even though they are not a government entity … I don't think that it will be an overstatement, they happen to have the most credible

research in education. And CAMPE is now an umbrella of almost more than two hundred NGOs working in education in Bangladesh. So again, what I'm saying is, that's the root of how it all started in 2003 and 2004. And they also had a fund. (DCM-3)

This DC member actually highlights the national implementation of EFA's Commitment 11, which was about the international community's additional funding through 'a global initiative'. This initiative sought to 'increase external finance' for basic education, facilitating 'more effective donor-co-ordination' and strengthening 'sector-wide approaches', all through the mechanisms of debt economics. Commitment 11 also advised of a global initiative for 'undertaking more effective and regular monitoring of progress towards EFA goals and targets, including periodic assessments'.[4] The interview extract highlights how CAMPE had become a nationally recognized source of research data that would support such monitoring and assessment of progress and performance of EFA in Bangladesh.

CAMPE, an advocacy and 'campaign network' (CAMPE, 2020), demonstrates a constructed and managed network of education actors. Education research and research-driven advocacy being its main strength, CAMPE now participates in PESoB governance directly. Particularly since PEDP II, the loosely coupled donors' group (ELCG) continued cooperation with this civil society network and vice versa. Later on, the DC convinced the government regarding the inclusion of CAMPE within PEDP's decision-making processes as a civil societies (CS) representative. One NGO leader and a founding member of CAMPE explained the history in brief:

> It was the donor group. Now, we [NGOs] were having different dialogues with the donors. And the donors were seeing that if the NGOs are here within this forum [PEDP III] besides [rather than competing with the] government, the discussion went to a productive and functional level and new ideas popped up. Then the donors convinced the government. And on the other side, government itself became convinced to create a provision for NGO's participation or say Civil Societies' participation. (I/NGO-SO-1)

'Convincing' is thus one empirical means through which global-local imbrication occurs, while the best-practice logic also has influence. The efficiency logic and associated performative drive are quite remarkable here. As a strategic move and a breakthrough, the DC convinced the government about the necessity of direct participation of NGOs in the PEDP system. While the NGOs were also eager, over the years, their participation in PESoB governance has become powerful as they eventually became networked and able to form strategic alliances with the more powerful networks (DC). Both of these networks are 'governance networks' (Klijn & Edelenbos, 2007; Torfing, 2007) that had an initial network effect that matured into a network governance effect. They were informal networks, performed network governance and over the history became institutionalized, giving rise to heterarchic governance (Ball, 2012, 2013). We will next consider the network governance effect.

The Network Governance Effect: Networks Governed through Meta Tools

We begin this discussion with a World Bank official's view on the role of civil society. Describing the nature of CAMPE's involvement, the World Bank official reported:

> CAMPE's core role is basically advising. Like CAMPE is a member of the [DPE] Working Groups. CAMPE has a representative in each working group. So, they can actually see how it is going on, in the supervision they also take part, and they also advise [the government] to do the things, [or to carry out a] couple of studies. Also, the government requested CAMPE to take part. Or CAMPE, they take their studies and regarding government, they decide that [whether or not the] government is taking care of [its roles and commitments]. (DCM-1)

While discussing CAMPE, this Bank official revealed some of the reformed operational units and management practices (meta tools) through which networks were activated and rendered effective within PESoB. The imbricative role of 'imaginations' was discussed earlier; in practice, it is through such meta tools that the global reach of heterarchies was imbricated within the national system. CAMPE's involvement in every working group exemplified network framing and associated management practicalities. It demonstrates how networks can be impactful not only through presence and proximity (Allen, 2009; Amin, 2002) but also in practice by establishing organizational mechanisms and tools through which such reach and presence are made official and effective (governance). However, we identified other powerful instances of imbricative 'practices of encompassment', which sociologically transformed reach into a long-term heterarchic presence that was characterized by 'superior spatial reach and vertical height' (Ferguson, 2006, p. 112).

Working Groups, Joint Consultative Meetings and Joint Annual Review Missions

Apart from working groups, a few other structural innovations were highlighted by another research participant. He talked about a Joint Annual Review Mission (JARM) and a Joint Consultative Meeting (JCM), which, respectively, are annual evaluative and formative assessment mechanisms where the government presented its EFA performance data to the DC in the presence of CS representatives for scrutiny against agreed-on indicators. This Bank official noted:

> Well, probably a major thing is trying to get the system more decentralized. And so more accountable at local levels. And then also we have tried to get civil society involved. Say, for instance, when we do our Joint Annual Review Missions, CAMPE is invited too. (DCM-2)

Instrumental to decentralization – a drive often linked to distributive and democratic values – CAMPE was now exercising a relative share in the authority practices such as working group monitoring, advisory and supervisory roles, and evaluation and research assistance. CAMPE's research gained the acknowledgement and esteem of the government itself. A matter of trust, this was also productive power and research authority developed through externally funded research; the result was imbricative in terms of added value by the introduction of a previously absent research culture within the system. Insightfully, networked advocacy and research funded by the World Bank (GPE) are what have transformed CAMPE from a loosely developed coalition of NGOs in the 1990s to a networked civil society (CS) representation in PESoB in the 2000s, and now with unparalleled research authority.

Pooled Funding

Yet another example of the imbricative role of funding was what the research participants referred to as 'pooled funding', another meta tool. While some donors disagreed[5] with one-container funding, in PEDP III, contributions eventually became fully pooled into one bank account as a part of SWAP imperatives. It was often called 'budget funding'; in actual fact, it was a 'yin-yang deal' (Freireich & Fulton, 2009). All the development partners now would put their donations (10–15 per cent of costs, at that time) into one fund that would then be blended with the government's contribution (85–90 per cent). This combined fund would then support the PEDP III programme on a 'money has no colour' principle: basically, money became unable to be tracked to providers.

Another DC member talked about these new mechanisms and their impact on DPE work in the following manner:

> What is fundamentally different in PEDP-III is, in PEDP-III we all are in 'Pooled Funding'. Which means that we gave all our funding to the Ministry of Finance. So, it all goes to the Ministry of Finance. Which means that when documents are being signed, they are signed not only with the Ministry of Primary and Mass Education [DPE]; Ministry of Finance also has a very big stake in this. So, Ministry of Finance is also on board. (DCM-3)

This unique funding mechanism made money 'identity-less'. Consequently, the financial contributions of diverse exogenous actors became linked to power and ownership that was not always congruent to their relative contribution. But most importantly it also demonstrated how a financescape (Appadurai, 1996) was constituted not only as a network (DC) but also through a history of incremental meta-governance of networks and convincing of 'authorities' otherwise regarding the necessity of tracking providers. However, within this financescape, what represented the practical power to govern was the construction and utilization of DLIs (disbursement-linked indicators), another financial meta tool with significant consequences.

DLIs and Results-Based Framework

The government's accountability to the DC-CS duet functioned through the introduction of DLIs, rubric categories for assessing DPE's EFA performance in PEDP III. The DLIs were used as indicators contingent upon the DC's clearance of annual disbursement of finances for DPE activities. This is the 'results-based framework', where expected results along given/agreed-on indicators were tied with the flow of money into the PESoB under the custodianship of the Ministry of Finance (MoF). This, despite being practised within a single national system, worked much like what Lingard and colleagues (2016, p. 2) have illustrated as 'data-driven rationalities and technologies of governmentality' that 'are tied to a form of biopower mobilised through numbers as *inscription devices*' (emphasis original).

On a different but important note, this involvement of the MoF is a structural reform that brings the PESoB under the rationalities of development economics. A high official from the World Bank further explained how areas for results-based monitoring of DPE's performance were negotiated and agreed on by the DC and the government together. Nine areas of activities for improvement (change) were identified for six years of PEDP's phase III, against which the DPE was to show evidence of its successful performance:

> So, we have nine [target] results for PEDP-III identified. All of us, together with government, for six years [of PEDP-III], we have identified these results areas. If they [government] achieve, they send us the proof, that they have achieved. Then all development partners, this [donor] consortium, looks though the achievement and then they [donor consortium] disburse the money [for the next annual phase]. (DCM-1)

Even though, apparently, the pooled fund for PESoB management in Bangladesh was locally managed/'gatekept' by the MoF, the DC's discretion to provide or negate annual clearance of that money against achieved or failed DLIs constitutes an example of the effective framing of heterarchic governance. As a meta tool, it was these DLIs that practically and inevitably linked the DPE's work to EFA's global monitoring framework. This is an illustrative example of how the global and the local become imbricated in practice and 'by reference to claims of superior spatial reach and vertical height' (Ferguson, 2006, p. 112).

On this note, one senior government official from the DPE provided an even more palpable explanation of how DLIs have become the rubric for the DC's assessment of government work. This official viewed DLIs as 'conditions'. He also expressed his mixed feelings about DPE-MoPME's inability to receive the grants directly and also about the fact that as the top authority for primary education in Bangladesh, they needed to apply for money to another ministry, namely, the Ministry of Finance:

> You know that the money of PEDP-III is in the form of Budget Support. The donation and aid money directly get into the government's treasury. So, it is Bangladesh Bank on behalf of Ministry of Finance as the reservoir. So, that money does not directly come to us from the hands of the donors. It goes to Bangladesh Bank. So, the ownership goes to the Ministry of Finance. We place a withdrawal application. The ministry of finance then disburses the money according to the allocation of the Planning Commission's books. So, getting this money depends on nine conditions that have been obligated by the donors. There are twenty-nine subcomponents. Of them nine subcomponents have been included within the DLIs. These are the nine indicators where we felt comfortable as achievable. (SGO-2)

This quotation provides a telling example of how networks function through organizational circuits and institutional mechanisms. It also highlights how conditions can have an imbricative impact. Indeed, networks do not float above and beyond or bypass the government. Rather it is through convincing, contracting, relating, rearranging and reforming at various levels, across time, that networks govern themselves and others and, in some cases, governments. Such processes had been imbricative in nature in this case in Bangladesh, and clearly, imbrications happened primarily through the introduction of networks as the culture of governance.

Discussion

Attending to recent emphases on context, evolution and history in understanding network governance (see Jacobson, 2016; Milward et al., 2010; Molin & Masella, 2016; Rhodes, 2017b; Torfing, 2007), this chapter has presented a sociological as well as a short historical account of the network-centric transformations that have occurred over the past two decades or so within the governance landscape of the PESoB. As far as governance is concerned, the chapter presented the argument that each network has its unique history in the course of which rules are formulated that exert influence and enable interactions (Kickert et al., 1997). Through such networks, negotiated matrices of collaboration develop and are institutionalized in various forms and to varying degrees (see Klijn & Edelenbos, 2007, p. 207; Rhodes, 2017b, p. 3).

Empirically testing such knowledge in the context of a less-developed nation, we have analysed the formation, evolution and institutionalization of networks as a mode of governance within PESoB by applying concepts such as 'network effects', 'network governance effect' and 'governance networks'. Despite policy and governance going hand in hand, our focus here was more on governance networks, a concept closely related to policy networks but not entirely so. Besides steering or influencing policies (policy network), networks can govern as well as be governed. Insofar as empirical evidence indicates, networks lose their governance potential, legitimacy and effect if they are not institutionalized as a matrix or system of assemblages for/of governance; governing policy can also be a major part of the system.

Dominant narratives on the rise and globalization of network governance have been written mostly in relation to the West, sometimes in a fragmented and often contradictory fashion. Alongside a few essential commonalities both in theory and in practice, debates and even outright negations in a more 'southern' setting such as Bangladesh indicate gaps in communication between regional literatures. In the context of this confusion (Börzel & Panke, 2008, p. 155), the importance of a comprehensive framework (see Molin & Masella, 2016, p. 494) has been coupled with a remedial emphasis on context-focused history (Torfing, 2007), which is what we have attempted here in this chapter.

Relatedly, contemporary second-generation research on network governance highlights a deeper and more nuanced approach to empirical analysis inter alia targeting specificities in formulation, development and functioning (see Kenis et al., 2009, pp. 24–6; Sørensen & Torfing, 2008, p. 14). Indicative labels such as multilevel governance (Ansell & Torfing, 2016, p. 2), governance of networks (Radnor et al., 2016, p. 51), designing and implementation of networks (Klijn & Edelenbos, 2007, pp. 207–10), metagovernance (Molin & Masella, 2016, p. 494; Torfing, 2007, p. 13), network governance effects (Wuyts & Bulte, 2012, p. 76), personal network influence (Heath et al., 2017, p. 108) and network/ing as governance (Mueller, 2010, p. 41) are a few of many concepts demonstrating this drive towards specificities. Such an approach calls for ontological and methodological reconsiderations that work with and beyond simply 'descriptive' and 'prescriptive' accounts of network governance (Rhodes, 2017a, p. 2). We have analysed the PEDP programme as a topological manifestation of a Global South policymaking world (Peck & Theodore, 2015) so as to capture agency, structure, flows and practices, while at the same time ensuring a balanced proximity to the interpretive truth that only empirical evidence can bestow upon the theory being used.

Predominant views on network governance, including in education, mainly stem from studies of policy networks and their power and efficiencies that essentialize new roles, rules and structures for governments. For reasons beyond the scope of this book, similar trends and transformations, particularly in the least-developed countries, have received only definitional, descriptive and superficial research attention to date (see Zafarullah, 2015) and very limited in-depth sociological analysis. In such contexts, network-oriented studies of education policy and governance are most often conducted exogenously and as such may not account for the history of contestations, negotiations, path/dependencies, hybridities and magical serendipities that provide valuable insights into how and why networks emerge and differ in modes and modalities depending on their history and 'evolution' (Jacobson, 2016; Provan et al., 2011). This chapter is a considered attempt to address that gap.

Conclusion: Some Points of Learning

The analysis and evidence presented in this chapter have demonstrated how understandings of networks can benefit from historical analysis. The chapter has also made visible an instance of the sociological dynamics through which networks are funded, framed, forged, intertwined, led, managed, institutionalized and carried out as mundane affairs along the various routes of history through to the present and immanent future. What learning and insights can we take from the analysis provided here? As our research and data indicate, system-level networks can be seen as products of agency, systemic imagination and operationalized governmentality.

Such networks cannot do without structural embedding and institutional galvanizing and some degree of authorization or authority – the legitimate right to exercise power. The networks that animated PEDP's SWAP arrangements were created, negotiated, managed and eventually institutionalized. They were made functional through managed work distribution processes, practised every day and put into a continuum of monitoring and evaluation. Clearly, from phase I to phase III, PEDP's journey had been one of self-actualization into an NAO – the orchestrator (Jacobson, 2016, p. 44). But to reach this stage, every block of activities took an evolutionary chunk of history, marking stages of inception, development and maturation but also often merger and institutionalization.

We identified three networks embedded within a flexible and dynamic array of units, tasks, rules, roles, inputs, outputs, outcomes and accountability mechanisms. The DC here acted as a lead organization in that a subset of the members coordinated its work and affairs. The CS network in its organizational form (CAMPE) acted as an NAO for its own network education NGOs. But then there was another quite distant network of global nature – GPE – that had funding involvement through the World Bank into the PEDP system. All three networks had interesting and overlapping developments, each influencing the others. For example, without GPE (actually FTI) funding, CAMPE would not have existed, meaning the DC would not have been able to promote civil society representation within the SWAP. This is what we have referred to as a constructed network effect, where exchanges in one relationship are contingent upon exchanges (or non-exchanges) in others. Most importantly, these are some of the processes through which the global and the local got closely imbricated to the extent that without the presence of the global the governance of the local now becomes inefficient, perhaps impossible. At its basis, such imbrications involved networks as immanent global forces and the local/national as the receptacles/ sites of influence.

The World Bank's lead in making the case of ELCG (PEDP II, loose network) and later DC (PEDP III, institutional network) presented the organization as something very close to a lead organization (Kenis et al., 2009, p. 24) in the history of networks within PESoB. We learned that the organization took initiatives to convince both the government and other donors of the value and necessity of networking through presentations and meetings, signifying its capacity of spatio-cultural making. The supporting rationales were grounded on the conditions of deficiency and ungovernability of much of the collaborative work between donors and the government. Yet, at the macro level, the discourses and imperatives associated with larger global commitments added context to this initial network drive; the context of context really mattered (Peck & Theodore, 2015).

Networks were governed; in fact, meta-governed. Working groups, JCMs and JARMS, pooled funding, results-based frameworks and DLIs were various forms of meta tools through which SWAP governed both the processes and products of networked collaborations and thereby the outcomes. As a part of meta-governance, we saw the transformation of 'competencies, compositions and the rules of the game' (design): think of DLIs, CS research, government's accountability, pooled funding, JCM and JARM here. We saw attempts to shape 'the political, economic and discursive framework' (framing): think of EFA, MDGs and SDGs and ideas such as SWAP. We also witnessed network management in the form of activation of specific actors (think of CS), as a way to keep the network on track. And this is what we have understood as a network governance effect. However, the final outcome of this historical evolution of effects was the SWAP umbrella that officiated and institutionalized itself as an emblem of the governance network, namely, heterarchies (Ball, 2012).

Indeed, the nature of roles and authority defining what one might imagine as government has morphed and become an entangled part of a networked dispositif (generally understood as apparatuses of power; combining knowledge, practices, techniques and institutions) of governance. In this current situation, the global and the national faces of power (authority), it seems, have entered into a symbiosis of governance relationships resulting in an expansion (alongside a concomitant delimiting) of relative scope and exchange of influence and authority. The dominant medium through which this symbiosis occurred is networks. An added new form of such global-national imbrications – much like a Möbius strip – is the civil society network, which is nationally rooted and pursues national development, yet is globally funded, oriented and ambitious.

We are in a moment of 'governance at large': governance from within and without and from below and above. But this does not mean that everybody will govern, rather marking the topological turn and rationality; only those capable of funding, orchestrating or joining networks will, regardless of geo-positioning, be able to govern. The question of democracy in this regard is often addressed through what has been referred to as expansive democracy (see Warren, 1992). The idea is to increase participation either through 'small-scale direct democracy' or through 'strong linkages between citizens and broad-scale institutions', while democracy's limits are to be pushed beyond traditional politics, and by 'relating decision making to the persons who are affected' (see Hajer & Wagenaar, 2003, p. 3). In this case, civil society is deemed as representative of and performing the latter. This certainly has a de-bordering effect on the nation-state.

On a concluding note, the emerging network governance literature traversed in this chapter has been helpful and illuminative in analysing and understanding the evolution of network governance in primary education in Bangladesh. Such an application demonstrated that a review and renewal of literature on governance networks can help appraise the institutional and structural contexts within which topological power and topographical authority get entangled and hybridized, and thus networks evolve, become legitimated and institutionalized. If 'complex and up-to-date information on most aspects of foreign systems of education' (Phillips & Schweisfurth, 2014, p. 1) is one central concern of comparative education, understanding how systems are governed in sociologically and historically contingent ways may provide deeper insights into how globalization and its derivative networks affect education systems in institutional, organizational and increasingly multidirectional and relational ways, as argued by Larsen and Beech (2014). In the next chapter, we consider the emergence and significance of social enterprises in governance in Bangladesh.

4

Social-Enterprising the Public Sector in Bangladesh

Introduction

In the previous chapter, we accounted historically for the rise and remit of heterarchic networks through a system-wide programme of governance within the primary education system of Bangladesh. Linked to the broader context of this transformation, various forms of partnerships surfaced as responsible for and responsive to the governance of educational services. While such partnerships in services, but often also in systems governance (see Chapter 3), have traditionally been imagined between the government and what we have known thus far as NGOs, our research traced the frequency of a 'social entrepreneurial' movement that signalled potential alterations within the NGO sector at large. These social entrepreneurial developments within the NGO sector are the principal focus of this chapter.

This hunch was triggered by and particularly evident in Teach For Bangladesh's (TFB) de facto social entrepreneurial functioning parallel to its official NGO identity (see Adhikary & Lingard, 2020). Intrigued by TFB, we probed deep into the possibility of a silent but sweeping transformation within the NGO sector. This chapter illustrates how such transformations were being led by another powerful imagination of a globally networked yet locally active organization, namely, the British Council Bangladesh (hereafter, BCB). We work with Appadurai's (1996, p. 4) conception of imagination, one that 'is neither purely emancipatory nor entirely disciplined'. Rather, he regards the work of the imagination as 'a space of contestation in which individuals and groups seek to annex the global into their own practices of the modern [intended for the local]' (Appadurai, 1996, p. 4). The efforts and network that the BCB led were directed to the NGO Affairs Bureau of Bangladesh (NGOAB), which is the national authority overseeing NGO activities and foreign charitable funding in Bangladesh and to which TFB was accountable.

Unlike the focus of the previous chapter, emphasizing the historical making of a governance network that acted more like a heterarchy (Ball, 2012a), this chapter's attention is mainly on a loosely coupled, comparatively fast-paced 'policy network' (Ball & Junemann, 2012) that functioned much like an advocacy movement. While in Chapter 3 the imagined and manifest 'world' of influence took the shape of a system-wide programme (Primary Education Development Programme (PEDP)/Sector Wide Approach to Programming (SWAP)) within the Directorate of Primary Education (DPE), the constructed 'world' illustrated in this chapter demonstrated an epistemic force within, and directed towards, the NGOAB. The BCB's 'policy making world' (Peck & Theodore, 2015) was about the creation of legislation necessary to establish social enterprises (SEs) as a formal and legally compatible organizational identity, along with ministerial structures necessary to support the growth of such organizations as a complete sector. Since NGOs were being taxed in Bangladesh, tax exemption or relaxation emerged as a mounting debate underpinning much-needed sustainable development that a social entrepreneurial future was expected to serve.

The BCB is an extension of the British Council Global (BCG). The latter being the global network, the BCB is an international cultural organization active in Bangladesh since 1951. During its foundation in 1934, the BCG was named the 'British Committee for Relations with Other Countries'. Considered an independent organization, the BCG is significantly financed by the British government (Savage, 2007). Currently a globally oriented non-profit charity, the BCG is meant to foster British culture, language and business around the world, and in recent years, it has shifted focus to 'social enterprises' (see BCG, 2019a,b). As a part of this move, the BCB has been actively pursuing social entrepreneurial policies and structures in Bangladesh since 2015. The goals are not only to expand social development businesses (including in relation to education) but also to facilitate a fully fledged social entrepreneurial sector in the country more broadly. In this chapter, we investigate the BCB's social entrepreneurial policy imagination for Bangladesh and the local enactment of that imagination through networking with an epistemic community and policy dialogue with the government. We approach BCB's local policy movement, again, from a spatio-cultural perspective.

The BCB led the imagined and manifest world (Appadurai, 1996) within which this social entrepreneurial policy movement was gaining influence. The organization brought together an aspiring network of epistemic 'experts' – incentivized 'sector specialists', as they were called – who helped it in the spatio-cultural framing of influence in anticipation of a nationwide SE sector (Adhikary et al., 2020). Deeply related to this persuasive momentum, some leading NGOs in Bangladesh were prefiguratively assuming social entrepreneurial identities, de facto, including TFB. Social enterprise is a powerful policy imagination of an 'elite' circuitry of global (new) philanthropists and impact investors (see Chapter 6). Within an emerging global policy culture, it is central to the organizational identity, model and policy agenda of TFB – an organization emanating from a globalized policy localism, notably Teach For America/Teach For All (Adhikary & Lingard, 2017).

This chapter shows how such an SE model is being imagined as a broad policy panacea inclusively for all service sectors in Bangladesh. Analysis revealed that SE policy was being actively pursued by an 'epistemic [policy] community' (Ball & Junemann, 2012) comprising glocal actors (Lingard, 2014a; Robertson, 1994) who leveraged a grounded footing within the larger policy landscape of the country. Nuancing such dynamics, we have captured the unique and fast policy sociology (Peck & Theodore, 2015) that empirically illustrated an emerging drive to transform NGOs to SEs or their hybridization in Bangladesh. TFB itself exemplified one such hybrid entity currently active within the primary education subsector of Bangladesh.

Analyses carried out in this chapter relate directly to the research question: How was 'social entrepreneurship' constituted as an overarching policy vector in Bangladesh, and what future did it signal for education? The research imagination underpinning this question arose from the network ethnographic interviews initially conducted, focusing on TFB and its founder. A few initial interviews led to the realization that an understanding of TFB would be systemically isolated and heuristically pallid without an examination of what was happening in Bangladesh regarding NGOs and SEs, which together helped constitute TFB's hybrid identity. The 'answers' to the posed research question were empirically supported by data from in-depth interviews, an influential policy dialogue event that was attended and associated policy artefacts.

Interviews involved leading policy actors from government, the NGO/SE sector and associated international organizations. These actors were found mobilizing and mediating considerable efforts and resources in the active persuasion of policies necessary for establishing SE as a comprehensive business sector. This intended sector was continually being 'imagined' as parallel to or even a replacement for the existing NGO sector in Bangladesh. TFB stood as a hallmark signifier of the changing scenario discussed in this chapter.

Methodologically, TFB emerged as a pathway to reach, analyse and understand the ongoing broader sectoral changes of which the primary education subsector was a substantial part and a target zone for entrepreneurial aspirations and interests, mostly through global partnerships.

Complementing Appadurai's (1996) argument that set the opening tone of this chapter, the analyses carried out here reveal how a network of global-local actors connected around very similar policy 'imaginations' and associated 'collective aspirations' vis-à-vis SEs. These imaginations and aspirations were then translated into 'evidence-based' advocacy events that powerfully activated a 'play of pastiche' through the spatio-cultural construction and utilization of international/ized 'reference societies' (Schriewer & Martinez, 2004; Sellar & Lingard, 2013; Waldow, 2012) and data-driven discourses of comparison (Grek, 2009; Hardy, 2015; Lingard, 2011; Ozga, 2009). Such efforts were participated in, debated over and often supported both by the central government and its long-standing competitors,[1] both old and emerging. These competitors, as the data revealed, included international (cultural) organizations and NGOs-turned-SEs[2] but also highly diasporic impact investors, policy consultants, employed researchers and legal advisors trained in Anglophone global universities and policy institutes.

Resulting from the efforts of these epistemic actors, a fast yet context-mediated 'movement' towards the establishment of an SE sector was set in motion. A perceived need for supportive legislation and an administrative wing (e.g. a new ministry) characterized the sectoral imagination around which data shaped discourses in events and meetings. All of these policy-seeking manoeuvres moved rhizomatically towards the NGOAB in the main. Demonstrating policy advocacy in practice, such dynamics unfolded empirically within organized and invited events, where the global and the national/local became imbricated. Empirically, such places of encounter were replete with epistemic charisma and field-specific expertise that drew their rationale again from a best-practice efficiency discourse. By studying one such event – a research-focused panel discussion – it was found that the essential *problématique* underlying this SE-sector policy movement involved three axes: sector development, essential legislation and tax relaxation.

Such conclusions have been reached through analyses performed in the following three sections. First, using interview data, we have sought to understand the apparent impasses in the way SE was imagined as a policy panacea to address social problems for and within Bangladesh, and what aspirations and interests made this imagination matter so powerfully. This is, again, the identification of the 'imagined community' and the associated landscape of collective aspirations – *imaginaire*. We also have highlighted the disjunctive cultural beliefs and political assumptions that informed competing policy imaginations around SE in Bangladesh. Next, we thematically analyse one policy dialogue event organized by the BCB to understand the nature of an ethnographic network (here an epistemic community) in action, the discourses and technologies[3] (Ball, 2006, 2015) that they used to steer policy. And finally, we conclude with an overview of the tensions characterizing this policy context.

The BCB and SEs in Bangladesh: A Contested Cultural Imagination

Social enterprise in Bangladesh is 'imagined' as a nationwide policy solution to existing and perceived social problems by a globally endowed yet locally active policy network (Ball, 2012). Composed of varied interests, such as international (cultural) organizations, NGO-turned-SEs, corporate legal services and research firms, this network demonstrated existential flows of global-local formations. Of these interests, the BCB displayed organizing capacity and took a deliberative lead (Ball & Junemann, 2012), assuming the role of network coordination. The government has been found to be receptive to a continuous process of policy influence manifested by the productive participation from networked organizations, few of which had substantial visibility and command within the global social entrepreneurial domain and associated governing infrastructure (see Chapter 6).

Initially, two international organizations were identified as working on specific goals and policies productive of social entrepreneurship in Bangladesh. Of them, the BCB appeared globally visible and was locally more deliberative and engaged. The other organization, GIZ, the German Federal Enterprise for International Cooperation, was not nearly so active. In contrast, the aspirations, interactions and work of the BCB enacted in practice the role of a lead organization. One senior official from an NGO-turned-SE and partner to the BCB's SE-policy work explained the emerging scenario in the following way:

> Different organizations are working in different ways. For example, some organizations do work through partners and they do not go for the implementation. For example, GIZ (the German Federal Enterprise for International Cooperation) is helping social entrepreneurs in Bangladesh.

British Council is also working. British Council calls itself a social enterprise. It is not an NGO. Since they are an international organization, they do not need to have NGO-Bureau approval. And British Council does not work using its own money. It takes money from UK funds and gets benefits out of that ... It takes fund from DfID.[4] It does business taking fund from DfID. And it is trying to explore further as to how it can do more types of social business in Bangladesh. And now it has turned into a social enterprise. (NGO-turned-SE senior official-1)

Two trends of activities formative of a SE sector in Bangladesh surfaced here, the milder version of which extended support to de facto social entrepreneurs fresh to the field of social innovations. While the GIZ represented this support trend, the organization's efforts did not involve coordinated steering of policy towards broader sectoral goals. Meanwhile, the BCB demonstrated grit in its meta-governance (Klijn & Edelenbos, 2007) of policy steering work. In fact, the organization culturally represented what it diligently propagated *as* and *for* policy – a global SE in itself. As a quango and an international cultural organization, the BCB stands as an example of SE that sought to imagine an educational future beyond the NGO box.

Not a traditional NGO, the BCB operates on DfID (the name of the UK department at the time) funding in the country as a 'cultural' quango. Locally, the organization explored business opportunities in Bangladesh at this point by working towards the foundation of a fully fledged social entrepreneurial sector. In theory, an SE-sector policy involves a nationally intended reform meant to override and cross-cut imagined social sectors, of which education is the central one in Bangladesh. Premised upon global entrepreneurial, (new) philanthropic and impact investment thinking, this is indeed a powerful policy imagination (Peck & Theodore, 2015; Robertson, 2005), and its localization (Santos, 2002) entails advocacy work within a pre-imagined field. One senior-level BCB official explained the organization's gritty stance in this regard, using impact investment vocabulary that constituted the SE-sector policy imagination:

What we are trying to do is really trying to get down to some of the nuanced, subtle features around how to grow social enterprises in this context here in Bangladesh ... And we are gonna focus on really where we see opportunity to grow social enterprises, where we think it can have the most impact in Bangladesh. (BCB-2)

'Opportunity' and 'impact' were key to the global SE-policy vernacular now resonating locally. Sliced from an inaugural speech by the BCG's manager for its

'Global Social Enterprises' wing, this quotation pointed at the transmogrification of global aspirations into meticulously local objectives with imaginable policy effects (Ozga, 2000). The very presence of such global actors within an otherwise local policy landscape certainly has an impact, foregrounding cultural encounter and coordination (Santos, 2002). This is a global imagination topologically carried and evident within the local. What Appadurai (1996) refers to as 'globally defined fields of possibilities' are reimagined locally on the basis of a globalized 'impact' logic that selects local interlocutors. The superlative 'most' prefixing the 'impact' again brings the efficiency motivation back into the analysis. Imagination puts to action the BCB's lead in agenda setting and policy steering and, most importantly, involving the government. Another BCB senior official added:

> Rino: Social entrepreneurial activities to be operative within this system require consideration of financial aspects, policy dimensions and legal elements.
> BCB-1: Ya! I am seeing that. Because British Council is leading this, Ok! So, we are kind of organizing policy dialogues. It is dialogue between these sector leaders, experts and sometimes some government officials. Additional secretary …
> BCB-1: Who did you meet at NGO Bureau? Did you meet the director general?
> Rino: …
> BCB-1: Ok! From NGO Bureau, the Director General [name deleted] is also involved with us. Minister of industries, minister of finance, Central Bank, [are also important, and] we are closely working on that.

The BCB's lead in coordinating the activities aspirational to an SE sector highlights the policy support important for the organization. Think of the self-description of the organization as an SE since 2015. Such considerations, in the context of Bangladesh, presented SE as a policy imagination collectivized and put to action by the BCB. By the time of data collection in late 2016, the organization had already demonstrated considerable progress in identifying the relevant government divisions and ministries that needed authorizing involvement in the process of co-imagining the policy. The emphases of NGOAB, its executive head and few other financial divisions enabled entry to the local policyscape related to social, entrepreneurial and economic governance of Bangladesh. Indeed, the local still mattered and quite obstinately so (Peck & Theodore, 2015).

However, despite the global embeddedness of social entrepreneurial policy and the British Council's promulgation and localizing role in it, one top official from the organization believed that SE was a home-grown phenomenon gone exemplarily global:

> Bangladesh has been a global pioneer in social enterprise. I have already mentioned of BRAC and Grameen. Two massive organizations in the field of micro-finance and social enterprise ... So the examples in Bangladesh have inspired millions. And paved the way for the growth of social enterprise worldwide ... Today there is a small but pretty vibrant social enterprise community in Dhaka. And a relatively larger social enterprise activity across the country. However, to date, there has been very limited quality evidence about the operations of social enterprise outside BRAC and Grameen. (BCB-2)

An interesting case in point, the projected local rootedness of Building Resources Across Communities (BRAC) and Grameen as a widely localized globalism adds interesting insights to de Sousa Santos's (2002) argument that anything that is global has its local roots. The unique feature here is that BRAC and Grameen are being imagined first as home-grown localisms, then as globalized localisms and finally reimagined back for/into Bangladesh as localizable globalisms. But in reality BRAC and Grameen were never unmixed localisms. Rather, they were 'glocalisms' – global-local imbricated – since the very beginning and still continue to be so. In fact, Annie Kelly, editor to the *Guardian*'s 'Modern-Day Slavery in Focus' series, defines BRAC's 'meteoric rise', emphasizing critiques from within the NGO sector of the organization acting as a 'parallel state accountable to no one' (Kelly, 2008).

The BCB senior official viewed two of the largest and oldest Bangladeshi NGOs – one led by a knighted recipient and the other a Nobel laureate – as pioneering examples of SEs with global circulatory impact. In practice, this is a reimagining and renaming of NGOs as SEs. Even though BRAC and Grameen had started and continued their work over decades as grant-reliant prototype NGOs, redefining them as 'social enterprises' exemplifies a process called 'referentiality', whereby international/national references are used as 'sources of authority' to legitimize intended 'practices, values and forms of organization' (Steiner-Khamsi, 2002, p. 70). Characteristic of global-local imbrication happening primarily at a cultural level, here we see an effort to reimagine local NGO activities as globally followed SE models. Empirically speaking to the concept of 'referentiality', this is 'externalization' of BRAC and Grameen as globally acclaimed models of SEs.

However, this de-territorialization of the imagination (Peck & Theodore, 2015) around BRAC and Grameen through renaming and then re-territorializing (see Schriewer & Martinez, 2004; Steiner-Khamsi, 2002, 2006) as SEs has been in practice in Bangladesh for a long time. Indeed, an SE-policy imagination is being de-bordered and then re-bordered here as a flowing cultural construct. This is an effort from the BCB to construct its own referential self (it is an SE), in terms of the local. One senior official from one of BCB's partnering NGO-turned-SEs explained such situational necessities as a case of 'old wine in a new bottle':

> Let me use a silly Bangla idiom 'notun botole purono mal' – old alcohol in a new bottle. This is innovation. You have an idea; people are seeing it. Why do people change the outer wrap? The products remain the same or close to the earlier version. It is just to attract people and that is the reason for working in a new manner. (NGO-turned-SE-1)

The projection of BRAC and Grameen as SEs is one key rationale underpinning SE-sector policy. The idea is that Bangladesh should expand and benefit from what the country has done through traditional NGOs, where reimagining NGOs as SEs becomes a home-grown and putatively wise imperative with opportunities that again need to be collectively reimagined. These externalizations of (re) imagined practices by using 'self-referential' discourses are particularly important when policies that are 'politically highly contested' are in the making (Steiner-Khamsi, 2002, p. 70).

We are considering this as 'reimagination' because the government department that directly oversees NGOs in Bangladesh did not view the latter as SEs. There were confusions and disagreements both from the political and bureaucratic arms of government regarding this issue. One senior-level government official clarified this tension in the following way:

> From *my Bureau*, sometimes it is the very general perception in the NGO Affairs Bureau that NGOs are to run the charity activities. If we find some NGOs that are doing businesses as well, then we feel that these sorts of activities do not match with the regulatory framework, or the order or the laws or the regulations which govern our activities. So increasingly we are coming across these situations. Many NGOs are running businesses as well. But there is no legal framework at the moment in my bureau, that is, to regulate them. So, this is a gap. Already I have highlighted this gap. That is, if it is an NGO that tries to run businesses, or do businesses then say how their activities should be governed? There should be

separate agency, or it would be the NGO Affairs Bureau, and I *imagine*, that is, a separate agency will take care. (NGO Bureau, senior official-1)

The use of the expression 'I imagine' captures how imagination and counter-imagination are characterizing the policy world within which SE is oscillating. This is indeed a disjuncture between two policy imaginations and associated cultural properties and local referents. The BCB and the policy network it leads imagine SE policy as supportive of business and enterprises owned by NGOs, while the government views the same as confusing, particularly for administrative and legal reasons. The whole policy dynamics here are based on the relative power of embattled imaginations (Appadurai, 1996).

The extract given earlier from the comment of an authority-level government representative clearly highlights the fact that what were presented by the British Council and related others as social entrepreneurial organizations and activities in Bangladesh were actually something intended and emerging or in the process of becoming. As far as regulation, legislation and structural requirements were concerned, there was 'no such thing as Social Enterprises in Bangladesh'. NGO activities were clearly defined as funded charity work with a predefined legal structure, organizational identity and governance mechanism already in place.

The reimagined development of SEs is something that empirically contradicted culture and regulations practised for decades by the relevant government authority, the NGOAB. The very question as to whether NGOs can/should do business emerged as central, not only for the state bureaucracy and government but also for the political elites that oversaw the former. For example, providing further nuances to this dilemma, one NGO leader partnering with the British Council to pursue SE-sector development policy exclaimed how the top political authority was also grappling with questions around NGOs' adoption of business motives and models. Based on his long experience within the NGO sector (BRAC) and with government bureaucracies (collaborative work), this research participant highlighted a policy moment characterized by confusion, tension and struggle that mostly arose from differences in policy imaginations:

[Sir Fazle Hasan] Abed[5] saw it [SE] a bit differently. He looked at Mahatma Gandhi as a social entrepreneur. It is not always that you have to have revenue from all your social good activities. So, you are working basically for societal change. For example, Hazard [Mohammed] Sallallahu Alayhi Wa Sallam was a social entrepreneur. He worked for the social impact. [Sir Fazle Hasan] Abed never focused on the revenue side when he mentions of the changes he brought into education and health sectors. But now he also has started. Now BRAC education is not free. Now they take a payment from the service seekers. And villagers are paying it. But Dr. Yunus[6] speaks directly of social business. But there are a lot of debates centring around this. And the debate is coming mainly from the government levels. The [very senior government figure] has gone severely against it [arguing], 'There should not be anything called social business. Do direct business either, everybody does business. Why social? You are basically doing business here.' (NGO-turned-SE-2)

Again, reaffirming Appadurai's point on the centrality of imagination in global cultural dynamics, the interview extract quoted earlier shows how SE as a sector policy is co/contra-imagined by competing authorities and interests, resulting in a disjunctive policy moment. Competing sets of ethical beliefs and religio-moral assumptions are disjunctively guiding the policy imaginations of the national political and bureaucratic elites on one side and a BCB-led network of 'sector specialists' on the other. This disjuncture manifests itself in the form of a policy condition characterized by powerfully nuanced interaction between the global/ized market-based policy imagination of SE and the local contextual authority factors associated with gatekeeping national culture, politics and administration.

The research participant quoted earlier goes to the extent of 'imagining' Prophet Mohammad and Mahatma Gandhi as social entrepreneurs. This clearly is an ethico-moral reconstitution as well as a cultural indigenization of a market-oriented policy. Based on such reconstitution, this participant rationalized the late Sir Abed's transformation from initial reluctance to focus on revenue to subsequent involvement in business activities. This example of BRAC and its larger transformative impulses are facing challenges from the government; they are both bureaucratic and political. Another top government official involved in NGO monitoring explained this critical disjuncture in a more nuanced way:

And you know BRAC; they are already working as a social enterprise. That is, they have lots of business initiatives and business undertakings. And BRAC is registered with NGO Affairs Bureau. But we do not deal with the business activities of BRAC. There is a sharp difference between these two [business versus NGO]. So, these are the issues that we are facing. And we are also in the grey area. We also seriously feel the need of clear definition of a social enterprise, legal and policy framework and government's position in terms of social enterprises. (SGO-2)

This interview excerpt highlights how the BCB's discernment of SE as an already existing de facto sector deserving government recognition and policy support is co-imagined yet countered by the government as a yet-underdeveloped reality that needs clarification and refinement. Processes of such co-imagination are imbricative by default because they bring the cutting edges of the global and the local in close contact, engaging them in a cognitive game of cultural appraisal. Open to learning from such appraisals, the government became critical of BRAC's business activities along ethical, legislative and administrative lines. Despite apparent unwillingness to compromise the traditional differences between business as usual and charitable NGO work, the essential importance of novel approaches to bringing such grey hybridities under definitional and regulatory deliberations surfaced.

Undeniably, imagination and its cultural properties are central to the imbrications of global-local relations. Following 'imagination', the empirical passage we have travelled thus far characterizes various moments of encounter of a policy movement as culturally disjunctive between key tensions. Such tensions represent not an impasse but a *problématique* of determining whether, how and what should be done to establish SE as a sector, whereby global-local investors and entrepreneurs can do business with a social purpose in mind. On one side of this tension is a network of glocal actors and organizations led by the BCB representing 'context-productive' (outside) forces and on the other is an apparent stringency of national policy elites, active as 'context-generative' (internal) mediators (Appadurai, 1996). How the negotiation of policy is carried forward through the interaction between these productive and generative forces is examined in the next section by studying one policy advocacy event.

The Placement of SE Practice: Panel Discussion as a Spatio-cultural 'Encounter'

This section presents a practical example of our methodological innovation of ethnographic networks in action. Data analysed here are derived from an in-situ encounter between the global forces of mobility (BCB network) and the local/national agencies of relative immobility (the government). Within such spatialities of 'encounter', we demonstrate how cultural appraisal performed in terms of data and field expertise at the local level intersected with a global SE imagination. It is through such spatio-cultural extensions that proximity and reach (Allen, 2009, 2011) of global forces (Massey, 2006) become moored and exert influence – touched down (Adhikary & Lingard, 2017; Ellis et al.,

2015) – in relation to the local conditions which we still imagine to characterize the 'nation-state' (Anderson, 1983).

The British Council commissioned baseline research on 'social enterprise' not only in Bangladesh but also in other countries with similar socio-economic conditions. Such countries relevantly included South Asian neighbours such as India and Pakistan, as well as Ghana as an African comparator. The organization then hosted a policy dialogue event where government officials, 'sector specialists', NGO-turned-SEs and corporate personnel were invited. During the policy dialogue event, an epistemic community presented the BCB's research output; on the basis of this, a panel discussion was undertaken and moderated by a senior BCB official. We view this policy dialogue event as yet another heterotopic place, where the placement of SE practice took one incremental step towards further development.

In this panel discussion, the director general (DG) of NGOAB faced questions, passed comments, listened to illustrations proffered by the epistemic community and engaged with the audience when possible. In the process, efforts were undertaken to render the BCB's policy imagination meaningful to the government gatekeepers, who, in turn, engaged in a manner that made it hard to realize the differences between the dominant, the residual and the emergent (Williams, 2005) vis-à-vis SE-sector policy. It is in this context that the ethnographic network presented itself at its best with an animated display of who they purported to be, how they talked, who they targeted, what resources they made use of, what activated and limited them and how this occurred.

The Ethnographic Network

The policy event analysed here was entitled 'Social Enterprise Landscape in Bangladesh: Launch of Research Reports'. The first author of this book was formally invited to the event as part of data collection as a follow-up to an interview with a BCB senior official. The event had two major segments: a research reporting session followed by a panel discussion. Two British Council research reports were disseminated at this event. One was entitled 'Social Enterprise Policy Landscape in Bangladesh' and the other was 'The State of Social Enterprises in Bangladesh, Ghana, India and Pakistan: The State of Social Enterprise in Bangladesh'.

The panel discussion was based mainly on the second report, which was a baseline survey of the Bangladeshi context. Forwarded by the director of BCB, these research projects and their reports were outputs of collaborative work between organizations such as the British Council, Overseas Development Institute (ODI), UnLtd for social entrepreneurs and BetterStories. Leveraging the principle of 'data = power', this research project was led and overseen by ODI with support from Social Enterprise UK (SEUK). While commissioned by the BCB for Bangladesh, BetterStories Limited led the project nationally (BetterStories, 2018b). This network of epistemic collaboration is indicative of its members' global diffusiveness yet locally decisive presence. The researchers were located in various global cities (Sassen, 2013) and yet were influential by collaborating with apparently domestic researchers from BetterStories Bangladesh.

A brief excursis about the nature of these organizations assists with understanding these relationships between the global and the local. A charity in England and Wales, the ODI is a leading independent think tank on international development and humanitarian issues. It is supported by grants and donations from global foundations, non-governmental organizations, the private sector, governments, multilateral agencies and academia (ODI, 2018). Similarly, self-labelled as 'the leading global authority on Social Enterprises', SEUK is 'the biggest network of Social Enterprises in the UK' (SEUK, 2018). A London-based charitable organization, UnLtd was founded by seven organizations that promote social entrepreneurship; these include Ashoka: Innovators for the Public, Changemakers, Community Action Network, Comic Relief, The Scarman Trust, SENSCOT and The School for Social Entrepreneurs (UnLtd, 2018). Finally, BetterStories, the local counterpart, is a foundation cum social impact business located in Dhaka, Bangladesh. It works to establish an SE ecosystem in the country. The two key actors are Minhaz Anwar (with the designation of chief storyteller (researcher)) and Muhaimin Khan (CEO; a young American Bangladeshi) (BetterStories, 2018a).

The panel discussion was designed particularly to foreground an SE-policy dialogue between the BCB-led epistemic community and the corresponding division head from the government, in this case the DG of NGOAB. However, the whole event was organized around the panel discussion, where the DG of the NGO Bureau was expected to join with the other panellists listed in Table 4.1. The panellists selected and invited by the British Council, excluding the DG, were open supporters and direct promoters of SE-sector policy and were actively engaged in pursuing the same. The British Council considered them as 'sector leaders and specialists', which the government later acknowledged. These so-called sector specialists and experts came from the sectors that were critically important for an SE-sector policy.

Table 4.1 Participants on the panel discussion

Participants	Information
Moderator: Mr Tristan Ace	Global social enterprises Partnerships and development manager The British Council
Panellist 1: Dr Ananya Raihan	Leading social entrepreneur ~Co-founder, d.net Bangladesh ~Ashoka Fellow
Panellist 2: Mr Minhaz Anwar (Conducted the BCB- commissioned research and presented the findings prior to participating in panel discussion)	Managing director and chief storyteller BetterStories, Bangladesh Limited ~Attended the Young Entrepreneurs Exchange Programme, the University of Oklahoma (two months in the United States) ~MBA, the Institute of Business Administration, University of Dhaka
Panellist 3: Ms Anita Ghazi Rahman-Islam	Corporate lawyer, The Legal Circle Advocate of the Bangladesh Supreme Court ~Barrister-at-law, LLB (Hons), the University College London (UCL)
Panellist 4: Mr Md. Ashadul Islam	Honourable director general The NGO Affairs Bureau of Bangladesh

Note: News about this policy dialogue is publicly available (see BCB, 2016; Dhaka Tribune, 2016).

The list of panellists (Table 4.1) and the globally diffused social entrepreneurial network in the background highlight the role of contacts – some were clearly hired – in the formation of an epistemic community, which was meant to augment or debate the British Council's policy imagination according to research, programming, legal and structural dimensions. From within this larger network of experts and researchers, the locally performative members were nodal players in the dialogue event. Led by the BCB, this locally active network now mobilized considerable time, effort and resources to foster an SE sector. The interests and remit of these participants were shaped by academic training and professional grooming, epistemically based in select US and UK institutions of legal and social entrepreneurial prominence. These involvements were indeed highly diasporic in terms of movement of individuals, knowledge and ideas.

Data Steering Policy: Similitude as the Cultural Logic

The SE community instrumentalized particular epistemic tools available at their professional disposal. Quantitative research was used to guide select discourses articulated during the panel discussion. Thematic analysis of the panel discussion transcripts exposed specific anchoring techniques through which the British Council official moderated the panel discussion. By using select data trends as evidence categories, the moderator scaffolded and navigated the relevant referential points and rationales that gave the panel discussion coherence as an SE event. This constructed frame of reference dovetailed the 'national eye' (BetterStories research on SE in Bangladesh) to the 'global eye' (mainly older research on SE in the UK) (No'Voa & Yariv-Mashal, 2003, p. 425).

The moderator began the panel discussion combining a bullet point summary with an overarching steering remark on the key findings of the quantitative survey which the BCB commissioned BetterStories to conduct. The projected developments in SE activities in Bangladesh were presented as something nearly indistinguishable from the UK context but also similar to what was occurring in neighbouring countries. These Bangladesh findings were then re-presented as identical to the findings of similar survey studies commissioned by British Council in neighbouring and African countries, such as Pakistan, India and Ghana. The expected effect was the realization that SE was something happening effortlessly at a global scale – most importantly within the neighbouring regions and their African counterparts. The following extract from the moderator's comments explains this construction of 'reference societies' (Lingard & Rawolle, 2011; Luhmann, 1990; Schriewer & Martinez, 2004; Steiner-Khamsi, 2006):

> One thing I found very interesting about the three surveys in South Asia is that many of the trends that we see there are actually similar in different parts of the world. And even in the UK some of the trends are also quite similar. Particularly the focus on the youth and the role that young people are playing in leading social enterprises. We see that consistently across the three countries here in South Asia. There is a really interesting question around why that is; is it because, perhaps, social enterprises and its model is less hierarchical? It allows for younger leaders to develop more quickly? These are really interesting things we are trying to explore more in detail. I think the fact that we have this larger number of women leaders within social enterprises is also really interesting. Again, we really try to understand why that is. It is something that British Council will be doing: we are embarking on a more in-depth report that will look into the role of women leadership in social enterprises. That's a study we will be kicking off very soon. (BCB moderator)

This introduction shows how research and data-driven evidence creation were deemed central to guiding policy processes and discourses. In fact, this is where a policy cycle effectively begins. More importantly, through such data projections, SE has been imbued with the status of an emerging culture. It also points at how the British Council was assuming the role of a research 'authority', not only in Bangladesh but also for similar other neighbouring and African countries, activating a process of 'externalization' (Schriewer, 1988; Schriewer & Martinez, 2004; Steiner-Khamsi, 2004). The isomorphic focus on 'youth' and 'women' expressed in the form of key findings set the overarching tone and theme for the discussions that were later picked up and recontextualized by the glocal discussants, who provided enhanced details through their experience and knowledge.

Most invitingly, the whole process of the panel discussion also ceded the assumed research authority and the associated discursive power (Ball, 2006) to members of the epistemic community by an underlying naturalized process of 'certification' (McAdam et al., 2001; Steiner-Khamsi, 2004). Certification is central to processes of political mobilization such as, inter alia, creation and transformation of actors and their authorization (McAdam et al., 2001, p. 13). To be specific, certification within global-local political processes means 'validation of actors, their performances, and their claims by external authorities' (McAdam et al., 2001, p. 145). Through the panel discussion, the British Council not only used research as an epistemic tool of influence (Shahjahan, 2016) but also assumed exactly the role of an external authority (heterarchy). Such authority comes from the ability and possession of resources to conduct, manage and disseminate 'research for policy' (Rizvi & Lingard, 2010, p. ix).

In the aggregate, the commissioning of research, the appointment of research professionals, the organization of research reporting, the homogenizing reference to the UK context and the designing of dissemination events presented the panel discussion and the associated glocal policyscape as a 'self-referential autopoietic system', or a 'self-referential society' (Luhmann, 1990, pp. 2–3). Luhmann's definitional reference to Milan Zeleny (1981) can further enhance the applicability of this 'self-referential' argument in understanding the British Council's policy manoeuvres:

> Autopoietic systems 'are systems that are defined as unities of networks of productions of components that recursively, through their interactions, generate and realize the network that produces them and constitute, in the space in which they exist, the boundaries of the network as components that participate in the realization of the network'. Autopoietic systems then are not only self-organising systems; they not only produce and eventually change their own *structures*; their

self-reference applies to the production of other *components* as well. This is the decisive conceptual innovation. It adds a turbocharger to the already powerful engine of self-referential machines. (Luhmann, 1990, p. 3; emphases original)

The British Council is a global SE and clearly wants to pursue policy and structural reforms conducive to the replication of what the organization has achieved, first in the UK through its fifteen years of work and then in other developing countries at an ambitious, global scale. The self-referential research of BCB re-creates its own self within envisioned subsystems (components). It is not only reproducing itself as an SE in Bangladesh but also reproducing within Bangladesh the policy system that it has created over the years in the UK and elsewhere through research-based policy advocacy. The organization has successfully mobilized significant effort and resources to create a local version of an autopoietic self-referential society in Bangladesh as and through the constituted epistemic community.

Numbers Influencing Imagination: An Opportunity Discourse of Youth, Women and Markets

The moderator's highlighting of the prominence of women and youth in social entrepreneurial activities in Bangladesh emerged as a key direction to policy thinking. It is beneficial to note for clarity that the focus on youth and women was and still continues to be central to EFA, MDG and SDG country imperatives; undoubtedly, the impact of this cannot be separated from the output of the British Council's current research findings. Moreover, NGOs and civil society organizations supported the government over the decades to pursue these international goals in Bangladesh. However, both the BCB anchor and the epistemic community constituting the discussion presented the prominence of women and youth as something counterintuitive but aligned to policy foci in the referenced societies. And it is through this overarching similarity discourse through data-driven comparisons that the BCB activated the 'play of pastiche' (Appadurai, 1996), while obstinately disregarding the challenges and obstacles rooted in differences:

> I am gonna construct the panel in the following way. I am gonna start off focusing on the positives. Let's forget about the obstacles and the challenges for the time being. And we are gonna focus on really where we see opportunity to grow social enterprises. Where we think it can have the most impact here in Bangladesh? I am gonna ask our panellists so that we can start off focusing on that particular question. From your own experiences, but also from what you

have read in our survey findings, where do you think the biggest opportunity is to really support inclusive economic and social development here in Bangladesh and the role that social enterprises can play in doing that? (BCB moderator)

First of all, the whole discussion was framed, here, around the meta-discourses of inclusive economic and social development. Secondly, an aura of appreciative similarities of opportunity was cast to shape the nature of questions to be discussed. Thirdly, the discussion was then given a referential structure of experience and research: experience of the certified epistemic community, and self-referential research conducted by BetterStories. All of this cognitive scaffolding was then geared towards asking one culminating question that would activate an apolitical and acritical search for market opportunities.

Panellists 1, 2 and 3, who are professionally and experientially promoters of SEs, were asked for the answers first. This was followed by concluding remarks from panellist 4, who was the government counterpart. Panellist 1, who was an Ashoka Fellow[7] and who co-directed a rapidly growing NGO-turned-SE in Bangladesh, parodied the moderator's remarks with experiential details:

> Thank you. First of all, about the research itself, if I take this piece of document referring to all of us, who are working within the social enterprise ecosystem, and beyond. So, congratulations to the team … so this time not to talk about the negatives, let me start with the opportunities. So, the opportunity that I see are the youth and the women's leadership. Because both in terms of the target market youth is very big in Bangladesh, 40 million plus, and in terms of entrepreneurship, the young generation is coming forward to work. And not only to make profit but also to get some impact on the society. I think these are the two opportunities that I see.

Panellist 1 considered the research report as an achievement in itself, hence the congratulatory reference in the third sentence. This achievement belongs not only to the researchers but also to what the panellist calls the 'social enterprise ecosystem' and 'beyond'. This discussant clearly brings to the surface the policy network of dependants and interests that work for SEs. This is what Appadurai (1996), after Anderson (1983), calls the 'imagined community', which today accompanies a 'landscape of collective aspirations'– *imaginaire*. Expansive in orientation, the imagined community now includes youth and women within their aspirational imagination supported by specific interventions. The aspiration is the target market of consumers, and entrepreneurs involve '40 million plus' persons. The centrality of the use of numbers was quite noticeable and continued to be so throughout the encounter.

Panellist 3, who was a corporate lawyer specializing in conflict resolution and start-ups, spoke of opportunities for SE from a sectoral point of view. A slice of the discussion went thus:

> Moderator: So, Anita, now I can come to you. Where do you see the biggest opportunity to grow social enterprises here in Bangladesh?
> Panellist 3: You mean which sector?
> Moderator: It could be an audience; it could be a sector.
> Panellist 3: For me I feel very passionately about social enterprises engagement education. But more in healthcare is needed there.

In contrast to panellist 1's driver/agency perspective, panellist 3 perceived opportunities in terms of sectoral orientation. The latter thought that education and training had the biggest scope (market) for opportunity. The health sector was then also highlighted.

However, panellist 2, who was a local business graduate and the lead researcher from BetterStories, provided a real-world yet comprehensive picture of what panellist 1 had earlier called a 'social enterprise ecosystem' as the greatest opportunity. He became quite effusive in expressing the market-oriented nature of the intended longer-term outcomes of the aspired-for SE-sector policy. This is where the numeric and calculative dimensions of market-oriented policy imagination played out at its fullest:

> So, I think, if we talk about some numbers, there are four billion people in the world that are not getting access to a lot of things. Not just education and health. But also access to financial services and access to information. So, I see a huge global market there. I was quite impressed by the fact that a lot of young people who are under 35 are looking into doing something that is not just for profit but also purpose. So, I believe there is the big opportunity. There are numbers, in the commercial sense, but also because they are driven by what is good for the society at large, I believe that they are going to make it happen. And the rise of support systems, including the impact investors, impact incubators and accelerators. And also, I see a lot of development partners are taking a lot of interest in this phase. So, the fact that in this room we have a lot of representation from a wide variety of development partners, private sector and support system, I think it is a testimony that there is this growing interest to support, to make it happen. So, I think we should all take advantage of that. (Panellist 2)

First of all, the imagination began with a global view. The re/imagination (as in 'I see', I believe', 'I think' and 'I am impressed') of a global market through numeric eyes appeared to be the key cognitive process in creating an image of an untapped sphere of social business opportunities. With the acknowledgement of education and health as already explored opportunities locally, this social entrepreneurial activist became aspiring in 'seeing' a huge global market. This panellist again highlighted the projected centrality of youth in the recognition, creation and capitalization of this market. Panellist 2 also illustrated what he called a 'support system', alluding to new global mechanisms and resources, such as 'impact investors, impact incubators, and accelerators' and also 'development partners'.

This is a comprehensive systemic imagination that reproduces and contains the other components of the self-referential autopoietic system (Luhmann, 1990; Zeleny, 1981): the social entrepreneurial ecosystem. This is how the process of 'certification' – the validation of (new) actors, their performances and their claims by external authorities (McAdam et al., 2001; Steiner-Khamsi, 2004) – was used to effect. Insofar as such discursive arguments and data were able to engage the government counterparts cognitively, this whole exercise surely had some policy effects (Ozga, 2000). However, all of these arguments were then aimed at the government representative (panellist 4), under the auspices of the BCB in front of the chosen audience.

Closely related, this certification process was also achieved by juxtaposing the government authorities on the horizontal platform of a panel discussion alongside other not-government individuals and entities. This horizontalization of the government and not-(so)-government normalizes a process of heterarchization of hierarchies by certifying exogenous forms of constructed authorities, namely, SE-sector leaders and support systems. Within the global/izing context of what he calls 'policy as numbers', Lingard (2014b), recycling Appadurai's (2006a) concepts and associated arguments, depicts such data-driven legitimization of heterarchies (Ball, 2012) as an inherent and continually expanding policy reality within overlapping global-local policy fields. It is through such processes that the heterarchies of transnational politics often legitimize, naturalize and utilize their acquired partnership and authority within national settings that consequently and visibly transform local government hierarchies into a co-player within a global policy field. Such transformations are captured through differential metaphors of the vertebrate versus the cellular:

> Appadurai juxtaposes a vertebrate, hierarchical, bureaucratic politics associated with the nation-state, which he says thrives on singularity *and* difference [i.e. government bureaucracy], with the emergence in the context of the global of

what he refers to as cellular, horizontal, networked politics which flow across nations. These networked cellular flows parallel what Thrift (2005) has called the '*cultural circuits*' of new global capitalism and in Vertovec's (2009)[8] terms function 'transnationally'. (Lingard, 2014b, p. 30; emphases added)

While traditional bureaucratic forms of government made and continue to make use of statistics/data to govern the populous by singularity (of/within the nation-state) and difference (from other nation-states), the new forms of heterarchies of global governance function via focusing data on similarities within pluralities. Yet most importantly, such governance happens at the cultural level as noted in Lingard's observation earlier. The interactions and tensions between these two activate and create scope for the processes of internationalization and externalization of policy reforms. The heterarchies constructed through certification (of aspiring, empowered, new glocal actors) and self-referencing (of the self, i.e., the BCB itself), here, collectively utilized research data to showcase the UK as having international best practice in SE (internationalization), while projecting local Bangladeshi NGO developments as SE work (externalization). Together, this set in motion what Steiner-Khamsi (2002) calls the 'indigenization' of policy reforms. This refers to a shift from 'externalization to internalization', as well as from 'internalization to indigenization', that is, a move away from 'lessons learned from abroad' to 'lessons learned at home' (Steiner-Khamsi, 2002, p. 71).

However, as a guided and organized process, the panel discussion demonstrated a horizontal/izing juxtaposition of government hierarchy (DG of NGOAB) with the glocal heterarchies that stem from the 'cultural' circuits of new global capitalism – the epistemic community and related support system. The government is analytically challenged to think in terms of and respond to questions in accordance with the names, parameters, conditions and categories that the presented data evoked. Emphasizing its increasing role under globalizing policy conditions, Lingard (2014b, p. 31) summarizes the power of naming and categorizing through data within any policy cycle:

> Indeed, knowledge has long been a tool for governing. This is Hacking's (1995) observation: that the technologies of governance through numbers and the creation of categories actually 'make up people' [named and categorized], and then have 'looping effects' back on to the social. Porter (1995) notes that 'numbers create and can be compared with norms, which are among *the gentlest and yet most pervasive forms of power* in modern democracies' (p. 45). As such, he argues, 'Numbers turn people into objects to be manipulated' (p. 77). Scott (1998) likewise sees numbers, data and categories as central to making the space of the nation legible for governing. (Emphasis added)

Here, we see the projected rise of 'youth' and 'women' as examples of how data as a process leads to 'making up' people as named instrumental categories. The associated 'looping effect' (Hacking, 1990) is practised and achieved throughout the panel discussion. Whether manipulation was necessary in the process of data creation and presentation requires further research.

Complex Issues and Surrounding Debates: From Definition to Taxation

Despite clear agreement between the moderator and panellists 1, 2 and 3 on the absence of any clear definition of SE in Bangladesh, all of these participants consistently expressed their 'expert' opinions about what the definition should be from their experience. Panellist 3 provided the definition from a legal perspective in the following way:

> Social enterprises? We do not have a definition of it. There is no ... There is noooo ... Since there is no definition, there is no law regarding it. There is no body which is required to list out or keep the list of how many social enterprises there are. So, this is a wonderful report that you have come up with. But I also agree that it is not for you to define social enterprises. Definition has to come from the government. Right!

To the epistemic community, this void around the lack of definition and statistics on SEs did not signify the absence of such practices in Bangladesh. Rather, the estimated numbers represented through specified criteria were utilized as evidence of the growth of SEs. It was estimated from the analysed and presented data that an astoundingly large number of 150,000 SEs were, at the time of research, operating within the country with further growth expected. Based on this estimation, which stood as evidence of real organic growth of SEs in Bangladesh, the government was entrusted with the responsibility of defining SEs and then providing pertinent legislation and policy support.

However, soon after her initial comments, panellist 3 herself stepped forward to define SE in the following manner:

> Now we are ... Ok ... what is a social enterprises? Let me come from my very simple legal straight point of view of it. It is basically an organization which is earning revenue and generating or putting back more than just its revenue into the project, right, but there is also limited feedback, where the members

are taking back some of the dividends back home. Right? I think that is a wonderful idea.

Basically, this panellist viewed SE as any organization that carried out income-generating business activities in order to support some form of social work. The individual then benefits from some of the dividend personally. Panellist 1 followed panellist 3's definition and added historical nuance to it. He defined SE as an historically evolved form of NGOs, a perspective that the government disagreed with:

> After the liberation [of Bangladesh], NGOs started working, and the model was very simple. You receive funds from abroad and you are doing particular tasks on the ground in healthcare, in education or even in microfinance. So, that was the beginning, and NGO Bureau was established to regulate NGOs, and there was an ordinance. The 1982 ordinance gave the guidelines for how to receive funds and how to report. In addition to the main registration, as a trust, or a company or a society, you had to have a second registration with NGO Affairs Bureau when you receive the foreign fund. Then it evolved, and many NGOs started to think that the fund is reducing from abroad. So how to keep continuing the good work we are doing? And then gradually they started to generate their own income. As Anita was saying, the model was developed that way – either they are generating the income and it remains within the NGO, they are spending it for social work or they are opening a new company with their shares and growing that dividend for their good works. So legally there is no social enterprises. Either they are private company, or they are NGO, or they are trusts. So now we come to that point. (Panellist 1)

The point intended here was that, in the context of foreign funding deficiency, large NGOs had to find ways to sustain their work. This resulted in some NGOs starting their own businesses using existing mainstream enterprise laws. This very hybridity was the seed of social entrepreneurial organizational thinking at the local level. The argument was that since the charity mode of NGOs was not sustainable, linkage with business activities required new organizational identity and associated government structures and policies. In the absence of such facilitation, the government should assume this responsibility as soon as possible.

Thus far, the arguments voiced seemed to be simmering about something that had not been fully addressed for a long time, and about which organizations were making their own decision. It was quite visible that the British Council, BetterStories and the panellists were reluctant to provide a direct definition;

in fact, currently, there was none existing for Bangladesh. However, panellist 1's statement loosened the knot a little. The debate was about NGOs[9] being treated as mainstream enterprises and businesses. Also: could there be anything done to incentivize such a sector in ways that would promote 'good' work and keep it encouragingly alive? As nothing from the government's end had been done thus far, the time had come for it to do something concrete. The central goal of the whole panel discussion, at this point, appeared clear – policies that would recognize NGOs doing parallel business as SEs and that the government could incentivize with tax remission needed to be implemented. The following remarks from panellists 3 and 1 summarized this central dilemma of the whole panel discussion:

> Because as I was saying, in Bangladesh the way we do it is by creating for profit and then a non-profit. Why are we doing this? Because if you are spending money on social good, you are spending money without the expectation of return. The key word here is taxation. Do you want to pay tax on it? No. Because if you are spending money for social good, you are not earning anything out of it. So, whatever the amount you are spending on it, you do not want to pay taxes. So, if you don't want to pay taxes on that certain portion. What do you do? You create a non-profit. So that's my answer. (Panellist 3)

Panellist 3's opinion clearly showed that there are specific ways that non-profit social activities with self-sustaining business support are doable and done in Bangladesh. NGOs are doing business under existing frameworks. But the need for a separate social entrepreneurial sector with specific laws and policy is premised upon a critical question: should SEs be taxed by the government? This dilemma was further clarified and brought to everyone's notice by panellist 1:

> If you come to the definition, if an NGO wants to receive [traditional] investment, that is impossible because they are not for profit. For investment, you have to be registered with the Companies Act not with the Societies Act. So, you can get grants. But if someone agrees to give you money from abroad, you have to pay 30 per cent tax outright. It does not depend on what is your annual balance. From the private company, if your annual balance is negative, you do not have to pay any tax. So, when you want to do something good, you are being taxed. And when you are making money and at the end of the year you do not have any profit, you do not have to pay tax. So, I think these are the areas we have to really look into so that you can really facilitate social enterprises or NGOs who are trying to do good things with investment. And many entrepreneurs I know

do not want to get grants. They want to get investment. I have been approached by many impact investors. I have been asking them, you see when I am making impact, I am spending more than a private company. And I may not be able to bring profit, which you are looking for. And impact investors are looking for profit, I mean the return on investment should be 30 per cent. Whereas in manufacturing company the IRR (Internal Rate of Return) 15 per cent is fine. So, the paradox is I have to make impact and I have to make IRR 30 per cent, whereas even if I go to commercial Bank an IRR of 15 per cent is fine to get investment.

The critical point here is how to facilitate and promote direct impact investment[10] to replace grants and donations. The expected incentive from the government is recognition of NGOs as SEs. Accordingly, SEs should not be treated as grant recyclers; rather, they need to be viewed as social investment utilizers, and for that, policy and legislation were necessary. Social impact and associated investments are areas that putatively deserve either a total tax remission or tax relaxation well below other forms of commercial investments, if, inter alia, youth and women were to be involved and encouraged towards social impact. Moreover, the basic profit motive of social impact investors was also to be supported in the process, as the situation seemed to have demanded this. However, the BCB moderator of the panel discussion, following this revealing discussion on taxation, wrapped up this argumentative stance by again referring to the UK's SE taxation model. He then put the ball firmly into the NGOAB's court:

> So social investment tax relief is probably 30 per cent in the UK. I think you are also referring to Big Society Capital.[11] So, this is the world's first Social Investment Bank. And I think the interesting feature about it is it does not directly invest in social enterprises. It invests in various social investment funds, as a result, to create sustainable social investment market in the UK. It is a very interesting model which I think is potentially quite effective. (BCB moderator)

The necessity was quite clear here: there was a need for the creation of a social investment market in Bangladesh, linking it to global networks of social impact investors and their foundations. Within this imagined future market, new global-local investors and actors needed to be provided with legal and policy support in encouraging ways. The question then remained as to how the government of Bangladesh was going to do this and when? On this note, the floor was then opened to the DG of NGOAB for response to these questions.

Consolidation: The Context Generative Mediates the Context Productive

The government representative from the NGOAB was the honourable DG. After all the discussions and question-answers had been completed, highlighting the projected SE turn, the associated actors and interests and the investment-taxation issue, the DG was given an open floor for comment. It appeared that the DG had done some preliminary work to promote the SE sector but not without having to face some context-bound difficulties. He explained how the context within the walls of the government mattered:

> Thank you. Basically, I think as opinions came up here, already the time is very ripe, this is the very right time to engage the government. And to promote social enterprises, definitely, is a very important thing. So, I think [it would be good] if there is a specific proposal in terms of taxation of social enterprises and also the funding. Already government has so many measures. For example, government has created a special fund to help out the women entrepreneurs. So, if there is a proposal for creating a fund for supporting social enterprises, and as you have mentioned, in different countries, different ministries are handling this job, it is also important to see who will be the lead agency. Whether, as I said before, Ministry of Industry or Commerce, or Finance Division. [NGO] Bureau cannot be the lead agency, because it should come under one particular ministry or division. So, these are the issues that we need to address first. Or at least we need to bring up with the government, that is, to create the environment or the landscape for the social enterprises. So, my suggestion is that, already I have discussed this with my colleagues who are working in the finance division; as I said before, that still they would like to see how does it grow. That is, how does it grow as a whole sector? It is their opinion that, if we go for the policy at the moment, that might hamper the organic growth of the sector. Let them grow. At some point we will step in and we will go for the policy framework.

The government here (as expressed through the words of the DG) is clearly aware of the globally oriented context-productive developments associated with the social entrepreneurial turn. The structural changes required to realize the intended outcome of this policy movement were fundamentally tied up with the highest-level administrative space of the Bangladesh government and on top, the political. A lead ministry or division in place of a bureau was required for the proposed policy and legislative outcomes to be achieved. This is where the 'context-productive' side of the whole SE-sector policy efforts and proposals were facing 'context-generative' mediation (cf. Appadurai, 1996). SE-sector policy is basically a global social investment policy, yet such investments were not totally alien to Bangladesh. This policy was now being pursued by the epistemic community that participated in the panel discussion led by the British Council. Now these policy proposals were filtering through the politics and culture embedded within the authority structures, with better support than before.

High levels of the bureaucracy seemed partially convinced on the ground that the social entrepreneurial practices must grow organically to an exemplary scale, although the BCB-reported research estimated a sizable number of over 150,000 extant SEs already in Bangladesh. The government also seemed to be concerned about the probabilities of SEs' efforts becoming redundant, given those of the government (competition). However, the DG also highlighted the absence and importance of guidelines required to formulate SE-sector policy in Bangladesh. He acknowledged the developments of SE sectors in UK and India and how these developments could become sources for *learning*. The DG considered these country-based experiences as learning opportunities and sources of guidance:

> I think if there are no guidelines or any framework, then it becomes very difficult to determine what to do. So, there is some sort of guidance or directions needed here. And, definitely, we can learn from the UK, because I see this is a pioneering country in promoting social enterprises or in creating special fund or this sort of things. So, Bangladesh can also take lessons from them. And also, from India and other countries who are working on this issue.

This extract, at least at the level of policy dialogue, shows how the British Council's efforts to constitute the UK as a reference society drew some success. We see a government official publicly willing to learn from the UK. This is a development that shows that due to globalization and associated diasporic learning opportunities, government officials have become more open to externalization efforts. The government now sees these developments and associated diasporic experiences as having positive impact on their understanding of action, agency and context for the betterment of their home country. The government's imagination and discursive display of ownership of the system (as in 'my bureau') is meeting global heterarchic counterparts, the impactful knowledge and experience of which are acquired through international and national events such as conferences. The honourable DG further explained:

In May this year, I had the opportunity to attend the AVPN (Asian Venture Philanthropy Network) conference. And I found that, especially the neighbouring countries are working – especially India is pursuing this issue aggressively. They are working seriously. So, we cannot sit idly and definitely we have to do something. The question is to make this concept familiarized with the government policymakers. That they will know that this is the new sector and quality people are working here. This is the survey report, and these are issues that you need to address. And definitely the NBR, the National Board of Revenue, should also be the important actor. Because they will develop the taxation policy and other related things. So, my suggestion and strong recommendation is that definitely the survey report will serve the purpose, and along with this, the sector leaders could put forward very specific suggestions. There is no reason that the government will not take it up seriously.

The DG here provided an example of how global philanthrocapitalist networks were inviting government officials to attend conferences where different social entrepreneurial ideas and practices were shared. From his experience of such conferences, the DG realized that important government authority personnel were not familiar with such practices and policies. Once this familiarization was facilitated, the government would accelerate the process. One important thing to note here is that, besides explaining the complexities threaded within the sociology of local bureaucracy and politics, the honourable DG provided concrete directions to the advocates of SE-sector policy reform regarding the involvement of the taxation authorities of Bangladesh, should the process need to be accelerated.

However, this discussion also demonstrates how policy instruments and suggestions can be influenced by what are perceived as authoritative data-driven perspectives on necessary steps and assessment of progress. Panellist 3 further fostered this influence when she proposed to 'draft a policy' on behalf of the government (note the use of first-person) on how this step was presaged by the collection of necessary data and relevant discussions, which had already been undertaken:

First, I would get the Banks, and alternative investment funds [on board]. I would get them during these panels and like to ask to them what are they looking for to the social enterprises? Secondly, I read somewhere that when you create awareness you get statistics and research. When you have that research report, you start policy dialogue. Once you do that you have law and you have change. We are already in the third stage. We have got all the pieces placed together, so have a draft policy and send it to the NGOAB.

The progression of proposed and seemingly completed steps was quite imaginative, given there were still differences in relation to how government understood SE. Panellist 3 argued that all pre-policy steps were completed, except for involving the national central bank and others. However, the most significant indicator of assumed authority was contained in the idea of drafting a policy for the government. This is probably one of the reasons policy cycles are becoming ever faster, something that Peck and Theodore (2015) have written extensively about in their authoritative volume *Fast Policy*. This also highlights how members of a constructed epistemic community often make definitive use of interpretation to make their case, promoting professional learning in relation to policy enactment (Hardy & Melville, 2018).

Imagination: Sentiments, Solidarity, Action and Encounter

In an interview with the *Saturday Evening Post* on 26 October 1929, Albert Einstein explained the purpose of imagination beyond its literal limits. Adding power to inner engagements, his take on imagination invokes an ex post facto sense of 'globalization'. For him, imagination roams and covers, seeking to enrich. When asked, 'Then you trust more to your imagination than to your knowledge?', he replied, 'Imagination is more important than knowledge. Knowledge is limited. Imagination encircles the world' (see Einstein, 1929, p. 117). On a few other occasions, he insisted that 'imagination enriches the world' and elsewhere that 'imagination embraces the entire world and all there ever will be to know and understand' (see Einstein, 2011, p. 12).

These statements are powerfully illustrative of global governmentality today. These proclamations construe globalization as occurring primarily at the level of agentic imagination (as in embracing and encircling the entire world); they also open one's eyes to a world-*making* ability (as in enriches) as the *creational* power drive (not creation itself) of 'globalization'. Being creational is certainly more powerful than being creative, since the former involves reordering human existence towards an imagined, better future.

Linked to our analysis in fundamental ways, these quotes offer explanatory purchase to Appadurai's (1996) 'imagined worlds' thesis on globalization, with imagination enlarged potentially by the new communication technologies. Appadurai (1996, p. 7) views imagination 'as the *staging* ground for action' and highlights the 'plurality of imagined worlds' (emphasis added). Such worlds in the plural are created by multiple capable actors with a range of creational contents in mind – therefore cultural but not culture itself – seeking to command imaginations that increasingly operate in ways that cannot be readily defined only by locality-based senses of human engagement (Appadurai, 1996, p. 5). Exposing further the nature of today's globalizing role of imagination 'as a property of the collectives', he views the same as 'a form of solidarity' (Appadurai, 1996, p. 8). The solidarized feelings seeded in such imagination forge 'communities *in* themselves' (Appadurai, 1996, p. 8; emphasis added). This is still the Andersonian thesis relating to the 'nation' mediated by the '-state' in the wake of modernity.

However, imagined communities in this time of modernity at large – globalization – are 'always potentially communities *for* themselves' (Appadurai, 1996, p. 8; emphasis added). Think of the networked epistemic community that the BCB fostered and commanded here. Indeed, not only did they share the same social entrepreneurial sentiment but they acted upon that sentiment undeniably for themselves (as in 'support system'). Here sentiments entwined with life's mission and occupational need, a theme we will return to in the next chapter in relation to the TFB founder. And this link between imagination and life's work is explicit in Appadurai (1996, p. 8), that is, communities resulting from such imagination are 'capable, of moving from shared imagination to collective action'. Such collective actions now have become professional work, particularly for those with 'powerful imaginations'. This is what Castells (2016, p. 2) refers to as 'placeless power' which functions by (a) 'the construction of meaning in people's minds through mechanisms of cultural production and distribution' and yet also by (b) 'coercion (the monopoly of violence, legitimate or not, by the state)', in combination. Some of the most impactful moments of such collective actions involving state and cult*ural* (newness) production are the ethnographic details we have sought to capture in this chapter.

When a transnationally imagined collective action intends global impact by changing nationally populated and managed system*s*, the change efforts must pass through authorized gatekeepers at the level of the state. Appadurai (1996, p. 8) contends that constructed 'sodalities are *often* transnational, even postnational, and they *frequently* operate beyond the boundaries of the nation' (emphases added). 'Often' as a temporal signifier indicates that transnational and postnational solidarities – think of the BCB network struggling with their government counterparts – are not exclusive realities. Also, the absence of a hyphenated 'state' after the 'nation' indicates that while the boundaries of the nation might be an imaginative category and culturally porous, the '-state' still remains an active agent of preservation. Indeed, Appadurai (1996) argues that today the nation and the state have become the projects of each other in the context of the multiple flows of globalization. 'Encounters' (Amin, 2002; Massey, 1994b), thus, are always between creational mobility and preservational fixity; the outcome is imbrications with cultu*ral* progression, be it of policy or of cricket. In this sense, the 'old wine in a new bottle' analogy that one NGO official alluded to in explaining the social entrepreneurial situation is not fully correct. There must be something new, something creative, at least in the purposive sense of imagination.

Analyses performed in the preceding section evidence the ways in which the administrative and political state were still important in the creation of the BCB's imagined world of social entrepreneurial policy. Seeking to affect or potentially overhaul an entire system of governance or service, the BCB had to bring the government in touch with the community of global reach. These are world-making efforts. Indeed, despite such imagined communities beginning to 'imagine and feel things together as a group', such 'communities of sentiment no longer work *only* at the level of nation-state' (Appadurai, 1996, p. 8; emphasis added) but do so insofar as national systems are the targets of cultural change. This does not mean that transnationally imagined yet locally organized forms of networked solidarity cannot bypass the government. Such forms certainly can, increasingly through topological surfaces where the presence of the state is felt way less than it is felt within a formally organized system or a sector (see also Adhikary et al., 2018).

In this chapter we have shown how social entrepreneurial policy was being localized in Bangladesh via a policy network. What was basically pursued in the previous chapter's example as 'partnerships' was taking a more specific and timely form of 'social enterprises' in this chapter. Here, we have demonstrated how this social entrepreneurial policy was being imagined and localized in the country by yet another glocal policy network held together by the BCB. In pursuit of a SE-sector policy, this policy network sought to influence the government structures that continue to oversee and gatekeep third-sector involvement in Bangladesh – the NGOAB. The mundane works (policy labour) of this network involved construction of social entrepreneurial policy discourses and their influential dissemination through policy technologies such as baseline research, survey reporting and organized events, all focused on the establishment of a nationwide SE sector.

The SE-sector policy was found to be intricately linked with the collective aspirations of actors and organizations, mostly global but others local with a hybrid nature. Such actors were nested in varied scales, spaces and sites[12] related to global philanthropy, social impact investment and associated policy research. Some of these network members apparently demonstrated legal and epistemic 'authority' derived from their professional expertise or educational qualifications obtained from institutions in the Anglophone West.[13] Often referred to as 'sector leaders' or 'experts', these actors practically steered policy through relevant research, legal knowledge and relevant professional expertise by engaging in policy technologies of negotiation[14] housed in organized events. This indeed is a process of 'heterarchization', both situated and networked, through which the SE-sector policy was actively co-imagined, respectfully contested and then rendered into a momentum of potential inevitability. Again, these are imbricative moments. The BCB, as an extended arm of the BCG, emerged as the leading global actor that had so far mobilized considerable resources and networked deliberations in pursuing SE-sector policy, making use of commissioned statistical research and its co-constructed univocal cultural interpretations.

Claiming certain statistical truths, the SE-sector policy has been discursively constructed through a commissioned survey. It was textually presented and then placed within an organized event, where a networked epistemic community appraised the policy, in the presence of government in front of a potential stakeholder audience. Ball's (2015, p. 2) argument that policies are primarily discourses and that such discourses in combination with technologies (e.g. survey, panel discussion) 'mobilize truth claims and constitute rather than reflect social reality' becomes insightful here. Bowe and colleagues' (1992, pp. 19–22) account of policy contexts has taken on a non-cyclical and imbricative order here. The 'context of practice' is claimed to be already in existence[15] (de facto) and therefore became a key rationale articulated within the 'context of influence' (panel discussion). More interestingly, a new mode of 'text production' (survey report and policy brief) sits between these other two contexts. Also, to be noted, the context of influence was evidently coinciding with the context of text production.[16] This can be viewed as a topological impact of globalization on policy cycles, where any element of the cycle can precede or follow the others depending on the way policy influence is designed and contexts are produced.

Although the policy was still in the process of becoming during the empirical operations of this research, both the networked and parochial nature of this policy drive invoked important insights regarding how policies in the least-developed world are currently being re/produced in ways that invite a glocal research imagination – particularly under the influence of neoliberal performative pressures. This imagination could not in any way be conceived as a segmented interplay between a rounded 'global' and a territorial 'local' in relation to policy. Rather, as has also been demonstrated in the cases of both TFB and PEDP in relevant chapters, such a glocal policy imagination can be epistemologically and ontologically conceived through a topological analytic, particularly in respect of considerations of globalization and governance as a matter of agency and cultural influence.

Conclusion

Clearly, the policy dynamics presented in the analysis provided in this chapter exemplify the new spatio-cultural making of policy and influence. The policy event examined is a heterotopic place, where the SE-sector policy was placed as a practice that swung between what previously existed and what was intended. The presentations and the panel discussion can nonetheless be viewed as topological surfaces, particularly insofar as they constituted and facilitated a relational field of emergence (Lury et al., 2012; Manning, 2009; Parisi, 2012). In practice, the culture of policy steering was based on reordering practices of numbering, categorizing, datafication, estimation and discourse, all of which sought to reconstitute NGOs as SEs but also others (e.g. quangos). Such cultural and spatial practices bring the power of new global philanthropic and social impact investment actors into close interactive 'reach' of those who govern the populous that the former want to affect.

The SE-sector policy in/for Bangladesh is a policy imagination primarily rooted in the UK version of social entrepreneurial policies and practices currently spearheaded globally by the British Council. Underlying this policy lead is the networked deliberation of a support system that powerfully includes impact investors, corporate philanthropies, market research organizations and social entrepreneurial think tanks (such as the head network). In the case of Bangladesh, this support system functioned at a distance, but also locally through the BCB (the hand network), initiating and managing policy advocacy technologies, particularly 'evidence-based' policy dialogues. The BCB and the glocal network active in Bangladesh were trying to convince the government to reimagine NGOs as SEs. This was an exemplary instance of what Nye (1990,

p. 166) calls 'soft power'. Evidently, this power was no longer coming directly from a hegemonic state but was orchestrated in the form of networked deliberations that made use of research data to render intended policy reforms meaningful, attractive or even inevitable.

NGOs and their activities in Bangladesh were being continually reconstituted by the British Council and its locally situated glocal collaborators as a historically home-grown phenomenon that needed to be re/viewed as SEs. These glocal collaborators and their common understanding of SE constitute a landscape of collective aspirations, wherein various actors and their differing interests coalesce to benefit from the envisioned SE sector in Bangladesh. Among these many different actors, the old and established (g)local NGOs appeared as the most powerful interests. In fact, NGOs are rapidly opting for a social entrepreneurial organizational identity and associated operational form, using loopholes within the existing government regulations regarding business enterprises and NGOs. The central debate around this SE-NGO dilemma points at the perceived need for tax remission for so-called SEs. This is where the case of TFB becomes particularly illuminating.

TFB represents in a de facto fashion what the BCB epistemic community proposed and pursued as SE-sector policy (see Adhikary & Lingard, 2020). It is a 'still-small' organization that had emerged in Bangladesh, particularly within the primary education subsector, as a local extension (hand network) of a global policy network (head network). TFB can be viewed as a manifestation of what Offe (1984, p. 190) describes as re/presentation of public policy through corporatist organizational arrangements of networked interests, as opposed to parliamentary representations, a process sometimes called 'deparliamentarization' of policy. Yet, this might also mean that new forms and functionings of parliamentary deliberations are in evidence. However, TFB's emergence is also marked at a time when the primary education subsector in Bangladesh (i.e. DPE) was also prepared to welcome social entrepreneurial and global philanthropic investments and partnerships through the upcoming PEDP IV programme (see Chapter 3). In the next chapter, we will examine TFB to see how this organization was imagined and locally imbricated through its policymaking world.

5

Governing Teacher Education as Social Enterprise through Teach For Bangladesh

Introduction

Chapter 3 observed the rise and remit of 'governance networks' in the form of a System Wide Approach to Programming (SWAP) within the Bangladesh Directorate of Primary Education (DPE), which promoted partnerships. Chapter 4 revealed a quango leading a movement-like policy network seeking to influence the NGO Affairs Bureau (NGOAB) in favour of a social enterprise (SE) sector and complementary policies. This chapter will revisit Teach For Bangladesh's (TFB) social entrepreneurial imagination and the way such an imagination imbricated the global and the local (see Adhikary et al., 2018; Adhikary & Lingard, 2017, 2020). We will demonstrate how such an imagination underpinned governmentality aspirations and manifested 'officially' in the form of an NGO with intended 'large-scale' impact.

We view TFB as a localized extension of a global policy network – therefore 'spatial' – sustained by locally nuanced efforts and 'encounters' that imbricated global 'social entrepreneurial' power and local governmental authority but also a social entrepreneurial disposition new to the existing culture of teaching and teacher education[1] and the governance of them. We will highlight this synergy between the social entrepreneurial and the bureaucratic national vis-à-vis power, spatiality and culture as a 'world of policy' (Peck & Theodore, 2015; Shore & Wright, 2011). Locally manifest and yet continuously in the making, this world of policy had its own imagined community (a recipient community), an *imaginaire* (aspiring network) and cultural content (images of discourse and practice) (Appadurai, 1996). This transnational, de-territorialized world of policy is constituted by, and works with, 'complex, partly imagined lives', which must 'now form the bedrock of ethnography'. These imagined lives are always simultaneously situated in conditions/contexts that are 'official or large-scale' and that 'represent the links between the imagination and the social life' (Appadurai, 1991, pp. 54–5).

Beyond the organization's NGO identity, this chapter presents TFB as a partial and de facto enactment of an SE policy that seeks to transform teacher education and recruitment in particular and the education system more broadly. Such arguments were first explicated as part of the doctoral research informing this book (see Adhikary, 2019). Expanding upon this initial work, the theoretical significance of this chapter lies in insights into how policy models gain mobility through networks and are 'imbricated' locally through hands-on efforts manifesting spatio-cultural encounters. In that sense, this chapter is empirically less about TFB as an organization and more about the role of networks in policy mobility, and how global-local/national imbrications were empirically demonstrable in the way TFB was both 'imagined' and 'enacted'. Here, we view policy mobility primarily in terms of imagination, networks, cultural flows and spatio-cultural formulations that such imagination manifests officially (Appadurai, 1996).

We have written quite a lot about TFB to date (see Adhikary et al., 2018; Adhikary & Lingard, 2017, 2019, 2020; Adhikary et al., 2020). While that body of literature was aimed at developing a more global perspective on the Teach For phenomenon, this chapter seeks to develop an understanding of policy mobility with emphases on imagination and common aspirations and their spatio-cultural manifestation through networked efforts. Here, we re-view the organization as an example of how a social entrepreneurial 'imagination' with local origins (Santos, 2002) attains official, large-scale acceptance (Appadurai, 1991) and how this involved various global-local imbrications (Lingard, 2021). We also reveal how imagination is enacted within a distant locale by an active network seeking to 'annex' social entrepreneurial capacities (discourses and practices) into the system of education. One additional question that we raise afresh besides what we have already dealt with is: how is TFB (or a similar organization) actually relevant to the transforming teacher education landscape of Bangladesh? We will address that question directly in the concluding part of this chapter.

Again, in approaching TFB in this way, we identify and explore the 'world of policy' that the organization has created as an emblem of modernity and that, to a certain degree, succeeded in annexing the local/national to it. The first step to that exploration is tapping into the agentic 'imagination' (Appadurai, 1996), in terms of both latent productive and manifest generative forms, and thereby tracing the social entrepreneurial essence of becoming, being and later official manifestations. We found that the imagination underpinning TFB had two dimensions: the 'productive imagination' dealt more with the formative self as a social entrepreneur, whereas the 'generative imagination' characterized the material context of imbricative practices. Imagination is central here since it is itself an imbricative process, and global-local imbrications happen first in the imagination of governmentality. We have also sought to ethnographically detail the locally manifest 'world' of TFB, aiming to link 'imagination' to the kind of 'social life' that designed and animated spatio-cultural encounters within which disjunctures facing TFB's local manifestation transmogrified (Lingard, 2021).

Imagination Productive: Imbricating through Universal Problems and Communities

The initial 'network ethnographic' (Ball & Junemann, 2012) online data collection on TFB revealed its founder as the key to an 'imagination' seeking to ameliorate problems and to its cultural fabric. The founder was interviewed in person on 5 October 2016 at her TFB office. This valuable interview allowed us to probe deep into the formation of a social entrepreneurial imagination, first in relation to herself and then in relation to her thinking on Bangladesh. The deeper expansive link between the entrepreneurial self of the founder and the *problématique* of education for the Bangladeshi 'poor' was of particular note and was itself a clear instance of an imbricative process. Such a deep imagination annexed the acquired global into the practices of modernity intended locally for Bangladesh through TFB. This section analyses the founder's imagination about her social entrepreneurial development and how it informed her thinking about Bangladesh's education as a *problématique*.

The founder of TFB is a Bangladeshi American who was born, brought up and educated mostly in the United States. Underscoring the shaping impact of Teach For America (TFA) on her world view, TFB can reasonably be argued as an experiential outcome of its founder's life in the United States. Insofar as the decision to extend the Teach For path from America to Bangladesh is of significance, the founder linked her personal motivation, cultural values, organizational vision and entrepreneurial orientation to the incidents, experiences and relationships in the United States. She stated:

> I am a Bangladeshi American. I was born in the United States. I grew up back and forth between Bangladesh and US. I think, growing up, I was very much aware of the fact that I was fortunate to receive a pretty good education there [in

the United States]. In Bangladesh, [for some time] I attended a private English medium school. But I was very aware that that [schooling] was [given] as a lot of luck, and [had] less to do with what I deserved and what I had earned. I've been born into a family that could afford those privileges. And it was not necessarily, anything else. And so, I think this idea of disparity and inequity was something that was a theme in my life just growing up.

These childhood memories and schooling experiences demonstrate the shaping influences that diasporic US nationality played in the way the founder imagined TFB as instrumental to addressing educational inequality. Diaspora and a perceived sense of elitism, combined with a feeling of privileged upbringing, characterized the founder's sense of identity. She acknowledged her parents' Bangladeshi origins while identifying herself as American. This hybrid subjectivity oscillated between its two-pronged rootedness in both the US and Bangladesh contexts. This is an example of reflexivity that influenced the way she imagined educational issues. In the way the founder now defined educational inequity, an imagined sense of commonality between the United States and Bangladesh can be noted. For example, in explaining her altruistic motivation supporting TFB, the founder spoke equally of her personal anguish derived from her 'car's rear view of street children' in Bangladesh and being 'haunted by' the lack of high ambition in one of her 'poor but gifted' TFA students in the United States (Machranga Television, 2013; May, 2013). Such equivalences in the imagining of realities – realism (Appadurai, 1991, p. 55) – actually equate the global United States with the local Bangladesh.

Said to have links to a minor part of the founder's childhood in Bangladesh, this theme of social disparity took on an American recontextualization mostly during her high school and TFA years in the United States. The childhood flashbacks of Bangladeshi street children were then rethought in terms of the disparities that the founder saw in her adolescence in a neighbourhood school in the United States and more so during her two-year TFA fellowship. As she exclaimed during the interview, this TFA experience transformed her notions of disparity into a desire to apply the TFA/Teach For All (TFAll) model to address educational inequity in Bangladesh. The following extract from the interview explains further the process of reflexive interpellation (Elster, 2017) involved here:

> And I became a [TFA] teacher in Southeast Washington DC. So, I taught mathematics to ninth graders for two years in DC. That also was pretty transformative experience for me. I went to high school twenty minutes away

from where I taught high school [as a TFA corps member]. And where I studied was a very white, relatively affluent community. But I went to a public school. And where I taught was of predominantly black, a low-end public school. But [what] the two public schools offered [were different]. And they were only twenty minutes away from each other! It was a life and death, day and night difference. So, I think that experience helped me understand better, and not just from an academic point, what inequity means for real people. And as a Bangladeshi American, I think I always thought, you know, are there applications to this in Bangladesh? (TFB founder)

The thin line between imagination and aspiration became thinner here. Perceptibly, the founder's own identity, sociocultural vocabulary and world view supporting TFB were deeply entwined with her diasporic background, her self-identification with the dominant, white well-off community (schooling habitus) and their gradual consolidation through her becoming a TFA corps member. Along with her life's temporal variations and territorial mobilities came a shift in her social imaginary (Taylor, 2004) and problem imagination (Bacchi, 2009; Webb, 2014). It is indicative here that, in the founder's view, the poor represented an imagined (Appadurai, 1996) and globally universal community-category, while their geographical and national positionings might vary (see Popkewitz, 1998).

This also demonstrates how a subjectivity rooted in a developing world socio-economic and cultural context becomes deconstructed and reconstructed as it longitudinally goes through specific experiences, affordances and influences of a First World global city life. That is, what is experientially local to her – in her imagination – can be rendered as further localizable to a new locale (Santos, 2002) and thus 'globalizable'. Indeed, global-local/national imbrication happens in the imagination first and by means of an apparently common cultural frame of reasoning. 'Poor' and thus 'poverty', regardless of whichever was imagined first, are examples of such categories of cultural frames of reasoning operative at the level of the imagination.

The founder's concern for poor children took a specific motivational and operational trajectory as a result of her TFA experiences. Such experiences also sparked in her a global governmentality (Foucault, 1991b) that made possible what Appadurai (1996, p. 31) calls a 'play of pastiche', involving weaving two completely different national, sociopolitical and jurisdictional settings in one imagining mind through problem thinking. Consequently, the founder identified TFA's recruitment efforts as her entry point to the imaginable TFB path:

> So, let's just fast forward [from childhood]. So, when I was graduating from my university [in the United States], I was approached by a recruiter from Teach For America which is when I first learned about this model. And although I didn't have plans to become a teacher, or plans to become an educator, the appeal of Teach For America to me was the opportunity to actually work towards this disparity that I had seen.

Through TFA, the founder consolidated her life's mission. TFA not only served as an occupational first step, in the form of a packaged and scripted model (TFA) (see Matsui, 2015) but it also provided a discursive framework, a value system, a set of programmatic tools and accompanying incentives to guide her imagination of the future. The assimilated aspirations and sentiments of TFA became the performative logic for the founder's life. Nevertheless, this aspiration was not primarily or only about the universalized poor community but also about her individual aspirations and life trajectory.

Clearly, it was not teaching but rather the social entrepreneurial side that attracted the founder to TFA. In other words, teaching became a means to an end; the end being her aspired career path as a social entrepreneur in service of a laudable (and broad) social mission, namely, addressing inequity in Bangladeshi schooling. Through TFA experiences and associated entrepreneurial learning, a looming governmentality developed within an otherwise unsure mind that aspired to 'make a difference'. As events and contingencies clicked for the founder, the TFA model gradually became the only possible way of helping poor children, in this case through education and in Bangladesh:

> So, I think when I was graduating from the university, I wasn't 100 per cent sure of what I wanted to do with my life. But what I did know was I wanted to do something that was meaningful [to me]. I wanted to do something that would 'impact' people. I wanted to do something different than what other people were doing. And I think that's why Teach For America was exciting to me. It's because it allowed me to get into the actual work. Get kind of my hands dirty. (TFB founder)

This wish to have an 'impact' upon people activated the philanthrocapitalist (Bishop & Green, 2016; Edwards, 2008) social entrepreneurial subjectivity and was to a degree professionalized through TFA. This was the root of her entrepreneurial spirit and associated problem imagination. The meaning of life and work to the founder now involved affecting other peoples' lives (governmentality), although in this case not in America but in Bangladesh. This experiential internalization (also assimilation) of an entrepreneurial governmentality and the associated socio-cognitive vocabulary gave rise in the founder to a specific kind of problem imagination. She was imagining the situation of disparity in education in Bangladesh in terms of her specific experiences in the United States.

The founder imagined TFA as a solution to educational problems in Bangladesh through a TFAll lens vis-à-vis TFB. The latent content of this imagination – imagination productive – originated and matured in the US context, while the manifest content –imagination generative – was reimagined in the context of Bangladesh. While so doing, the founder aligned her own self and actualized her occupational thinking in terms of the aspirations, emotions and logics internalized from the TFA experience. She deemed such experiences as an entrepreneurial learning opportunity (see Mair, 2010) to govern lives in Bangladesh (as in 'actual work' and 'getting her hands dirty'). It was this entrepreneurial imagination in American terms that led her to establish TFB in the United States as a limited liability company[2] first, prior to starting TFB in Bangladesh for reasons explained later.

What we see here is the extension and expansion of imagination as a result of a very particular diasporic experience (Appadurai, 1996). TFB started in the individual imagination first, became matured through particular aspirations and experiences and then became manifest through efforts and actions, first in the United States and subsequently in Bangladesh. Imagination and action were mutually inclusive in this process of reflexive transformation (Rhodes, 1997), as the founder further elucidated:

> I moved to Bangladesh after finishing teaching in 2011. I decided at the end of that year that I was going to start Teach For Bangladesh. And I registered the company in February 2012 [in the United States]. And I worked independently. We registered in the United States as an LLC. It's a limited liabilities company. And then acquired a non-profit status in the United States. And then we also registered in Bangladesh as a non-profitable trust. There is a very standard procedure to set up a company [in the United States]. Right? You fill out some forms. LLC is registered with the Virginia Commonwealth, and non-profit status is given by the IRS. It's the Internal Revenue Service. It is the tax authority within the US. So, we got a tax-exempt status. But anyway, we started Teach For Bangladesh back in 2012 and we joined the Teach For All network in October or November of that year.

This excerpt directs attention to how the entrepreneurial imagination of one individual achieved, step-by-step, organizational shape. Empirically, the foundation of TFB was a planned and interwoven manifestation of imaginations and aspirations of an entrepreneurial mind. The founder took gradual steps in forming TFB. She registered TFB in the United States while she was back in Bangladesh. The US version of TFB followed the Virginia state jurisdiction as a company for which attaining tax exemption[3] was important. The manner in which the founder highlights the tax-exempt issue presents this matter as an important concern of social entrepreneurs.

Another probable reason of strategic significance for establishing TFB in the United States first was that global social entrepreneurial impact investments were impossible at the time to be channelled into countries such as Bangladesh, where the relevant legal frameworks and administrative structures were absent. It was our understanding that such funding (investment) for so-called SEs could only be transferred to jurisdictions that had SE as a legally supported sector (e.g. the United States and the UK). During data collection in 2016, Bangladesh did not have formal protocols to allow non-profit charitable organizations to function as 'SEs', let alone receive such quasi-investments. According to the NGOAB documents, the social entrepreneurial funding that TFB received from Porticus Global was first received by the TFB-USA and then transferred to the TFB-Bangladesh as an NGO grant in strict compliance with the NGOAB regulations.

However, the market embeddedness and philanthrocapitalist nature of TFB's establishment are evident in the organization's beginnings as a 'company' and the emphasis being on achieving tax-exemption status. What started as a company in the United States synchronously transformed into a non-profit trust and later an NGO in Bangladesh. The entrepreneurial and business vocabulary used by the founder points at the shaping of her imagination by a business framework culturally grounded in the broader US context. This is an insightful case of how diaspora and an associated transformational imagination now play a key role in constructing global entrepreneurial subjectivities, related aspirations and their re-operationalization with/in distant local jurisdictions.

TFB as a De Facto SE: A Generative Imagination

The productive dimension of the founder's social entrepreneurial imagination was linked to her biographical experiences in the United States. A generative imagination unfolded once the same organization had to be rethought in terms of Bangladeshi culture and context. The very idea of SE had to be mediated through the local/national and in practical sociological terms. The founder provided a rationalized perspective on SEs, which bore clear correspondence with the discourses and practices that overlappingly characterize philanthrocapitalism, venture/new philanthropy, impact investment and SEs. Yet, such discourses, as we shall discover later, had to be rethought in terms of what was happening in Bangladesh in similar directions. We begin this discussion by alluding to the founder's idea of SE:

> My understanding of social enterprise is that it is around investors who want ... [social impact]. So traditionally what do you have? Investors investing in for-profit business; the way they measure the return of their investment is, 'Are you making money?' Right? And so, if you are investing with social capital in mind, then you might also be wanting to see money. Maybe if it is [a] for-profit venture, or if it is a not profit venture, you don't care about the money. But in addition to that what you want to see is that there is social impact. That's a part of the dividend, that's a part of the revenue. (TFB founder)

According to the founder, the key ideas related to SE are: investors, social impact, enterprise venture and measurement of return, while the enabling and imperative logic is social impact. An SE is seen to be primarily about investment and the actors who are capable of making such investments. Regardless of an investor's focus on financial dividend/returns, such investments are viewed by the founder as non-traditional in their focus on social welfare and therefore deemed as altruistic and welfarist.

Here, dividend is reimagined and argued to be measured in terms of social impact and vice versa. That is, impact is measured in terms of whether and how measurably lives are being affected by the investment and associated programmes. TFB is a recipient of one such impact investment, which was applied for and subsequently granted by Porticus Global.[4] However, particularly in relation to the TFAll movement, the founder explained how she viewed impact in and through her localized practice:

> So, in Teach For All's case it is the impact defined by each organization. And for us, we talk about ending educational inequity. That's what we mean by impact. And so, the way in which we do that is through the student achievement in the classroom: [meaning] how much are the students learning, how much are they growing? And it's through the leaders we are building through our fellowship and our alumni movement. And so, Teach For All is working to help accelerate the impact of each organization, their effectiveness in doing these things, by

sharing expertise, sharing counsel, almost like consulting [appropriate] for various aspects of our organization. That's kind of how Teach For All works.

Impact for TFB involves several layers of problem imagination and locally meaningful interventions. At the broadest thematic level, impact for TFB is addressing educational inequity, something TFAll propagates. At the school/classroom level impact for TFB is enhancing students' learning achievements and outcomes (actual results). Then, at the systemic level, impact is given a movement like force meant to change the entire education system; this change, as it is envisaged, is to be driven by the potential leadership for which TFB fellows are trained.

However, the last sentence of the previous extract is particularly important as an exemplar of global-local/national imbrication through measures of impact. Despite TFB's self-portrayal as independent of TFAll, the latter's advisory role in the acceleration of impact of TFB essentializes monitoring and measuring of impact, as well as the stimulus for continued improvement. Because what is acceleration without time-framed measurement of developments and their speed? TFAll's imagination productive becomes manifest through TFB's generative imagination as ideas such as educational inequity, students' achievement and leadership are operationalized by reframing impact in terms of the contextual specifics of the local. The 'independence' that TFB enjoys de facto is a guided one. The purposes and goals set by the organization function within the bigger ideational and ideological umbrella of TFAll. The question as to how TFB is reportable or even accountable to Porticus Global is also insightful here in terms of impact.

Impact Imagination and the National Sectors (NGOs and Primary Education)

Entrepreneurial leadership is at the heart of the systemic impact to which TFB is oriented. The entrepreneurial mode of leadership that the organization proselytizes, through its alumni movement, involves all social sectors within a nationwide approach. The founder explained that the leadership training for the fellows was meant to have long-term effects in all sectors, including education. The idea is that the recruits, being high-achieving graduates, warrant future senior positions in their respective fields from where they will lead the future of education. Once given the social entrepreneurial leadership training, these fellows will be able to support TFB's future developments. The following statement from the founder clarifies further:

> I am talking about the leadership part. So, we want these people [fellows] to become the long-term leaders of Bangladesh in education and as well as outside of education. The solution has to be a combination of both [teaching and leadership] ... So, what we need is the people [fellows] who are doing this programme, who are building the skills, who then need to go into policymaking. They need to go into research tasks.

The fellows are not essentially meant to be teachers or educators or even educational specialists in the longer term. Rather, they are expected to be leading a movement of change makers. Indeed, this is not only change in relation to educational inequity; it is also change of the fundamental structures of educational management and leadership. This is a vision of inter-sectoral social entrepreneurial activity with a specific focus on education. The founder explained her views of long-term impact in the following way:

> And there should be more entrepreneurs, who should take those lessons and figure out how to do it. We need our fellows to get into the health care sector and figure out how does health combine with education. How does legal aid combine with education? And how does housing affect education. How does nutrition affect education? So, what we want to create is generations of change makers. Right! And so, that's how we are hoping to have that long-term impact through the short term, demonstrating [that] it's possible.

Clearly, the view of social entrepreneurial impact delineated by the founder is not only (education) system wide; to be accurate, it is also an all-sector long-term approach to change in governance. More importantly, this is an issue that invites democratic deliberation from all possible fronts, TFB being one. However, in achieving the aforementioned short-term goals and long-term social entrepreneurial visions, the founder underscored the inevitability of quality organizations and exemplary institutional practices. Exemplifying the notion of 'relentless pursuit' as found in TFA practices (see Thomas & Lefebvre, 2018), but also in TFB's media work (see Adhikary et al., 2018), the founder emphasized organizational best practice:

> I talked to you a little while ago about the quality of institutional practice. So that's very important. We don't want to be just another NGO; we want to be a [accented] very, very high performing organization. So, what that means is

everyone within our organization, from me to fellows, to our cleaning boy, needs to operate with high levels of professionalism and attention to excellence.

In this extract, a defining feature of the NGO-SE nexus is identifiable. Such comments imply that SE is equal to N(GO)+1. That is, unlike traditional N(GO)s that supplement governments' efforts in addressing social issues through grants, SEs innovate, modulate and become the symbol of 'best practice' in one specific social area/domain. Social entrepreneurial spirit is meant to be intensely competitive and infinitely perfectionist, regardless of the culture they work for and within (see Blumenreich & Gupta (2015) for insights on Teach For India). The idea is that any social entrepreneurial undertaking has to be a proof of success and that success has to be better than all others – a proud niche. On this note, Thomas and Lefebvre (2018) have shown how such overdriven, almost zealous, practices can be dangerous and often involve various forms of symbolic and real violence, while this power-drive can also provoke productive possibilities (see Foucault, 1991a, p. 194; Gaventa, 2003, p. 2).

Relatedly, and as highlighted in the previous chapter, one major finding of the research underpinning this book was a globally endowed but locally active policy movement from NGOs to SEs and associated debates. Among many, one such debate was around the cultural rootedness of SEs in Bangladesh. Some argued that social entrepreneurialism had its initial foundation in Bangladesh in the work of such figures as late Sir Fazle Hasan Abed[5] and Dr Muhammad Yunus[6] through their NGOs and thus had already existed for decades in Bangladesh as a culture. Others, including very influential members of the political and bureaucratic elites, argued that NGOs should not be equated or intermingled with business practices. The founder's view of this NGO-SE nexus was more attuned with the former argument. She thought that in the context of Bangladesh, one really did not need to look outside of the country to learn social entrepreneurship; it was already there in Bangladesh:

> I don't think that I see social entrepreneurship as a separate thing [from NGO]. Really, that, you know, I think, especially as a Bangladeshi, social entrepreneurship is something that has been happening in Bangladesh for decades and decades after decades [indicating as a culture]. Whether you talk about Abed Bhai,[7] or Yunus Bhai or anyone else. Really! Social entrepreneurship has been happening in Bangladesh from the beginning of time. So, I don't think I have ever thought like learning separately about a new idea of social enterprise. I simply see it as someone who is trying to innovate and set up a new idea or set up a new system that has a social impact.

TFAll itself is an SE; its network partners must be SEs as the associated funding is sourced by impact investors mainly and the goal is social impact. These are the characteristic tenets of philanthrocapitalism and its global social entrepreneurial policyscapes. As a part of this global social entrepreneurial milieu, as the founder rightly said, she did not have to learn social entrepreneurship; as a matter of fact, she was living a life as such already. But her approach to the late Sir Fazle Hasan Abed and Dr Muhammad Yunus as pioneers in SE knowledge apparently put an 'equal sign' between NGO practices and those of SE. Her perception of leading NGO figures in Bangladesh was premised on the logic that anyone trying to innovate and create a system for addressing and governing social issues is a social entrepreneur: a combination of a transformative and an innovative approach to SE.

This view is important because, besides primarily acknowledging NGOs as SEs, it also creates room for any other types of organization that would systemically serve a social purpose, including for-profit businesses (NGO+1). This view is in complete unison with that of Bill Drayton, deemed the father of the idea of SE (see Koo, 2013; Ludwig, 2012). It is important to note that the social entrepreneurial movement in Bangladesh is often represented by NGO leaders (including Sir Fazle Hasan Abed and more recently Dr Ananya Raihan) who were trained as Ashoka Fellows in Drayton's US-based Policy Institute. These are examples of how the global-local/national often become imbricated through education and training.

Impact Imagination and the Government

TFB's transformative vision of a social entrepreneurial future for the education sector and teaching in particular essentialized specific imperatives for the government. In the founder's opinion and as far as local support was concerned, the government emerged as the principal site of and support for such transformation:

> For us, it was very important to have the government support us from the very beginning. We don't see this in any way as opposing the government. Rather, we want to work in collaboration with the government ... And given the fact that the vast majority of the primary schools in Bangladesh are government primary schools, and because we wanted to walk within the mainstream, it was important that we have permission to operate within the government public school system.

The founder's description of the government's support for TFB also signalled some of the reforms that a social entrepreneurial future would entail for the government. Bangladesh is a relatively low-resource country, yet its government runs one of the largest education systems in the world with a relatively low percentage of GDP spent on education. In this context, the TFB founder thought it important that the government of Bangladesh rethink its budgetary allocation for education and particularly teacher education. In further nuancing TFB's mandate for systemic change, the founder underscored the necessity of the government's prioritization of funding education in an efficient and effective way. In her view, scarcity of funding apparently created the deficient situation within the system that TFB sought to address. At the bottom, her argument was 'you get only what you are ready to pay for':

> Bangladesh has one of the lowest per capita GDP investments in education in the world. If we look at our percentage of spending in terms of GDP, it is one of the lowest in the entire world and even in the region. What does this show? It is possible [to provide high-quality education for poor children]. But you have to reallocate your resources or reprioritize. The question is, what is needed to make this happen? If we realize, that, ok, what we need is higher-quality teachers, higher-quality training and better compensation, then we act as pressure point to help [government] change some of those things [by] showing them that this is possible if you [government] are willing to prioritize [education].

TFB is an organization funded and guided by various philanthrocapitalist actors (see Adhikary & Lingard, 2017). What it tries to demonstrate to the government, and thereby act as a pressure point for, is that given proper funding, social entrepreneurial interventions can ensure high-quality education, even for the poorest communities. And this is exactly what Building Resources Across Communities (BRAC)[8] has achieved over the decades as an NGO. So, something must have become unsettling or anachronistic with NGOs, their structure and functioning.

Mannan (2015, p. 59) in his anthropological insider's account of NGOs in Bangladesh has identified three distinctive stages of NGO evolution: from the 'gestation period' (1971–5), to 'the consolidation stage' (1975–90), to 'the NGO industry in the age of globalization' (1990–present). Among many major transformations, the third phase came with a gradual decline in donor support, while the support provided came increasingly with conditions such as abandonment of social mobility approaches per se and adoption of a market approach to social programming. This drive also involved popular encouragement to buy NGOs' services and products – this is, the social entrepreneurial spirit – while the public were increasingly constructed as responsible for their own development (see Mannan, 2015, pp. 84–5).

TFB's World of Policy: The Ethnographic Network

We view TFB as a potential policy, reassembled locally as an ongoing modular programme of empirically discernible practices and discourses (see Adhikary et al., 2018, 2020; Adhikary & Lingard, 2017). It is not a culture but bears cultural potential and implications in the character of an intended policy by having a systemic as well as a professional reform agenda. Although the formation of TFB and its sustained functioning may have links to a 'universe' of relationships and resource exchanges, to understand the TFB world, we sought to follow the material manifestation of the founder's 'imagination' in Bangladesh (see Adhikary & Lingard, 2017, p. 11).[9] Peck and Theodore (2015, pp. xv–xvi) correctly, in our view, argue that despite the increasingly 'de-bordered' nature of policy imaginaries, the 'achievement of policy outcomes remains a stubbornly localized, [and a] context-specific process'.

Accepting this realism, what mattered most was the locally active and systemically effective aspirational community – the network of grit – which worked on the ground, day in and day out, incessantly designing and enacting successful 'encounters' (Massey, 1994b), continuing through to today. Incremental successes achieved through such encountering moments were the ethnographic stories we have summarized here (see Adhikary (2019) for more details), while unsuccessful moments were no less revealing. We have referred to such locally active/effective networks as ethnographic networks. In every topology (e.g. a network) a certain combination of elements must remain flexibly yet relationally constant in terms of effects. From within a nodal universe of actors and organizations, we found a world-making network responsible for the transmission and translation (vernacularization) of a powerful 'imagination' locally, involving a recipient imagined community (Anderson, 1983).

In initial work, we created a universe-like map of all the people, places, organizations and resource-sharing involved in such a network (see Adhikary & Lingard, 2017, p. 10). Despite risking empirical superficiality and partiality, and depending on the availability of valid demonstrative data on the internet, such a map was helpful for framing a preliminary understanding or a bird's-eye view of what might be involved in the 'incremental' processes of an intended policy. Much like a battle map, it helped strategize the next move, where the opponent was a potential potpourri of data. However, the next move initiated an ethnographic journey towards depicting more firmly the nature of this policy world, and interviews were crucial to this end and characterized a more ethnographic approach from this point. Initial impulses became more substantive as we felt we could 'follow' the imagination of the founder to elicit the material manifestation of a locally emerging world – an intended yet emergent 'world of policy'. This was a world that involved a specific cultural content – practice and discourse steering policy intentions – that was simultaneously globalizable/localizable and therefore understandable in terms of globalization.[10]

That is, to understand TFB as a global policy locally remade, we found it necessary to appraise the organization in relation to the structural and agentic apparatuses that enable, partially or fully, its take-up in situ. For, without local embedding or even institutionalization, such developments as TFB are purely ephemeral. Without a situated perspective, a development such as TFB might seem like those comets that flicker for a moment within the universe, only to vanish as quickly as they appeared. A comprehensive understanding invites an examination of how TFB as a spatio-cultural entity was gradually assembled within the system of governance we traditionally refer to as the nation-state. Empirically, the nation-state still mattered/s and will continue to do so – even as an illusio (Bourdieu & Wacquant, 1992, p. 116). Yet, clearly, the way the nation-state works has changed and will continue to change.

Before any panopticon reality of governance is 'imagined' and can occur, the apparently omnipotent global and the seemingly recipient/generative local (also productive in a few powerful cases) must imbricate in the realm of a cultural programme. It is due to the differences in cultural programmes that the global and the local/national still 'encounter' each other in multiple ways and directions (Larsen and Beech, 2014). Imbrication happens through the play of pastiche. By imbrication, we do not mean that something completely different emerges out of the global-local interplay; rather, it is the relational coexistence of the global and the local/national within a locally constructed 'world' of practice and discourse that matters. In this world, the local must coexist with and in relation to the global to operationalize the influence the global carries when juxtaposed against the local.[11] And such value must be incrementally worked within and through the existing system of local/national governance to be impactful at any level within any given sector.

In the case of TFB, the new dimensions of the alternative programme continually sought the 'dominant' value in relation to the 'residual' (government) and the 'emergent' (i.e. transforming NGO practices) (Williams, 2005). In their relational symbiosis, the global tended to claim the privileged[12] 'best practice' status and thus sought to culturally subordinate (cf. Santos, 2002) the existing (i.e. not-so-efficient teacher education and education systems). In this sense, the 'disjunctures' that Appadurai talks of are mainly cultural disjunctures, and without such disjunctures, the global and the national would not even exist. In fact, the global is non-existent without the mobility of global processes (forces, connections, imaginations), and their effects and presence are felt within both the national and the local. However, in the case of TFB, we found certain practices, mindsets, protocols and arrangements transmogrifying such disjunctures. Additionally, the local and national helped constitute and affected the global and vice versa. Furthermore, some global effects bypassed the national context and had a direct topological impact on localities.

These locally practical dimensions – often broadly supported by existing structural arrangements at various scales or by much worked on hybrid arrangements explained in the last two chapters – constituted the conditions of/for coexistence or symbiosis between TFB and relevant pockets of authority and reception within the Bangladesh education system. We found common aspirations of powerful actors, existentially critical funding, relationships of power and authority, magical technologies of reach and connectivity, auto-epistemic instrumentation and social mediatization as imbricative of the global and the local contributing to the easing of cultural disjunctures underpinning the TFB model. In all such dimensions and associated processes, asymmetries in relationships of power and resources constituted empirically the very conditions of conformity, agreement and flows, while transmogrifying disjunctures.

Aspirations

TFB's localization in Bangladesh would not have been possible without the support from an aspiring network of globally expansive and nationally significant actors and their organizations. Local high-profile actors with resources and authority from government and non-government sectors, and particularly those having global reach, experiences and orientation, comprised this locally effective community of social entrepreneurial aspirations. Most of these individuals received their higher education in the Anglophone West and were either protagonists of entrepreneurial dispositions or champions of corporate innovations. For example, the first advisory, motivational and financial support for the TFB founder came from the founder and chairman of BRAC, the late Sir

Fazle Hasan Abed. BRAC is a Bangladesh-based I/NGO and is considered the world's foremost NGO[13] in terms of number of employees; it has programmes in eleven developing countries and international offices in both the United States and the UK.

Formerly, BRAC was known as the Bangladesh Rural Advancement Committee. But recently it changed its name to Building Resources Across Communities – indicative of its broader reach and more global orientation. BRAC runs successful education-, health- and gender-focused programmes in countries experiencing unrest, such as Afghanistan, Pakistan and others. It also has large-scale business involvements through BRAC enterprises, which is a conglomeration of thirteen businesses[14] and four investment ventures, including BRAC Bank.[15] The late Sir Abed was a conjoint believer of business and NGO work for addressing poverty (Harvard Business School, n.d.). The TFB founder exclaimed:

> Our first donor was Sir Fazle Hasan Abed. And BRAC. When Abed Bhai heard of what we were trying to do, he called me into his office and he said you know 'tell me about this programme'. He knew Wendy Kopp (TFAll/A founder) and he had known Teach For America from a long time ago. In fact, he had helped name Teach For All when she [the founder Wendy Kopp] was starting out. He has always wanted there to be a Teach For Bangladesh. So, when he heard that we were trying to do this, he was really excited, and you know BRAC's board approved the first grant that we got in, I think, September or October 2012. So anyway, our first money came locally.

This interview passage underscores how the global and the local are interwoven through relationships. It also demonstrates how global entrepreneurial individuals connect and support each other, particularly when allied programmes spawn within commonly accessible vicinities. The motivational link here was commonalities in interest and aspirations facilitated through connections between Wendy Kopp,[16] the late Sir Abed and the TFB founder. Clearly, such actors demonstrate eloquence in reaching out and extending dedicated financial and advisory support when moments of unison emerge. These diasporic long-distance relationships across global cities involve many forms of connective mobility that occur between face-to-face meetings and telephone calls. Importantly, all of these three actors identify themselves as social entrepreneurs, a common 'imagined' category that brings the global and the local together, since there is clear dependency or friendship founded upon a social entrepreneurial imaginary imagined globally but with local intent.

To add to this social entrepreneurial linkage, the late Sir Abed had specific training about social entrepreneurship from Ashoka, United States. Visibly, what connects these 'social entrepreneurs' is the commonalities in programmatic imaginations for personal and social benefit within a specific social-agenda-field involving an imagined recipient community (e.g. the poor in Bangladesh). This connectedness on the basis of homogeneity of beneficial goals (aspirations) and expertise (purpose), despite distant situatedness, creates the *imaginaire* – the landscape of collective aspirations (Appadurai, 1996) that connect global cities affecting developing country sites (Sassen, 2007, 2013).

Funding

TFB's funding sources comprise a network of corporate philanthropic individuals and organizations. The first phase of TFB activities was funded by a BRAC grant under Chairman Sir Abed's patronage. The second phase of TFB's 'Leadership Development Programme, Phase 2', the NGO Bureau registered name, received a US-based fund transfer of $418,500 sent from TFB (532 Walker Road, Great Falls, VA22066, United States) (NGO Bureau document, dated 10 July 2015), registered as a 501 (c)3 non-profit in the US state of Virginia. The sender was the chairman of the board of TFB, Quasim Rana, the TFB founder's spouse.

Further research through NGO Bureau documents revealed that TFB-USA was funded by the Hong Kong–based Porticus Asia Limited (PAL). PAL is a wholly owned subsidiary of Stitching Porticus, Amsterdam, the Netherlands (NGO Bureau Document, 22 July 2014), with global offices located in the UK, North America and Germany (see organization website, https://www.porticus.com/en/home/). It is an international organization that manages and develops the philanthropic programmes of charitable entities established by the Brenninkmeijer family entrepreneurs. Brenninkmeijer is a German Dutch family and the owner of 'C&A' brand, an international chain of clothing stores. Porticus donated, as indicated in the document signed by Philip Booth (regional director Asia, Porticus), 130,000 euros to TFB-USA (NGOAB Document, 22 July 2014). The fund was transferred to TFB-USA first and then channelled back to TFB-Bangladesh.

Relationships

The guidance for the identification of appropriate and supportive government personnel for help also came from highly diasporic personal relations from

BRAC. The founder talked about how she took advice from one of her close acquaintances from BRAC in identifying the right person from the DPE to seek government approval for TFB's educational programme:

> So! Let's see how did it begin? You know Muna [pseudonym] Apa [elder sister], who I went to for advice. And I asked her who should we meet? And I think maybe it was her, who first introduced us, or suggested the name of the Dhaka DD, deputy director of the [DPE]. I guess it was a 'her' at that time. But these offices change quite frequently. So first we went, I remember, to this office in Mirpur, and we explained what it was. And she said, 'Okay, those were lots of good ideas, but it's never going to work, because you are not going to be around.' And I said, 'Of course I'm going to be around.' And she said, 'Okay if you can make it work, well, we are open to trying it.'

Dr Muna, the then director of one of BRAC's many institutes, is again a highly diasporic and globally oriented individual who received her self-financed PhD and MA, respectively, from University of Cambridge and London School of Economics. She referred the TFB founder to one specific deputy director (DD) who was in close relationship with the BRAC personnel and was then in charge of the Program and Evaluation Division of DPE. Although the founder could not recall the actual government person during the interview, this senior official was identified during another interview with the very government officer in question. Dr Mazharul Islam (pseudonym), also educated in the Anglophone West on government scholarships, explained how he supported the TFB founder:

> Of course! They [TFB] are most important. Because they are coming up with creative and innovative ideas. Government has in mind not to put an obstacle. You know TFA, [I mean] Teach For Bangladesh. There is this [uttered the TFB founder's name]. You know that lady you asked. Wrote me. Once she was frustrated. We people gave her support. And supported her morally. She is very close to me. If you ask her and you want to know about me and my support to her. We are in the government. We want to establish some bridge not to ignore the others' contributions. We do supplement, we do acknowledge. So, government was sincere about it. The invitation of resource. Resource in terms of money and manpower, technology and others. So, some people are coming up with very creative and innovative ideas. This is the supportive or congenial environment to promote this initiative successfully. This is the positive environment that Bangladesh is now nourishing. Now we are in a position, we have in mind to work in a team. We already recognized that education is a team effort. (SGO-1)

This quote from this government senior official shows how alignment in belief, mindset and necessity can have real outcomes. It demonstrates how the interviewee imagined the imperative role of government as a facilitator for entrepreneurial programmes, particularly given the importance of the resources (money and knowledge) that they brought into the country.[17] His enthusiasm is noteworthy in the sense that most other DDs interviewed gave a slightly unfavourable and often times (post)colonial view of such initiatives as TFB. The second half of this quotation is a clear description of how the government had become welcoming, particularly to social entrepreneurial programming, as the latter brought in money, creative ideas and resourceful individuals. The 'nourishment' of such initiatives and the enabling 'positive environment' have now been created by the government reconstituting educational management into 'a team effort' (see Chapter 3). Culturally, this government official now contained the global within his local subjectivity, and he imagined the local/national supportively in terms of the global entrepreneurial.

Technologies

The technoscape of TFB mainly facilitated the mobility of knowledge, people and finances enabling reach, presence and engagement of the global within the local and vice versa. Know-how and strategic experience were shared through different cutting-edge information and computational technologies, where 'best practice' were imperative and communicated as redemptive and thus indicated superior 'practice'. Most notable was TFAll's institutionalized global learning network named 'online partner learning portal' (TFB official Tweet, 21 October 2015), which aimed to facilitate instant connectivity and share digital content and experiences between distant TFAll partners. Such techno-aided spatialities – topological surfaces of cultural reordering – are by default imbricative since what matters most in such platforms are engagement in appraisal and acceptance. We see here, of course, the ways in which the new communication technologies and enhanced computational capacities facilitate the new spatialities of globalization and communications within and across them. This is Spivak's (2012) well-taken point that globalization in one sense at least exists on our computer screens.

Quite intuitively, the nature of knowledge flow was mostly Teach-For-network based. Official visits by Wendy Kopp (TFA/ll founder) and Brett Wigdortz (Teach First, UK founder) to Dhaka marked this Teach-For centrism. The former highlighted a fundamental homology between all nations' educational problems and TFAll model's universal applicability. This occurred at a BRAC-hosted event involving sessions and meetings with TFB fellows and officials followed by school site visits. TFB's visits to the Teach For India Summer Institute, designed to foster learning from the latter, provided another example of Teach-For centrism (TFB official Tweet, 21 May 2015). Fast transportation technology and advanced computational capacities were the conditions enabling such diasporic flows of knowledge. Expert visits to local sites (TFB official Tweet, November 18, 2015), international learning trips (TFB official Tweet, May 12, 2015), global conferences (TFB official Tweet, October 28, 2018) and in-person exchange of digital resources (TFB official Tweet, 21 October 2015) characterized a topological environment, wherein construction of the 'best' determined the value of practices.

Epistemic Diaspora

Teach-For reliance – indicative of the global – was further marked in TFB's recruitment of managers and directors from TFA and Teach First alumnae. Such employment offered international airfares complemented by a high salary. For example, Katelyn Runyan-Gless, a TFA alumna from the United States, was the leadership director at TFB at the time of data collection. Similarly, Richard Wood, a Teach First alumnus from the UK, was the leadership development manager (TFB official Tweet, 22 October 2015). He was also acting as the Winter Academy director, in addition to conducting regular academy sessions.

TFA curriculum experts (e.g. Patti Sica, a TFA alumna) also designed materials and ran sessions at the Winter Academy. Such employment practices and leadership roles demonstrated the flow of leadership and managerial knowledge, a manifestation of the global ideoscape of TFB. These roles also exemplify distant but direct connections and participation associated with the global TFAll in the make-up and functioning of TFB and, most importantly, the training of the recruited fellows. Their direct presence within the local office and 'academies', which are actually places of cultural training and appraisal, interweave the global and the local on a long-term basis. Such UK- and US-based employees and their long-term leadership and educative roles within local TFB sites of graduate preparation ensure the direct reach and presence of TFAll knowledge culture within the local training practices. In a sense, these 'foreigners' represent the global 'best', set against the perceived, existing and deficient local. These are also examples of long-term mechanisms of 'encounter' established between the 'fantastic' global and the 'fascinated' local/national, who are now engaged within processes of epistemic inclusion/exclusion (Appadurai, 2001).

Social-Mediatization

TFB has been particularly proactive in the media, ranging from traditional daily newspapers to modern social media. In such media content, the TFB founder, the fellow teachers and the programme have been given considerable recognition with notes of thanks. Prominent daily newspapers and their online versions highlighted the self-sacrificing nature of TFB practices. For example, the *Daily Prothom Alo, Notun Barta, Dhaka Tribune,* the *New Age, Open Equal and Free,* the *Daily Star* and *Voice of America* (Bangla online version) have published such stories. This is archetypal to what Ahmann (2015, pp. 3-4) describes as 'story telling' constituting an 'overarching humanitarian narrative' to 'invoke a call for action'. Although such stories were locally retold, their rootedness in the United States indicates their global/local character: stories have impact in the way they command imagination and acceptance.

TFB thanked Voice of America for broadcasting the inaugural event for the Winter Academy 2014, where US Ambassador Dan Mozena described TFB as a 'Third Movement' (neither public, nor private). This was further augmented by Professor Gowher Rizvi (the international affairs adviser to the honourable prime minister of Bangladesh, and a professor from Harvard), who added that TFB was a hallmark example of educational development for both the government and private entrepreneurs (VoA, 2014). The TFB founder was introduced to Professor Gowher by the former's friend, who was also a 'social entrepreneur' running youth development projects in Bangladesh (TFB founder, 5 October 2016). Again, the identities of such individuals of power and prestige are two pronged, one rooted in the local/national politics, and the other intimately linked to US academia and politics. What is interesting here is the global representation and local presence and performance of such individuals of power and prestige.

Another example of such individuals was the US Ambassador Dan Mozena. Besides speaking for TFB and promoting it on several occasions, the US ambassador gave official promotional interviews praising TFB (Mozena, 2014). Such videographic promotional practices were meant for garnering public acceptance and are still publicly available. A similar video titled 'Supporters of Teach For Bangladesh' features Sir Fazle Hasan Abed (chairperson, BRAC), Munawar Misbah Moin (group director, RahimAfrooz Bangladesh Ltd) and M. Azizul Huq (MD, GlaxoSmithKline Bangladesh) explaining the role of TFB in building and developing the nation through education.

What we see here is a mobilization of a constructed media network seeking to make TFAll's global policy meaningful and attractive to Bangladeshi locals (see

Adhikary et al., 2018). The involvement of figures of formal authority, political power and global fame deepens processes of 'mediatization' (Fairclough, 2000) and 'vernacularization' (Appadurai, 1996) of the policy. Indeed, such media practices animate the affective dimensions of policy (McKenzie, 2017) within today's topological media environment of globalization. They also recognize that the world of politics is, among other things, an effect world (Berlant, 2011). They constitute a 'policy message system' – a network of topological surfaces – full of in situ or reported moments of cultural encounters indicative of the complexity of global, national and local relationships. Appadurai (1996, p. 13) rightly argues that 'imagination is now central to all forms of agency' enabled by new technologies and stretching beyond the imagined community as only the nation.

Highlighting the role of affect in such mediatization surfaces, we have conducted an analysis of TFB's social-mediatization efforts by analysing specifically the organization's Facebook page (see Adhikary et al., 2018). This revealed TFB's Facebook activities as an example of how social media has become a powerful new platform for policy mediatization. This is also a developing world example of a (global) policy rewritten (locally) as audio-video bytes. Our analyses revealed three ways in which TFB sought to influence recruitable graduates but also the local government and public, via Facebook. First, it created opportunities for recurrent reading, hearing and seeing the policy in practice as animated by 'stars', 'spectacles', 'glamour' and 'statistics', all of which regularize a sense of heroic bodily feeling-as-vernacularization. Secondly, it sought to inform and reshape the social imaginary and associated problem imagination of the graduates and locals to whom this message was directed. And thirdly, it involved what might be described as a 'post-truth' way of engagement via the excessive use of emotional stimulus, manifesting an understanding of the affective aspect of policy and politics.

TFB and Teacher Education in Bangladesh

Let us now look back at TFB in terms of its local/national relevance and remit as a de facto SE (see Adhikary & Lingard, 2020). TFB was allowed to work within the primary education system of Bangladesh as an alternative model with limited scope and under government accountability systems, particularly that of the NGOAB. As a part of its declared commitment, TFB must continue to be active in changing the education system if it is to remain true to its stated goals directly linked to TFAll's impact. This means that the organization must at some point access some of the apex structures that govern the primary education system of Bangladesh, if a system-wide impact continues to be the target. Despite the fact that TFB's success in seeking support and permission from the DPE was remarkable, its initial efforts to enter into the PEDP's system-wide governance structure (see Chapter 3) failed. One of the Donor Consortium (DC) members talked about TFB's unsuccessful attempt to secure a seat in the Joint Consultative Meeting (JCM) and Joint Annual Review Mission (JARM) meetings:

> [TFB founder came to us with] two main agendas: one agenda was that obviously they were seeking funds … And again, they also wanted to gain access in the main primary education scenario and that landscape, which means PEDP III … even though I realized that they were going to DPE regularly for a variety of reasons … But they wanted to gain access in those crucial PEDP III meetings. For example, in JCMs, Joint Consultation Meetings … we have JARM Joint Annual Review Mission, were we review the whole [PEDP] programme … So, they [TFB] wanted to know how they would be able to gain access to those meetings. And of course, what I told them probably did not make them that happy. (DCM-2)

This interview excerpt makes it clear that systemic transformation is TFB's ultimate goal. This meeting with a DC representative is one instance of a failed 'encounter', even as it is a telling one. However, even though TFB failed to enter the apex of system-level decision-making, the organization's relevance as a teacher education reform sits in complete alignment with the path that JCMs, JARMs and their Disbursement Linked to Indicators (DLIs) paved for teacher education reform in Bangladesh (see Chapter 3).

The reason why DLIs are important is that the implementation of some of them was directly related and conducive to what TFB does and also aligned with the systemic vision of the organization. It is through some specific DLIs that teacher education reforms were brought to sector-wide focus in Bangladesh and were planned and implemented. Of the nine DLIs pursued by the DPE, three were directly linked to TFB's scope and nature of work. These were:

DLI 2: Teacher education and development
DLI 5: Decentralize school management and governance
DLI 7: Teacher recruitment and deployment

According to the DPE's PEDP III document (MoPME, 2015, p. 7), the Bangladesh government had had some success in meeting all of these DLIs. For example, teacher education and development were given a central priority by the DC and therefore the government. The consortium had done research on behalf of the government to assess the current status and need for teacher education. Based on the findings, the government agreed to eliminate the existing Certificate in Education programme for in-service primary teachers and replace it with an eighteen-month diploma. One senior government official talked about this transformative context:

> Now we have shifted from Certificate in Education to Diploma in Primary Education. That was twelve months, the new one is eighteen months. With these changes, we expect that the learning achievement of the children will be increased. (SGO-2)

The World Bank participant provided deeper historical detail about how this focus on changing teacher education was initiated and was then led by the DC as a follow-up to PEDP I and II and associated research. This high-level World Bank official considered this reform focus on teacher education as linked to global discourses that shape local policies, practices and provision of teacher education. He added:

> These are the findings of the research; these are the findings of implementation of PEDP I, II, and these are also global understanding. So, government then had several teachers' training [facilities]. One was PTI – Primary Teachers Training Institutes. So, we [donors] did assess what this training covered. We thought that though they were giving the training, this training was not enough. Second, there is something called Refresher. Refreshers training, you need for the new teachers. Refreshers were not there. Now there were not enough PTIs to train all the new teachers. A lot of teachers are actually teaching for the first two, three years without any training on teaching method or anything. So, we thought that … PEDP III targeted that; let's think about this training. They require more and better [teacher] training. So, we are doing an assessment, how this diploma is going on. Based on this assessment, we are sort of redesigning the programme. Our expectation is we will try to have this diploma provided by a lot of other agencies in different parts of the country. (DCM-1)

This extract nuances how teacher education was given top priority by the DC after the beginning of PEDP and which had been augmented since then in terms of research, training and reforms. Evidently, the consortium was still taking the lead in assessing the needs and in framing solutions. As a result, the number of primary teachers training institutions was going to be increased, while the former Certificate in Education had already been enlarged to an eighteen-month Diploma in Education. Additionally, pre-service and refresher teacher training were given serious consideration as essential for effective and productive teacher education. All such important initiatives, however, were no longer imagined to be provided by the government only. Rather, based on their assessment, the consortium now deemed it important to have teacher education provided by various extra-government providers in different parts of the country.

This is where different forms of broad-based partnerships (see EFA, MDGs and SDG frameworks) become essential. To meet the 'global standard' in teacher education, the most available alternatives to government facilities would be their long-standing competitors, I/NGOs, which were continually evolving, taking hybrid quasi-market identities as SEs. A leader of one significant NGO in Bangladesh talked about how they had already identified similar gaps in teacher education in the system and had started working in that direction:

> I put my emphasis on the professional development of the teachers. Education is something that is on continuous modification. And we talked about the global changes. It is a continuous process. We need to prepare our teachers on that. It is not a matter to be done only through a certificate or diploma. Teachers need on-site support. Teachers face academic problems and they have professional needs. These need to be supported. Now we have courses – namely, the refreshers course which runs by rotation. Some of these courses are not customized according to the teachers' own needs. They [government's diploma] have a common modular course. This hinders teachers' professional development. (I/NGO-SO-2)

Of note, the education of both pupils and teachers was viewed here as linked to continuous global changes. It was also observed during research interviews that such educational thinking in terms of global priorities and developments had increasingly become a culture among NGO leaders. With such a mindset, NGOs were easily and readily getting access to the agenda and direction that the DC pursued through the PEDP; NGOs were directly involved therein via CAMPE (see Chapter 3). Accordingly, the NGOs thinking ahead promptly ensured they were ready for the future or even reimagined it.

In the earlier extract, the speaker not only knew where the government was going in the future vis-à-vis teacher training (refresher training) but was also reimagining the possible gaps in that future. These imagined gaps – need for refresher training, on-site support and professional development – were areas upon which TFB programmatically focused. That is, TFB did a fast-track 'refresher' training of recruited graduates and sent them directly into classrooms to model apparently better and more professional teaching. For the case of TFB, this specific focus on teacher education had a direct global orientation (TFAll/Porticus Global). Yet, such focus areas and associated discourses and practices of TFB were clearly in synchrony with the global discourses and reforms that PEDP actors enacted.

Inter alia, this is what made TFB relevant and acceptable to the DPE authorities. What TFB did and represented as a policy model was actually what PEDP had created an environment for, although not yet fully developed. TFB's funding link with Porticus Global and network link with TFAll brought the same global priorities and discourses now enacted through PEDP. The main difference between TFB and local NGOs was that the latter usually had more than two decades of local history of transformation and donor grant usage, while organizations like TFB were rather recent and funded by philanthropic organizations, depending on common aspirations and compatibility. However, both these types of organizations were going to compete for a role in teacher education as such education became more liberally and widely available in Bangladesh. The emergence of TFB was thus linked to the context of PEDP's focus on teacher development and the involvement of NGOs and/or SEs in the governance of teaching services. The deregulation of school leadership and management in future will further open up an immense service sector for teacher education to global philanthropic patronage and SEs. Structural reforms enable many changes.

TFB and Global-Local Imbrications: Linking Imagination to Mobility and Fixity

At this point, the nature of our ethnographic exploration demands consolidation. In this chapter, first, we examined the genomic and formative 'imagination' behind TFB by analysing psycho-biographical data collected through an interview with the founder. We demonstrated how such imagination took its 'official' character and 'large-scale' inspiration by, respectively, capturing what we have analysed as the 'imagination productive' and the 'imagination generative'. Then, we delved into the locally manifest 'world' (Peck & Theodore, 2015) of TFB seeking to identify how the 'imagination' linked with the kind of 'social life' that characterized tireless struggles within spatio-cultural encounters designed and participated in to address disjunctures.

This 'world'-making sociology is what we have conceptually advanced and ethnographically studied with specific focus on the changing spatialities of culture. This is ethnography of heterotopic places (Foucault, 1986): place considered as engaging moments of a relational temporality (Massey, 1994b); as placements of practices (Amin, 2002); as moments of intertwined spatial histories; and indeed as moments of encounter (Massey, 2006). Some such engaging and telling moments were possible to be directly experienced in the case of the British Council Bangladesh network delineated in Chapter 4. But in the case of TFB, the organization itself and its founder guided the tour through the world it created, often glimpsing déjà vu moments of encounter from a not-so-distant past.

To understand such moments, think of all the advisory, donation and legal support the founder secured from various actors but also the disjunctive challenges in the form of high-profile meetings, restless waiting, uncertain convincing and stubborn legal compliances that the founder mentioned during the research interview. The network of actors and organizations that directly mattered in such numerous moments constituted locally what we call here the 'network of grit'. The sociological basis and purposive manifestation of this network of grit was the imagined and unfolding world of policy. Details revealing such networks and moments were ethnographic in nature. Interviews made it possible to reveal the power of imagination and feelings of a quasi-real experience. A heterotopic reality also involved the researcher 'walking the same path' for a second time, guided by clues from interviews and events and seeking to map and make sense of an imagined world.

Much like sutured scenes of a movie, such details clipped moments of encounter involving 'relations which stretch[ed] beyond the global as part of what constitutes[d] the local, the outside as part of the inside' (Massey, 1994a, p. 5). And this was the linking between imagination and social life, not in a prefigurative fashion but for defining the purpose itself as it unfolded ethnographically. Data and theory modulated our research imagination, giving rise to the idea of 'imbrication' that reaffirmed the importance of cultural dimensions in studying education policy, perhaps any policy. 'Imbrication' was a concept we came to talk about long after the whole research was completed and substantially written about; it was a research finding, not our goal. With our usage of imbrication, we are trying to capture the complex multidirectional relations between the global, national and local, moving beyond the dominant trope in much globalization and education policy research of focusing exclusively on top-down global impacts and effects (Larsen & Beech, 2014; Lingard, 2021; Piattoeva, 2019).

Indeed, the founder leveraged a network of grit to localize TFB. Despite the fact that relationships of power and resources transmitted, carried and moved policy, the stabilization (fixity/touch down) of the mobile policy underpinned hands-on work of spatio-cultural significance. It was always eventually a cultural encounter between 'placeless power' and authority of 'place', therefore ordaining (see Santos, 2002) the global/universalized outside in relation to the local. Boaventura de Sousa Santos (2002, p. 15) rightly argues that culture is, by definition, a social process constructed at the intersection between the universal[ized] and the particular (see Beech & Rizvi, 2017; Takayama, 2011, 2019) and defining culture by default means defining frontiers. For what is convincing without frontiers? It is in that intersection where imbrication occurs involving a process of evaluation and ordination. Global-local imbrications happened both in movement (think of the imagination that drove mobilities of various sort) and in fixity (consider the locally manifest world of policy here). Yet, mobility and fixity had to be given a degree of permanence by some form of legislative cement, involving local, authorized officials in this work. Thus, the nation-state still matters even as global processes affect both the national and the local and are also in turn shaped to some extent by them (Sassen, 2007).

Empirically, considering TFB, localization meant global-local imbrications through incremental processes of spatio-cultural encounters, enabling the reach and remit of 'informal authority' and resulting in annexation of a set of practices and discourses within the mundanity of a system requiring transformation. We have defined such incremental cultural making in terms of spatialities and particularly in relation to a renewed understanding of 'place' as part of immanent forces (space). Related, and vis-à-vis ethnography in the context of globalization, Gupta and Ferguson (2001, p. 41) have highlighted the centrality of culture 'attaching causes to places and the ubiquity of place making in collective political mobilization. Such place making, however, need not be national in scale'.

Conclusion

Similar to the other two globalizing actors (and their worlds of policy) that we presented in the previous two chapters (i.e. the World Bank and the British Council), TFB demonstrated that moving or travelling is one thing and getting locally stabilized is another; the latter is necessary for impact. While both mobility and fixity are essential for the localization of a globalizable reform/

policy, anthropologically, we view an intended policy as a cultural endeavour with a specific set of practices and discourses of presumably superior value. Most importantly, sociologically, these culturally explainable practices and discourses must be enacted on the ground to be localized and sustained meaningfully as a change in relation to process, product and people (manifest world). Furthermore, such sociological dynamics can be studied ethnographically, depending on access to the actors and resources of power and spatialities of culture. When a national system is involved, the local matters.

Understanding such (g)local-sociological dynamics in spatio-cultural terms is illustrative of the global within the local (Burawoy, 1991, 2000, 2009; Sassen, 2007) and is ethnographically feasible without being beholden to the global-local binary or to the nation-state as the sole anthropological domain of cultural globalization. Methodologically, it is now possible to perform ethnography without resorting to a traditionally understood ethnos of territorial culture (Gupta & Ferguson, 2001); yet 'without ethnos' does not imply ethnography minus culture. Ethnography beyond culture (understood in the traditional territorial sense) does not mean the elision of the centrality of culture or the nation-state. Both ethnos (people) and culture (ways of life and frames of reference) matter even more, as we rethink ethnography de-territorially, broadening the research imagination beyond the nation-state and thus beyond methodological nationalism.

Viewing policy mobility in terms of cultural dimensions thus opens up new ethnographic possibilities that do not rob the nation-state of its remnant remit in the management of the human condition and culture (think of the roles governments have played, or failed to play, in managing the COVID-19 pandemic). Travelling for policy is slightly different from travelling in the usual sense of reaching and staying somewhere for a while and then returning to the traveller's original base, once the goals have been achieved. Today, policy travels to impact and transform for aspirational reasons, involving powerful actors and resource circuitry beyond the remit of, but always simultaneously associated with, the nation-state. A globally mobile policy travels to local sites to influence and impact, yet also to stay, to generate, and in the process, such recontextualization changes globally mobile policy. This is why we would argue the necessity to move beyond both methodological nationalism and methodological globalism.

6

Learning from Researching Teach For Bangladesh as Social Enterprise

Introduction

The theoretical, methodological and empirical outcomes presented in the previous chapters are situated between education policy research and the alternative future that we have just stepped into. The 1950s Anthropocene[1] (Rafferty, 2009) considered in tandem with today's pressing concerns of climate change and sustainable development present a trilemma – choose two from openness, speed and stability (Zakaria, 2020, p. 16) – to a post-pandemic world. Meanwhile, an overwhelming thickness of techno-global texture commands the future of the developing world be raised to an even higher level of significance in education policy and policy research. Globalization has affected education policy and policy processes, hitherto limited within the domestic chores of a given country – the 'modernity trap' (Cowen, 2014, p. 6). On cultural as well as performative counts, such challenges to education policy amplified as a transformative future-thinking have begun to guide the workings of 'extra-national forces' (see Silova et al., 2020, p. 3).

In the first instance, following the end of the Cold War, education policy research had to challenge methodological nationalism. This perhaps resulted in the dominance of methodological globalism in policy sociology in education research (Clarke, 2019). The more recent rise of anti-multilateralism, new nationalism and ethnonationalism among right-wing authoritarian populist politicians (e.g. former US President Trump and UK Prime Minister Johnson) has challenged this either/or methodological nationalism/methodological globalism binary. Rather, we would argue that we now need to move beyond this binary. The nation-state was never in decline despite talk of post-nationalism, but rather the challenges of the various processes of globalization reframed the way it worked in political and policy terms. Restructuring of the bureaucratic state was at one level at least a response to those pressures. New public management saw a reworking of classical bureaucracies, while subsequent modes of network and heterarchical governance conjoined new political frameworks and new modes of working with real impacts on education policy in relation to both production practices and discursive framings (Rizvi & Lingard, 2010; Wilkins & Olmedo, 2019).

In the analysis provided in this book, we have challenged a view of globalization and education policy within nations as simply needing to focus on top-down global effects on national systems of schooling. Rather, as with Larsen and Beech (2014), Piattoeva (2019) and others (Lingard, 2021), we would argue that the new spatialities of globalization must be seen to work in multiple directions and across various spaces and places. Furthermore, while globalization, advanced by the affordances of the new technologies and enhanced computational capacities (Williamson, 2019), has constituted the globe as a commensurate space of measurement through International Large Scale Assessments and outcome measures in respect of the UN's SDGs, and seen some convergence of education policy, this convergence is only in respect of policy discourses, not actual policy manifestations. That is, policies in practice are always framed in path-dependent ways with further local mediation in the moves to enactment. Our analysis of Teach For Bangladesh (TFB) has shown the fast movement of a global policy idea and its path-dependent take-up in Bangladesh with broader implications for the mode of governance in that nation, especially in respect of the place now of social enterprises (SEs) in relation to the functioning of NGOs.

All policy documents in some way work in a constitutive manner in respect of time. They constitute a past, a present and an imagined future with the focus being mainly on present-future developments. Policies also construct narrative storylines about their temporal positionings and aspirations. This is the case in respect of TFB and for SEs more broadly. We acknowledge the different temporalities affecting the fast mobility of policy models around the globe and those temporalities framing both their path-dependent mediation and enactment. Today, however, we are positioned in a broader temporal era, namely, that of the Anthropocene and the climate emergency, which carries significant implications for education, education policy, imagined futures and educational research conducted in this context (Rappleye & Komatsu, 2020).

One response to the future in this time of the Anthropocene has been acknowledgement of the finiteness of the resources of our planet, linked to a proposed infiniteness of cultural cycles (see Rappleye & Komatsu, 2020). The discursive structure of such future thinking centres around one main stem – that our inability to think beyond modernity, ethnonationalism and nation-state, impedes our future and we need an overhauled cultural reorientation to be able to reinvent and instil new fundamental assumptions to govern our basic view of life – our social imaginary (Taylor, 2004; see Rappleye & Komatsu, 2020). The preparedness for this infinity of cultural production, Rappleye and Komatsu (2020) would argue, is the solution to the finiteness of available resources. In that context, Rappleye and Komatsu have written very instructively about the pressing necessity to rethink comparative education research in the context of the Anthropocene and current pressing climate emergency. That condition has driven home the significance of both national and global responses, as has, of course, the COVID-19 pandemic, which nonetheless has appeared to strengthen some manifestations of nationalism, including what can be seen as vaccine nationalism. In this context, we need to rethink the purposes of education and thus of comparative education policy research.

These tectonic shifts in the Anthropocene have heavily affected education policy and its practices (see Manzon, 2018, p. 94), particularly in less-developed countries such as Bangladesh, which aspire to a high degree of development. The more the world has become transnationally 'ordered', the greater the impact of such ordering on the nationally organized governance of education and its policy.[2] As we have demonstrated empirically in earlier chapters, the practical expression of transnational ordering and global capitalism (including philanthrocapitalism) can be understood vis-à-vis the rise of networks and heterarchies (Ball & Junemann, 2012). Indeed, we have documented the workings of both policy networks (Ball, 2012a) and governance networks (Torfing, 2007), the latter being more formal and permanent than the former in the case of Bangladesh (see Chapter 3).

As the most germane recipients, government actors of education policy in Bangladesh are not immune to this impact, and today think and act more in facilitative, participatory and partnership-based ways (cellular relations) than in sole authority terms (vertebrate relations) (Lingard, 2014b). This means that rather than focusing on the nation-state and its actors (sociology), a focus on following policy itself (Ball et al., 2017, p. 15) is more illustrative of how education policy occurs 'differently' today – 'associologically', in Bruno Latour's (2005) terms. Since our research revealed SE as an epochal cultural essence, which gave purpose to the networks that animated the three cases we identified and studied, in what comes next, we will briefly conceptualize SE to then reflect on what we have found in Bangladesh. Finally, we will present what we have learned about policy mobilities in relation to Bangladesh's primary education sector and its possible futures.

Researching SEs, Global-National Networks and Education Policy in Bangladesh

The research that informs this book began with its initial focus on Teach For Bangladesh back in early 2015, while late 2016 fieldwork demanded a zoom out to a broader research agenda, namely, the localization of social entrepreneurial policies in education. As domestically relevant data on power, politics and persuasion excavated the erratic links between nationally situated policies and global presences, our organizational gaze on TFB enabled engagement with the idea of 'social enterprises'. Research interviews were intense and longer than anticipated, and the resulting discussions on systemic transformations revealed how TFB was but one signifier in the social entrepreneurial saga that had only begun to be enacted nationally. The phonetic charm of SEs felt unwittingly glamorous and seductive as articulated by its proponents in the research interviews. For others, it seemed like a headwind against the seeming scleroticism of traditional bureaucracy. In the interviews, the messianic ubiquity of a social entrepreneurial spirit evoked a potentially dazzling future against a moribund past and present. Methodologically, we would make the point that data derived from research interviews is not only the words used but the ways they are delivered, and the nature of the relationality with the interviewee. To understand SE in the context of Bangladesh also requires knowledge of how it operates globally in relation to what is now widely referred to as new philanthropy (NP) and impact investment. These are matters we turn to next.

New Philanthropy, Social Entrepreneurship and Impact Investment

A new era of capitalism has reinvented philanthropy that now acts as a transformative force in the global framing and governance of social problems (see Bigham et al., 2016; Walker, 2017; Salamon, 2014; Wiepking & Handy, 2017; Adelman, 2009). Including in education, this NP (see Ball, 2012; Ball & Junemann, 2012; Olmedo, 2017; Santori et al., 2016) differs from traditional charitable practices in that the NP involves the donor/giver in directly controlling or regulating the usage of the money donated. In this case, the management of money donated depends largely upon the governance aspirations and personal proclivities of the donor (Tompkins-Stange, 2016).

This entails a directive role for the 'giver' in matters of choosing interventions, designing programmes and monitoring management (Nielsen, 1996, p. 11). Besides individual and organizational philanthropies, multinational corporations now seriously focus on their corporate social responsibilities (CSR), which have been supported by the global construction and growth of new philosophically focused secondary infrastructures (e.g. Porticus Global) that has evolved into an industry in itself (Ball, 2012a, p. 50). Through CSR and individual philanthropic programmes, companies are seeking to perform a kind of 'socio-moral duty' that was previously assigned to governmental organizations, civil society organizations and state entities – the moralization of the market (Shamir, 2008, p. 4).

A large portion of new philanthropists, who think and act globally, have accumulated their fortune from the Silicon Valley and the dot-com boom. These philanthropists promote a particular approach to solving social problems globally (Morvaridi, 2015, p. 4). Often referred to as a 'Silicon Valley Consensus' (SVC) (Morvaridi, 2015), this new approach seeks to identify and solve global social issues based on entrepreneurial innovation, corporate managerialism and technological advancements. SVC claims that private donations and philanthropic contributions channelled through networks of public-private and philanthropic-civil society partnerships are more efficient in addressing social problems than government-led processes (Morvaridi, 2015, p. 5). On the basis of this argument, there has been a 'renaissance of philanthropic foundations', mostly in the United States, but also across European and other countries (see Anheier & Leat, 2006; Ball & Junemann, 2012; Tompkins-Stange, 2016). Linked to this is the professionalization of fundraising activities at a global scale that have taken the form of a 'global megatrend' (Cagney & Ross, 2013, p. 8).

Understandably, NP is more than innovative projects: it is also about global governance of social issues, significantly in relation to the developing world. Particularly in education, the systemic-transformative aspect of NP lies in its deeper 'strategic' motive of convincing governments about the value of philanthropy-supported innovation in solving social problems (Ball & Junemann, 2012). Strategic philanthropy, as Ball and Junemann (2012, p. 51) argue, is actually a means to get governments interested in innovative social projects. In this regard, 'new philanthropy' is deemed as a real opportunity for philanthropists to persuade governments to take up nationwide upscaling of innovative private programmes that have shown considerable success in the demonstration stage (e.g. TFB). Such initial demonstration phases, often called start-ups, are typically carried out by social entrepreneurs/enterprises (think of the TFB founder). This SE-NP dependency is expanding and being globalized in the same way as international law includes more and more countries (think of Teach For All (TFAll)); and finance, goods and services are becoming more mobile (Anheier, 2007, p. 117). Anheier (2007) argues that NP has become largely transnational, and it follows the patterns and processes of globalization. This means NP is spread globally through specific policies, policy networks and their localized practices (see Ball & Junemann, 2012; Ball et al., 2017; Olmedo, 2017).

The localizing hands of new philanthropists, social entrepreneurs, are those individuals who initiate, lead and even globally manage SEs. Alvord et al. (2004, p. 262) have identified three categories of SEs: (a) profit-oriented business entrepreneurs who combine commercial interests with social impact by making use of business skills and managerial knowledge in creating enterprises that can accomplish social purposes besides commercial profit-taking (Emerson & Twersky, 1996); (b) entrepreneurs who innovate for problem-solving by planning and promoting new social arrangements and mobilizing resources targeting a specific social problem (Dees, 1998); and (c) SEs who catalyse long-term social transformation with an understanding of the present problems and their link to the long-term future (Ashoka Innovators for the Public, 2000). Thus, there are three broad and oftentimes overlapping categories of SEs – the entrepreneurial, the innovative and the transformatory (Leadbeater, 1997, p. 53). Individual social entrepreneurs innovate and follow business models using their management knowledge and leadership abilities of a corporate kind in the social realm. The difference between business entrepreneurs and social entrepreneurs lies mostly in their focus and scope of action. The former profit from traditional businesses, while the latter target social problems to be solved in the main through business-like social innovations or supportive direct business in some cases. We stress that social entrepreneurs are very varied; in many cases, social entrepreneurs profit in indirect and often opaque ways.

All of the aforementioned aspirations, involvements, transactions and intended transformations are captured in the term 'impact investment' (Allman & Nogales, 2015), also known as 'social investment' (Hemerijck, 2017). Impact investment comes in the form of debts or equities (shares/stakes). They can have any geographical reach and situatedness and tend to globalize innovative services that combine an expected margin of profit-returns with a measured degree of social impact (Allman & Nogales, 2015, p. 3). Allman and Nogales (2015) postulate further that the most dominant thread of social impact funding goes to the formation of SEs and mostly to the developing world. Impact investment involves the investor's evaluative engagement in the performance and impact that the supported SEs are expected to produce. Thus, impact investments are inherently 'evidence-based', necessitating the SE to 'build data on the type of interventions' that are required to have 'a positive development impact'. Impact investors by default expect to 'examine and share learnings on the combination of products and services, the type of designs, the pricing and distribution models, and the accompanying services that will result in positive societal impact on the targeted population' (Allman & Nogales, 2015, p. 4).

Impact investors are the key driving force of philanthrocapitalism. The oldest and most globally influential investors work with intergovernmental institutions.[3] Usually such investors have a specific mission and seek commercial-style investment with very low capital costs over a long period. The second layer of impact investors includes the charitable organizations. Such organizations usually range from non-profit institutions[4] that rechannel donated money as investments to organizations[5] that garner funding from profitable private-sector enterprises to make impact investments (Allman & Nogales, 2015, p. 5). While these are high-range impact investors, the middle-range comprise high-net-worth individuals who channel their own capital directly to SEs. Such giving is often called 'catalytic capital' that supports 'early-stage ventures' or funds 'business plans that materialise into companies' (Allman & Nogales, 2015, p. 5). Finally, there are also direct for-profit impact investors that are usually corporations and businesses. What we have been talking about here are the cultural circuits of global capitalism, indeed philanthrocapitalism (Thrift, 2005). Today, the financescape of social impact investment has become complex and globally powerful.

Impact investment is often criticized for its sole focus on impact measurement (input in relation to output) and neglect of effectiveness (Then et al., 2017). Its efficiency logic and possibilities facilitate marketization and economization, not only in the non-profit sectors but also in the social sphere more generally (Eikenberry & Kluver, 2004; Kehl & Then, 2012). Centralizing their focus on education as a space for profit-making within the global financial market, impact investors and venture philanthropists are changing the nature and ecosystem of educational funding (see Santori et al., 2016). Santori and colleagues (2016) have identified five categories of such 'eduplayers' active within this new global investment space for education. These are: specialized non-profit investment ventures (funds sectoral change programmes), specialized financial advisors, specialized education private equity investors, specialized incubators and accelerators and specialized funds.

What we have described thus far in this section constitutes the neoliberal economic firmament of philanthrocapitalism that today strongly influences the developing world of policy and governance in education. Teach For Bangladesh and the British Council's social wing were two of the very first and few instances of immediate philanthrocapitalist policy experiments in Bangladesh, while the role of the World Bank had been more of an historical and preparatory one since the late 1990s.

TFB, Past and Future: Social Entrepreneurializing Primary Education in Bangladesh

For a less-developed context such as Bangladesh, the global rise of NP and venture capitalism carries strong social entrepreneurial reverberations. In earlier chapters we have presented how three overlapping networks of actors and organizations have pursued social entrepreneurial policies, manifesting three different forms, speed and intensity, both in relation to and within the national governance landscape of Bangladesh. We have conceptualized these in terms of imagined (Appadurai, 1996) and enacted policymaking worlds (Peck & Theodore, 2015), wherein spatialities were constructed, managed and engaged by actors and organizations with hybridized national and global dispositions and networks. Involving and seeking to mediate hierarchies, these actors appraised and negotiated aspirational policy imaginations that had specific cultural dimensions meant to be progressively different from those imagined within Bangladesh.

Before we elaborate further, we feel it important to address the research questions, the answers to which are meant to be the learning outcomes from the research reported in this book. Here we make consolidative remarks on the empirical policy lessons we acquired by studying TFB and the context of contexts (Peck & Theodore, 2015) that surrounded it in relation to SE (British Council) and to older forms of impact investment partnerships (World Bank and the Donor Consortium).

An important research question (as outlined in Chapter 5) was: How did TFB constitute and locally institutionalize TFAll/America's global teacher education reform policy in Bangladesh? It was found that beyond its organizational identity as a local NGO, in a de facto fashion (Adhikary & Lingard, 2020) TFB represented and worked with and for a social entrepreneurial policy imagination (Appadurai, 1996), originally situated in global cities, particularly in the United States (Sassen, 2007, 2013). The founder of TFB, aligned to her diasporic upbringing and professional development within an American social entrepreneurial circuitry of philanthrocapitalism (Bishop & Green, 2008; Olmedo, 2016), constituted and acted upon a policy network – a globally imagined community of practice, an *imaginaire* of global philanthropic aspirations (Appadurai, 1996). From a bird's-eye or logocentric view, this constructed global community looked like a dense global net (web) (see Adhikary & Lingard, 2017, pp. 10–11), within which Porticus Global, Teach For America (TFA)/TFAll/TFB and Building Resources Across Communities (BRAC) acted as a network that persevered in its stated mission of seeking to influence public education governance and provision. This could be construed as something of a 'network of grit' as indicated earlier in the book. These actors are primarily funders and proselytizers of a social entrepreneurial mode of educational governance.

This 'net' of philanthropic actors mobilized ideational, financial and connective support to the organizational making of TFB first in the United States as a limited liabilities company and then in Bangladesh as an NGO. This 'net' also demonstrated how global flows of resources in the form of money, people and ideas (Appadurai, 1996) constitute and are contingent upon the connective, aspirational and circulatory power of global entrepreneurial imaginations. However, apart from this imagined yet purposeful 'net' making, more practical and locally embedded policy labour (Ball et al., 2017) was also performed by TFB. It was through such organizational interstices that influence occurred, touched down, remained anchored and exerted strong influence. One instance where the founder had to show considerable grit was in seeking government approvals necessary for TFB to be annexed within the primary education system. It then acted as a globalizing 'microspace' of influence (Ball et al., 2017; Cook & Ward, 2012). We have viewed this as the 'work' of the network.

Coming to the cultural construction and popular dissemination of TFB as a policy and practice, the second research question asked: How does TFB culturally constitute and disseminate TFAll/America's globalized teacher education reform model through media? It was found that TFB's media construction of itself as a policy and practice demonstrated a developing-world example of a global policy 'rewritten' locally as audio-video bytes (Appadurai, 1996; Lingard & Rawolle, 2004), illustratively with specific signifiers and emotions. In TFB's cultural construction of itself, Facebook emerged as an engaging interactive platform – a topological surface (Lury et al., 2012) for policy 'mediatization' (Fairclough, 2000). Evidently, such social-mediatization (see Adhikary et al., 2018) practices activated culturally global social entrepreneurial imaginations, discourses, sensitivities and practices related to TFA/All/B and affectively canonized the actors who acted upon such cultural dimensions.

The research data and analyses revealed three ways in which TFB sought to influence policy via Facebook. First, it created opportunities for recurrent reading, hearing and seeing the policy in practice as animated by 'stars', 'spectacles', 'glamour' and 'statistics', all of which regularized a sense of heroic bodily feeling-as-'vernacularization' (Appadurai, 1996). Secondly, it sought to inform and reshape the 'social imaginary' (Taylor, 2004) and associated problem imaginations (Bacchi, 2009) of the local populous, government and particularly youth. And thirdly, it involved what might be described as a 'post-truth' way of engagement via the excessive use of emotional stimulus (Keyes, 2004; Suiter, 2016; Sismondo, 2017), manifesting the affective aspects of policy (Berlant, 2011; Massumi, 2002; McKenzie, 2017).

Such social-mediatization of the TFB model also demonstrated an instance of the becoming topological of (policy) culture, since Facebook acted as a topological surface (Lury et al., 2012; Thompson & Cook, 2015), wherein both the influential policy actors and the target recipients[6] became connected to interact and negotiate meaning in relation to a situated practice (Amin, 2002), the TFA/B reform model. The TFB Facebook page demonstrated an instance of a virtual heterotopic place (Dehaene & Cauter, 2008; Foucault, 1986) and a field of co-emergence (Lury et al., 2012), wherein specific reform practices had been placed for collective appraisal and thereby creation. Again, all of this 'net'ing, 'work'ing and 'social-mediatizing' was facilitated by purposive 'flows' of resources constituting power of/to influence, steer and eventually make policy. These flows included diasporic individuals and their imaginations, large finances, social entrepreneurial ideas, professional media work and advanced technologies (Appadurai, 1996) but also underscored the rising and often manipulative power of the flow of data (Zuboff, 2019).

Nonetheless, these flows demonstrably owed their mobility forces to the collective aspirations of global owners, seekers and mobilizers of such resources. It is again due to the orchestral capacity and unifying role of such collective imaginations and aspirations (Appadurai, 1996), vis-à-vis a social entrepreneurial mode of governance, that TFB became institutionalized and embedded in Bangladesh. In the process, the local and the global involved each other through flows that brought the topological power of 'resourceful reach' to the mediating topographical state as they became imbricated (Lingard, 2021). TFB here functions as a hybrid organizational conduit (Ball & Thawer, 2018), acting as a pipeline enabling flows towards local receptacles of governance. In other words, it is an interstitial microspace of influence through which the global topological came into continuing touch and continuous interaction with what was authoritatively national and topographical in education in Bangladesh. Indeed, this exemplifies a reordering of influence and respatialization of governance as and through globalization (Held et al., 1999), implicating cultural continuity and productive expansion.

Insofar as state support in the local institutionalization of TFB was concerned, few of the participating government officials shared the same social entrepreneurial policy imagination as TFB. Such senior government officials, a few with substantial educational experiences in global cities, represented a glocal (Ball et al., 2017; Lingard, 2014a) social imaginary that constituted 'national' governance of education proactively in terms of global partnerships. However, this glocal imagination of partnerships, as data analysis revealed, originated and deepened within government officials through a history of reforms that implemented globally agreed-on commitments and development goals in the country. Such implementation embedded various forms of public-private partnerships and GO-NGO collaborations, particularly within the primary education subsector but also increasingly within the NGO sector. These two sectors, respectively, became the foci of two further research questions with specific attention to the historical and ongoing transformations in relation to social entrepreneurial discourses and practices.

Coming to this wider context, another research question addressed was: What changes in the local education policy landscape in Bangladesh create the policy conditions that mediate and enable the emergence and work of SEs such as TFB? It was found that the primary education subsector of Bangladesh (PESoB) has experienced a shift from government to networked and heterarchic governance (Ball, 2012), again, through the practical manifestation of a global policy imagination rooted in globally defined commitments and development goals that benchmarked public-private partnerships and GO-NGO collaboration. Social entrepreneurial governance backed by corporate/global philanthropy is increasingly leading the trend of such collaborations and partnerships. This global policy imagination was glocally represented and path-dependently implemented through a series of structural adjustments led by the multilateral banks.

In Bangladesh, such structural adjustments involved the construction of a funders' (development partners) network called Donor Consortium, a globally funded network of local education NGOs named CAMPE and the respatialization of government structures in line with new public management and subsequently networked heterarchic principles. Most importantly, the whole PESoB was brought under one sector-wide approach to educational programming and financing. All of these transformations were cross-temporally (across the varying temporalities of the global, the national and the local) situated across a reformative history of a phased programme called Primary Education Development Programme (PEDP), the fourth phase of which is ongoing. Under this networked and heterarchical mode of PEDP governance, priority was given to global-local partnerships, particularly in matters of teacher quality, education and recruitment, areas on which TFB is focused. In the ongoing PEDP IV, data analysis revealed the role of new philanthropies and social entrepreneurial governance of educational services has real salience for future policy agendas.

However, it was also noted that the historically evident steps and actions that brought the PESoB to its current state of affairs (Latour, 2005) highlighted the dominance of use of data. Primary education is now being glocally governed by data through various indicators and evaluation processes that tie the Bangladesh government's performance in development goals to its access to globally mobilized funding of various sorts. Such funding comes not only through the Donor Consortium but also via global funds, such as the Global Partnership for Education, a networked organization that has TFB's funder Porticus Global on its governing board. Indeed, the governance of primary education has experienced a real sense of transformation that is practically glocal and futuristically globalizing. As data revealed, concrete policies and guidelines for allowing global philanthropic funding and associated social entrepreneurial governance practices in education are underway in PEDP IV. However, TFB being one de facto social entrepreneurial organization, yet still registered as an NGO, the transformations within the NGO sector vis-à-vis SEs became a subsequent and important focus for our research.

Consequentially, our final research question was: How is social entrepreneurship constituted as an overriding policy in Bangladesh, and how is it linked to the work and future of TFB? We discovered that another third network of actors led by the British Council Bangladesh (BCB) was locally active and mobilizing a considerable amount of globally flowing resources (money, individuals and knowledge) to impact in particular the NGO Affairs Bureau (NGOAB; see Adhikary et al., 2020). By influencing the NGOAB, this network sought to formulate legislation, guidelines and a policy environment necessary for the establishment of SE as a fully fledged business sector in Bangladesh.

In BCB's efforts through a supportive epistemic community to convince the government, the production and utilization of commissioned quantitative research and associated data and analysis were evident.

The presentation of SE as a policy panacea for Bangladesh (see Adhikary et al., 2020), in this case, was a policy imagination proselytized by the BCB. This organization constituted and coordinated the network of grit, an epistemic community (Adler & Haas, 1992; Olmedo, 2017), the members of which conducted research, presented and analysed the findings from legal, structural and operational perspectives and utilized those findings in self-organized policy-dialogue events, wherein government counterparts participated in co-appraising such recommended practices. Thus, social entrepreneurial sector policy is now in the process of being embedded and the necessary policy labour is being performed by yet another microspace of influence, which is locally active but glocally formulated and which made use of heterotopic spatialities (events) to influence the government towards such cultural goals.

To conclude, these research-questions-based findings highlight something wider in scope and implication. We started the empirical investigation through TFB and reached through it the emerging new philanthropic imagination of governance, notably SEs. This TFB focus also brought to the surface many global, local and glocal actors that constituted TFB, not only as a networked space of policy influence but also as a locally embedded microspace for practical policy persuasion work. The power of this microspace lies in its demonstrated ability to bring the reach of heterarchic new philanthropic powers to those that still mattered most in the implementation of a social entrepreneurial policy imagination in education in Bangladesh, namely, the government.

The same social entrepreneurial policy imagination was pursued by two other microspaces of influence of differing scope and modalities, led by two other global and globalizing organizations, namely, the World Bank and the BCB. What emerged as common among these spaces was that there was always a networked space of influence (the net) and a history of work, short or long term with variable success, at embedding influence locally (the work). In the process, the authority of the government was evidently being shared with such global networks and institutional forces at various levels, giving rise to heterarchical governance.

Yet, most importantly, these three microspaces of influence combined nuance what Peck and Theodore (2015) characterize as a 'fast-policy condition'. Within the limits of this research and vis-à-vis the persuasion of a social entrepreneurial model, Bangladesh undoubtedly demonstrated a globalizing policy condition.

This was characterized by 'the intensified and instantaneous connectivity of sites, channels, arenas, and nodes of policy development, evolution, and reproduction', which now define not only governance (Peck & Theodore, 2015, p. 223) but also policymaking through governance (Alexiadou & Bunt-Kokhuis, 2013, p. 346) and governing of governance itself (Torfing, 2007). We see the emergence of 'fast-policy fields' (we found three), which are 'much more than a zone of bilateral transactions' and are 'made up of dense networks of hierarchical and lateral relations, and multiple nodes of translation and reinvention' (Peck & Theodore, 2015, p. 223). Our research findings on the ways TFB, the World Bank and the BCB have demonstrated their policy influence and a fast policy condition. These findings fully resonate with Peck and Theodore's (2015, p. 223) observation about globally mobile policy models:

> In order to earn the status (and influence) of a 'model,' global policy models invariably command an extensive audience, many of whom will be actively engaged in the *work* of complex adaptation rather than simple mimicry, while these *circuits of extralocal influence and multipolar mutation* will also themselves be characterised by *different degrees of resourcing, different forms of advocacy, different geometries of power, and so on*. Once again, this is why fast policy refers less to a quantifiable state, more to a social condition. (Emphases added)

While Peck and Theodore (2015) studied such fast policy conditions comparatively between two different jurisdictions, the research reported in this book illustrated the same focusing within one developing world policy landscape highlighting the rise of philanthrocapitalism. This was done through the identification of a cultural base, SE, common to the three overlapping networks. The focus on culture allowed us to detect processes and spatialities of global-national-local imbrications across the three interwoven policymaking worlds; and cultural imbrication (spatialities) preceded structural imbrication (institutional embedding).

Reimagining Comparative Research in Education Policy in Bangladesh

Our research was conducted in Bangladesh at a time when old ways of policy and governance had apparently outlived their effectiveness, and new ways were emerging. It is precisely because of this temporal framing that our 'reimagination' of education policy in Bangladesh is enabled. Today, it is not an overstatement that policymaking in education in Bangladesh is no longer imaginable without the consideration of mobilities and networks, and the social entrepreneurial future that such networks potentially enable. Emerging policy mobilities research makes timely sense of the empirical worlds of policies we have studied in Bangladesh. However, our ethnographic journey generated novel insights, which we share here.

Broadly speaking, two overlapping trends of work on policy mobilities mainstream the network literature that explain imbrications of changing and morphing relationality and territoriality in educational policy and governance. One deploys a political science approach to studying networks, using social network analysis, and the other directly 'follows the policy', adopting a broadly ethnographic extended case method (ECM) to policy mobilities (Gulson et al., 2017, p. 225). While these works are undeniably prototypical and command the largest engagement in research on policy mobilities, we accept Gulson and colleagues' (2017) productive critiques that the former approach invites further insights on how networked relations are held together (we add why to that) and the second approach invokes further reflection on the speed and intensity of the movement of policy.

While in substantial ways, our research builds upon empirically supported theoretical 'imagination' on policy mobilities (Ball et al., 2017; Ball & Junemann, 2012; Gulson et al., 2017; Peck, 2011; Peck & Theodore, 2015), to reimagine the same in and for a least-developing context, we have put sincere efforts into addressing some of the critiques alluded to earlier – not only because ongoing development is necessary in an emerging field but also to appreciate the democratic ethos that placing attention on speed and intensity would enable. Consideration of speed and intensity facilitates the placement of the ethnographic present informatively between the active past and immanent future. Speed and intensity are functions that certainly can be a solid basis for comparable insights, as well as insightful comparisons. They are, however, unrevealingly barren without a comparative scope. To generate such a comparative view, we sought to accommodate a few methodological innovations that would address to some extent the critiques stated earlier.

With a backdrop of globalization processes, a theoretical-empirical dialogue invited a cultural dimension in relation to global-national-local flows that would demonstrate a suturing effect in regard to the movement of a reform policy. If multiple instances of policy mobilities were able to be identified pertaining to a single cultural essence, they could beneficially be compared in relation to speed, intensity and causal cues taken from the local. Through an anthropologically oriented global 'cultural' approach to the power of an agentic and expansive imagination (Appadurai, 1996), we sought to interrogate the hard-territorial foundations of the so-called modernity trap in relation to the 'cultural' circuitry (Thrift, 2005) of philanthro/capitalism. Indeed, TFB was a harbinger of philanthrocapitalism.

TFB, BCB and World Bank all demonstrated that governance today involves cultural flows carried, cast and sustained in and through assemblages of 'things' (Latour, 2005) both human and material. It was evident that without reach and presence (Allen, 2009, 2011) governance is fissiparous (also see Gulson et al., 2017), and it is meaningless without a cult*ural* programme (not yet culture itself) (Lury et al., 2012). While power works and flows relationally, it also lies in the ability to constitute and control reach, proximity and presence, which are what today's heterarchies muster in relational and material terms, while the influence is cognitively cultural (see Chapter 2). Policy mobilities in the context of Bangladesh are no exception to such insights as policymaking today is quasi entrepreneurial and has been globalized.

In this context, adding a cult*ural* perspective to governance in researching agentic or network collaboration can benefit more nuanced comparative understandings. Söpper (2014, p. 54) argues that while a governance approach illustrates the structure, quality and intensity of any collaboration in existential ways, adding a cultural view enables insights into why the collaboration takes a particular form depending on the deeper aspirations that underpin collaborations. Moreover, a cult*ural* approach also enables nuanced analyses by activating comparatively the empirical and cultural differentials that mediate processes of participation, activation and mobilization in collaborations (Söpper 2014, p. 54). Think of the culturally differing ways the World Bank, TFB network and BCB worked on the same social entrepreneurial policy at various levels within the system. Here, our focus is not on culture as a noun but rather on the adjectival use of it – cult*ural* – so that we could identify and make use of differences, contrasts and comparisons (Appadurai, 1996, p. 12).

Hard structures have governed thus far through human bodies (Foucault, 1991a) and territorial imaginations (Anderson, 1983), but one double-edged reality of modernity has always been the political wardenship of collective imagination and cultural habits, a form of governance under epochal challenge. Research on policy mobilities in Bangladesh now needs to consider this rapturous time that already has broken the shackles of limiting 'imagination' territorially through the affordances of the new communications technologies which have enabled global imaginations (Appadurai, 1996). Today, anybody with the right set of relationships, resources and networked connectivities can generate impact through the power of their innovative ideas (i.e. systemic imagination), however strong ethnonationalist forces and sentiments may be. We felt it important to introduce the role and power of 'imagination' into our understanding of policy mobilities. Policy mobility occurs within a manifest 'world' of a potentially productive entrepreneurial imagination that contains the cultural blueprint for impact. Besides imagination, the manifestation requires onsite ground work, inevitably involving challenges, competition and collaboration.

Appadurai's anthropological work on global cultural flows was particularly helpful for our research in capturing aspirations, imaginations, flows, cultural making and collaboration. His concept of 'imagined worlds' helped us rethink what Peck and Theodore (2015) advanced as worlds of policy or policymaking worlds. These scholars rightly reject the notion 'that policymaking worlds are racing toward convergence – unilaterally driven by steamroller models of best practice, or "flattened" into a neoliberalised monoculture' (Peck & Theodore, 2015, p. xvi). Rather, they seek 'to make the more subtle point that those policymaking worlds are becoming more intimately and deeply interconnected than ever before' (Peck & Theodore, 2015, p. xvi). They continue,

> Furthermore, a related proposition is that this condition of interconnectivity is itself subject to historically distinctive forms of acceleration and intensification. Continuous monitoring and learning, continuous promotion of best-practice models, continuous inter-referencing of policies, especially at moments of path-altering 'reform' – all these are features of reconstituted policy worlds. And in the terms we are exploring here, they are reconstituted fast policy worlds. (Peck & Theodore, 2015, p. xvi)

The intimate interconnections that we have seen between the policymaking worlds, which TFB, BCB and the World Bank created, were historically revealing. We have seen acceleration and deceleration in policy efforts by actors, depending on accumulated failures followed by moments of decisive success. While intensity most often depended on the strength of the actors in relation to the resources at their disposal, serendipity also had effects. We also have witnessed how continuous monitoring and learning, promotion of best practices, intra- and inter-referencing using data and encountering moments of epistemic or amicable persuasion all oscillated around social entrepreneurial policy reforms. These indeed were 'reconstituted fast-policy worlds'.

Additionally, the changing nature of the social that Latour alludes to carries implications for the way sociology and sociology of education policy ought to function. We see methodological purchase in Latour's conceptualization of the social and his associated take on sociology. Thus, for us a topological analytics must acknowledge a sociology, which works less as 'the "science of the social", but [more] as the tracing of associations', where the social is 'but a type of connection between things that are not themselves social' (Latour, 2005, p. 5). This is a move away from 'sociology of the [traditionally] social' to the 'sociology of associations' that Latour (2005, p. 5) refers to as 'associology', which also acknowledges the non-human as actors in the social. Latour's account of the social as association and connections also is able to account for global-national-local manifestations of the social.

As we have noted throughout, our research sits within both comparative education and policy sociology in education. As with much comparative education, we have provided a detailed case of policy and governance developments in education in a specific nation-state, here Bangladesh. However, under the changing conditions of globalization and the ever-changing and interwoven relationship among the national, local and global, we have demonstrated how the nation-state remains significant in policy terms but no longer is a tightly bordered container and today works in different multi-scalar and multi-spatial ways.

Education policy is no longer under the sole jurisdiction of the nation. Education policy discourses, and policy models (such as TFAll), now move across the globe and mutate in path-dependent ways as they touch down and interact with national and local policymakers and practitioners and competing policy imaginations. Additionally, there has also been the emergence of what we might see as a global education policy field. For rich countries, this has been constituted through international large-scale assessments (ILSAs); for nations of the Global South, this policy field has been constituted more by UN agendas, today specifically the SDGs and related outcome measures. In these nations of the Global South, the impacts of conditionalities attached to aid funding and the effects of globally mobile policy ideas have also helped constitute this global field.

Comparative education today, as we have attempted to show throughout the book, needs to deal with this global policy field but also the ways globally mobile policy models touch down and morph in national and local contexts, yet also must acknowledge the continuing significance of local and national actions, which help to some extent both constitute and mediate the global. We have suggested at various stages the need, methodologically, for comparative education to develop research methodologies beyond the methodological-nationalism/methodological-globalism binary. We have also been very aware of No'Voa and Yariv-Mashal's (2003) exhortation to comparative educators to avoid any possibility of comparative education becoming simply a mode of governance in its almost fetishized fascination with ILSAs and global comparative performance indicators. We accept their position that comparative education should remain an academic field of research focused on fostering understanding and also fostering 'reconciliation between history and comparison' (No'Voa & Yariv-Mashal, 2003, p. 433).

Concluding Comments

Following Peck and Theodore (2015), we have researched how TFB as a global policy model (TFAll) touched down in Bangladesh, in and through specific global and national networks, giving rise to heterarchic arrangements of policy and governance. Additionally, we have emphasized TFB as a de facto SE. In proffering this analysis, we have drawn on literature on policy mobility, globalization, the Teach For phenomenon, comparative education, policy sociology and education, and spatial geographies of mobility and globalization. The latter include emergent global fields, new scales of policymaking and new topological relations. Throughout, we have attempted to document and deal with the complexities of relations in policy and governance terms among global, national and local effects, suggesting that these work in very complex, multidirectional and interweaving, contingent and overlapping ways. We have used the concept of 'imbrications' to pick up on these contingencies. We have also attempted to research and document bottom-up, locally focused engagement with global forces, connections and global imaginations (Burawoy, 2009) and in so doing have tried to grasp some of the messy and contingent ways that global policies touch down in specific locations. We are in line here with Carney's (2019) call for more of this kind of research in comparative education, paying attention to local, bottom-up interventions.

Our research is in line with that of Friedrich (2014), Ellis and colleagues (2016), Lam (2020) and Thomas and colleagues (2020), which emphasize Teach For entities as social entrepreneurial vehicles of transformation of public governance. As a point of difference, we emphasize culture and imagination. Here, the Appaduraian distinction between culture and cultural applies in better understanding the transformative dimensions that such developments carry in distinct sites. Such cultural dimensions are implicated within the aspirations that manifest through constructed worlds of engagement, which Appadurai

(1996) characterizes as *imaginaires* (collective aspirations). In our analysis, we have focused on the ways in which TFB as a de facto SE has become part of a much bigger transformation occurring in governance in Bangladesh and more broadly. Here, we have researched and documented the ways in which NGOs in Bangladesh have been, perhaps potentially, transmogrifying into SEs, with the broader goal of restructuring the governance of primary public sector schooling. This is a process that is currently under way and evolving in and through government policies and legislation.

Of interest to us is that one could sustain a defensible argument that the concept of SEs had its beginnings in Bangladesh in the work of the late Sir Fazle Hassan Abed and his BRAC organization, founded in 1972. What is interesting is how this concept has been de-territorialized and travelled globally as a globalized localism (Santos, 2002) touching down in many other nations of the globe, including those in the Global North. Our analysis has shown how the concept of SE has been re-territorialized in Bangladesh in respect of the changes we have illustrated throughout. We find these iterative de-territorializing/re-territorializing phenomena fascinating, and it clearly has mediating and translational effects of both context productive and context generative kinds (Appadurai, 1996).

The analysis presented throughout this book has a strong emphasis on imagination in framing the conceptual understanding of global-national-local forms of governmentality that today manifest *in* and *as* networks and heterarchies. All of the three worlds of policy that we have ethnographically investigated demonstrate this central role of imagination in the ways policy agendas were thought about and enacted. In particular, the role of diasporic imagination was central in the making and mediation of global-national-local imbrications in and through travelling policy models. This was particularly the case in relation to TFB. Such imaginations were important in their ability to enhance the ethnographic effect of the sociology we have undertaken here in this book.

Our research began with a network ethnography of Teach For Bangladesh. We then moved to more grounded ethnographic research, following Burawoy's extended case method and the methodological insights from Peck and Theodore (2015), and it was from that point that we found three interlinked network cases entertaining a common cultural essence. This confirms the ongoing significance of local ethnographic work and reflections about it (Vavrus, 2021) but also the pressing need today to understand that the local and the national are both affected by the global and these effects work in multiple directions and in multiple ways. That is, the global is partially constituted by the local and the national and vice versa. Just as Appadurai has argued that with the flows of people around the globe today, the nation and the state have become the projects of each other in nation-states, we might say that today the global, national and local are the ongoing projects of each other. National and global responses to the COVID-19 pandemic have driven home the global connectedness of people but at the same time have demonstrated the fragility of global dispositions within nation-states, reflective of the strengthening of ethnonationalism, including making national borders less permeable within some but not all nations.

We have struggled in the book to go beyond methodological nationalism and methodological globalism, while acknowledging that this is an ongoing and yet inchoate project. This project is of significance today in the academic fields of comparative education and comparative educational policy sociology in education. In order for this project to unfold inclusively, methodological, theoretical and empirical approaches need to avoid exclusionary epistemologies and embrace a more inviting approach to multiple positionalities and perspectives. Among other things, this would enable and support theorizing by scholars from the Global South and reject any notion that the Global South is simply an empirical landscape for mining and theorizing by those in the North. Indeed, essentializing of the Global North and Global South must be avoided, and the hybridity of much theoretical and conceptual thinking needs to be acknowledged and encouraged. We recognize, nonetheless, that there are always asymmetrical power relations between nations positioned differently geopolitically and between differently positioned researchers, particularly graduate students from the Global South and their advisors in Global North university settings.

While we offer a research-based account of Teach For Bangladesh and its emergence as an SE, we have situated that account in a bigger context of NGOs becoming SEs and the desire for that type of organization to restructure the public sector in Bangladesh, including schooling. We have, however, attempted more than this in striving to make methodological and theoretical contributions to both comparative education and comparative policy sociology studies. We hope the approaches adopted in this book have application in other path-dependent schooling systems and for research about them which acknowledges the ever-changing imbrications among the global-national-local. The increasing prominence of networks and relationships stretched globally is promising a future in which, indeed, as Latour (2005, p. 6) prophesizes, 'we are no longer sure about what "we" means; we seem to be bound by "ties" that don't look like regular social ties'.

Notes

1 Teach For Bangladesh: Rethinking Comparative Policy Research in Education

1 See Wendy Kopp's (Kopp, 2008, 2011; Kopp & Farr, 2012) work on Teach For All and Teach For America.
2 Building Resources Across Communities (BRAC) was founded in 1972 in Bangladesh. It is the largest and number one NGO in world.
3 Not an INGO but has NGO-like programmes in Bangladesh.
4 'Fellow teachers' is the term used in Bangladesh. We acknowledge that 'teacher fellows' is a more felicitous descriptor.
5 The first author taught TFB fellows in this master's programme for two years as a lecturer.
6 For further insights into the Teach For phenomenon in Norway and New Zealand, please see Nesje (2016) and Crawford-Garrett (2017, 2018), respectively.
7 We prefer the concept of teacher education to the more reductive teacher training.

2 Theorizing Policy Mobilities in Education

1 Put in a simple way, topology is the prioritization of direct relationships, connectivities and reach over physical locations and distances in constituting as well as understanding sociocultural processes of influence. The topological emphasizes relations over locations.
2 Foucault (1986, pp. 24–6) defines 'heterotopia' ('other places') as a temporal condition wherein an individual or a collective arrives at 'an absolute break with her/their traditional time'. Heterotopias are also understood as places of 'nowhere', 'privileged', 'sacred' or 'forbidden', since they do not correspond to the quotidian rhythm and norms of everyday society. These are places of 'deviation' where diversity and difference 'in relation to the required mean or norm' of a given society are placed, supported or punished. Vis-à-vis the current globalizing conditions, they can be viewed as a 'treacherous terrain' that points to 'various institutions and places

that interrupt the apparent continuity and normality of ordinary everyday space' (Dehaene & Cauter, 2008, pp. 3–4).

3 Think of Education For All as a globally intended practice and how it is always referred to in terms of the conference site (where the practice was placed) and time of the event, notably Jomtien, Thailand (1990).
4 Thinking of others' culture.
5 Placeless in the heterotopic sense, not in a literal sense.
6 See also Peck and Theodore (2015), Wright (2011) and Sassen (2003) in relation to education policy.
7 Leverage does not denote 'domination and authority' only. A form of power, it also includes manipulation practices of both public and private entities that involve 'the indirect reward-based inducements' and 'seduction' that attend 'the possibility of rejection and indifference' (Allen, 2011, p. 291).
8 See literature on 'boundary spanners' and 'network capital' (Ball et al., 2017; Ball & Junemann, 2012).
9 By *représentations collectives* Durkheim (1995, p. xviii) refers to 'shared mental constructs with the help of which, human beings collectively view themselves, each other, and the natural world'. A landscape of collective aspirations represented as such is a unit that is culturally governable.
10 Also known as 'impact investment' (see Allman & Nogales, 2015).
11 Venture philanthropists are intermediary entrepreneurs who want to be hands on, bringing innovative ideas to scale by investing their time and energy and thereby helping the richest get the best out of their philanthropic dollars (Bishop, 2007).
12 More than texts and utterances, discourses should be understood as 'ways of thinking and sense-making and as behaviours, relationships, interactions and arrangements of signs and material objects'; discourses are not just what are said, they are practices and can routinize practices (Thomson et al., 2013, p. 157; referring to Foucault, 1982).
13 The theoretical foundations of this approach have been discussed in the theory section of this chapter.

3 Changing Governance of Primary Education in Bangladesh

1 For more on the World Bank, please see Mundy and Menashy (2014).
2 Aligned to the Dakar Framework.
3 See discussion on the enhancement of donor coordination for EFA in the *Dakar Framework*.

4 See discussions on working groups, DLIs, JCMs and JARMs as examples of such mechanisms in practice.
5 For unidentified reasons, the Scandinavian donors involved left the Donor Consortium at the time of data collection.

4 Social-Enterprising the Public Sector in Bangladesh

1 Such as the NGOs and corporate entities.
2 In Bangladesh, prominent NGOs have started identifying themselves as social enterprises.
3 Similar to Appadurai's (1996) idea of 'image' as a verb.
4 Department for International Development.
5 Sir Fazle Hasan Abed KCMG (27 April 1936–20 December 2019) was the founder of BRAC, one of the world's largest non-governmental organizations. He was awarded a knighthood.
6 Muhammad Yunus (born 28 June 1940) is a Bangladeshi 'social entrepreneur', banker, economist and civil society leader. He was awarded the Nobel Peace Prize for founding the Grameen Bank and pioneering the concepts of microcredit and microfinance.
7 A US-based global organization, Ashoka: Innovators for the Public defines and pursues system-level change as 'impact resulting from the social entrepreneurs, ideas and networks' (Wells, 2010). With this aim, it selects and trains individuals, namely, Ashoka Fellows, with potential and innovative ideas for system-level changes. Such fellows are expected to network with successful entrepreneurs who support attempts to convert an innovative solution into a self-sustaining institution (Harley, 1985). While Ashoka's funders are Western charities and wealthy individuals (Ashoka, 2018), it has advisory relations with the World Bank.
8 Vertovec (2009, p. 4) argues that transnationality is the workings of networks.
9 Referring specifically to NGOs that are struggling to survive in the face of a decline in foreign funding and aid but trying to do good work by raising funds through additional businesses.
10 This is where new philanthropy comes in.
11 This was David Cameron's neoliberal policy framework as UK prime minister (see Lingard & Sellar, 2012).
12 Global cities.
13 Mostly the United States and the UK.

14 Such as the panel discussion or the research presentation followed by questions and answers.
15 That is, 150,000 SEs already active in Bangladesh.
16 The BCB is requested to write a draft policy.

5 Governing Teacher Education as Social Enterprise through Teach For Bangladesh

1 Please see topological analytics in Chapter 2, where we have theoretically demonstrated and argued that globalization basically references a spatial reorganization of governance at large, and it occurs as/through power effects (reach and imbrication), combining cultural flows and spatial formulations.
2 While the idea of social enterprises is one that has circulated globally, we would argue that knowledge of such legislative frames establishing these enterprises has also circulated globally, including special tax status of such enterprises.
3 This was increasingly becoming a key debate within the NGO sector of Bangladesh (see Chapter 4).
4 Porticus is a philanthrocapitalist organization that manages and develops the philanthropic programmes of charitable entities established by Brenninkmeijer family entrepreneurs.
5 Founder of Building Resources Across Communities, formerly Bangladesh Rural Advancement Committee (BRAC). BRAC's non-formal education model is widely used across the globe. Sir Abed was a believer in market/business driven social programming.
6 A Nobel laureate and founder of microcredit programmes and the Grameen Bank in Bangladesh.
7 Meaning elderly brother in the sense of close colleague or mentor, rather than as a relative. This new culture of collegiality was introduced from the 1980s onwards in the work of NGOs, particularly with the rise of BRAC.
8 BRAC is a Bangladesh-based NGO active in education both in Bangladesh and in several other least-developed countries.
9 Also see the conclusion of Chapter 4 for further elaboration on this.
10 We entertained the anthropological possibility that globalization is understandable fundamentally at the cultural level.
11 However, this manifests differently when the local/national itself is more powerful than the global representation within. Think of Teach For China here (see Lam, 2020).
12 As in brilliant, saviours, efficient and so on (see Adhikary et al., 2018; Adhikary & Lingard, 2017).

13 Annually ranked by Geneva-based NGO Advisor. Since 2016, BRAC has never missed the top ranking.
14 http://www.brac.net/enterprises#who_we_are.
15 http://www.brac.net/investment.
16 The founder of Teach For All and Teach For America (see Kopp, 2011).
17 See Chapter 3 to understand the context of dependency on external funding.

6 Learning from Researching Teach For Bangladesh as Social Enterprise

1 A broader perspective of time when the earth system reacts to human action in such ways that we no longer have a stable and indifferent framework in which to lodge humanity's desires for modernization (Latour, 2018, p. 18).
2 For example, the 1990s EFA and consecutive rounds of MDGs and SDGs have strong influence. See Chapter 3 for more details.
3 The International Finance Corporation (IFC), a member of World Bank Group, is known to be the largest Impact Invertor ever. It is funded by World Bank member countries. Such other examples are Norway's Norfund and the UK's CDC Group (see Allman & Nogales, 2015, p. 5).
4 Such as Acumen Fund, EnterpriseWorks/VITA and Relief International.
5 Such as Soros Economic Development Fund.
6 TFB Facebook page has 43,781 likes and 43,668 followers with a five-star rating as of 20 September 2018.

References

Adams, J. S. (2016). The spatial organization of society [Review of *The Spatial Organization of Society*, by R. L. Morrill]. *Economic Geography*, *47*(4), 555. https://doi.org/10.2307/142645

ADB. (2019, 9 October). *Poverty: Bangladesh* (Bangladesh) [Text]. Asian Development Bank. https://www.adb.org/countries/bangladesh/poverty

Adelman, C. (2009). Global philanthropy and remittances: Reinventing foreign aid. *Brown Journal of World Affairs*, *XV*(II), 23–33.

Adhikary, R. W. (2014). Relating development to quality of education: A study on the World Bank's neoliberal policy discourse in education. *KEDI Journal of Educational Policy*, *11*(1), 3–25.

Adhikary, R. W. (2019). *Globalization, governance and Teach for Bangladesh: Understanding social enterprises in education policy*. The University of Queensland.

Adhikary, R. W., Hardy, I., & Lingard, B. (2020). Social enterprise as a policy panacea: Panel discussions, data and the cultural formulation of policy in Bangladesh. *Globalisation, Societies and Education*, *18*(2), 194–207. https://doi.org/10.1080/14767724.2020.1711708

Adhikary, R. W., & Lingard, B. (2017). A critical policy analysis of 'Teach for Bangladesh': A travelling policy touches down. *Comparative Education*, *54*(2), 181–202. https://doi.org/10.1080/03050068.2017.1360567

Adhikary, R. W., & Lingard, B. (2019). Global-local imbrications in education policy: Methodological reflections on researching the sociology of Teach for Bangladesh. *London Review of Education*, *17*(3), 252–67. https://doi.org/10.18546/LRE.17.3.02

Adhikary, R. W., & Lingard, B. (2020). Teach for Bangladesh as a de facto social enterprise: What is it and where is it going? In M. A. M. Thomas, E. Rauschenberger & K. Crawford-Garrett (Eds.), *Examining Teach For All: International perspectives on a growing global network* (1st ed., pp. 117–37). Routledge. https://doi.org/10.4324/9780429331695

Adhikary, R. W., Lingard, B., & Hardy, I. (2018). A critical examination of Teach for Bangladesh's Facebook page: 'Social-mediatisation' of global education reforms in the 'post-truth' era. *Journal of Education Policy*, *33*(5), 632–61. https://doi.org/10.1080/02680939.2018.1445294

Adler, E., & Haas, P. M. (1992). Conclusion: Epistemic communities, world order, and the creation of a reflective research program. *International Organization, 46*(01), 367. https://doi.org/10.1017/S0020818300001533

Ahmann, C. (2015). Teach For All: Storytelling 'shared solutions' and scaling global reform. *Education Policy Analysis Archives, 23*(0), 45. https://doi.org/10.14507/epaa.v23.1784

Ahmann, C. (2016). '… And that's why I Teach For America': American education reform and the role of redemptive stories. *Text & Talk, 36*(2), 111–31. https://doi.org/10.1515/text-2016-0006

Ahmed, M. (2013). The post-2015 MDG and EFA agenda and the national discourse about goals and targets: A case study of Bangladesh. *Network for International Policies and Cooperation in Education and Training*.

Ahmed, M. (2016). *Non-formal primary education: A subsector policy and strategy study*. SHARE Technical Assistance Team.

Alamgir, M. (2020, 3 June). Bangladesh budget 2020–21 for coronavirus-battered education sector unchanged. *The Daily Star*. https://www.thedailystar.net/bangladesh-budget-2020-21-for-education-sector-unchanged-1912649

Alamgir, M., Hossain, Md. S., Sabina, K., Islam, Md. S., Hossain, Md. M., Akter, Y., Hasan, Md. M., Wahedi, M. S. K., Khan, Md. O. A., & Hossain, Md. I. (2014). *Annual primary school census – 2014*. Monitoring and Evaluation Division, Directorate of Primary Education of Bangladesh.

Alexiadou, N., & Bunt-Kokhuis, S. van de. (2013). Policy space and the governance of education: Transnational influences on institutions and identities in the Netherlands and the UK. *Comparative Education, 49*(3), 344–60. https://doi.org/10.1080/03050068.2013.803750

Allen, J. (1999). Spatial assemblages of power: From domination to empowerment. In D. B. Massey, J. Allen & P. Sarre (Eds.), *Human geography today* (pp. 194–218). Polity Press; Blackwell Publishers.

Allen, J. (2009). Three spaces of power: Territory, networks, plus a topological twist in the tale of domination and authority. *Journal of Power, 2*(2), 197–212. https://doi.org/10.1080/17540290903064267

Allen, J. (2011). Topological twists: Power's shifting geographies. *Dialogues in Human Geography, 1*(3), 283–98. https://doi.org/10.1177/2043820611421546

Allen, J., & Cochrane, A. (2010). Assemblages of state power: Topological shifts in the organization of government and politics. *Antipode, 42*(5), 1071–89. https://doi.org/10.1111/j.1467-8330.2010.00794.x

Allman, K. A., & Nogales, X. E. de. (2015). *Impact investment: A practical guide to investment process and social impact analysis + website*. Wiley.

Alvord, S. H., Brown, L. D., & Letts, C. W. (2004). Social entrepreneurship and societal transformation: An exploratory study. *Journal of Applied Behavioral Science, 40*(3), 260–82. https://doi.org/10.1177/0021886304266847

Amin, A. (2002). Spatialities of globalisation. *Environment and Planning A, 34*(3), 385–99. https://doi.org/10.1068/a3439

Anderson, A. (2013). Teach for America and symbolic violence: A Bourdieuian analysis of education's next quick-fix. *The Urban Review, 45*(5), 684–700. https://doi.org/10.1007/s11256-013-0241-x

Anderson, A. B. (2020). Expanding the research terrain: Teach For America and the problem with one-dimensional research. *Teaching and Teacher Education, 94*, 103080. https://doi.org/10.1016/j.tate.2020.103080

Anderson, B. R. O. (1983). *Imagined communities: Reflections on the origin and spread of nationalism*. Verso.

Anheier, H. K. (2007). Introduction. In H. K. Anheier, A. Simmons & D. Winder (Eds.), *Innovation in Strategic Philanthropy: Local and Global Perspectives* (pp. 3–6). Springer Science & Business Media.

Anheier, H. K., & Leat, D. (2006). *Creative philanthropy: Toward a new philanthropy for the twenty-first century*. Routledge.

Ansell, C., & Torfing, J. (2016). Introduction: Theories of governance. In C. Ansell & J. Torfing (Eds.), *Handbook on Theories of Governance* (pp. 1–20). Edward Elgar Publishing. https://doi.org/10.4337/9781782548508

Antecol, H., Eren, O., & Ozbeklik, S. (2013). The effect of Teach For America on the distribution of student achievement in primary school: Evidence from a randomized experiment. *Economics of Education Review, 37*, 113–25. https://doi.org/10.1016/j.econedurev.2013.08.004

Appadurai, A. (1991). Global ethnoscapes: Notes and queries for a transnational anthropology. In R. G. Fox (Ed.), *Recapturing anthropology: Working in the present* (pp. 48–65). School of American Research Press: Distributed by the University of Washington Press.

Appadurai, A. (1996). *Modernity at large: Cultural dimensions of globalization*. University of Minnesota Press.

Appadurai, A. (2006a). *Fear of small numbers: An essay on the geography of anger*. Duke University Press.

Appadurai, A. (2006b). The right to research. *Globalisation, Societies and Education, 4*(2), 167–77. https://doi.org/10.1080/14767720600750696

Appadurai, A. (2020). Globalization and the rush to history. *Global Perspectives, 1*(1), 11656. https://doi.org/10.1525/001c.11656

Appadurai, A. (Ed.). (2001). *Globalization*. Duke University Press. http://read.dukeupress.edu/lookup/doi/10.1215/9780822383215-001

Arranz, N., & de Arroyabe, J. C. Fdez. (2013). Network embeddedness and performance of joint R&D projects. In T. Ehrmann, J. Windsperger, G. Cliquet & G. Hendrikse (Eds.), *Network Governance* (pp. 33–50). Springer Berlin Heidelberg. https://doi.org/10.1007/978-3-7908-2867-2_3

Ashoka. (2018). *Ashoka at a glance*. https://www.ashoka.org/sites/ashoka/files/Ashoka_At_A_Glance.pdf

Ashoka Innovators for the Public. (2000). *Selecting leading social entrepreneurs*. Ashoka Innovators.

Ayres, A. (2014, 28 October). *Bangladesh: Capitalist haven*. Forbes. https://www.forbes.com/sites/alyssaayres/2014/10/28/bangladesh-capitalist-haven/

Bacchi, C. L. (2009). *Analysing policy: What's the problem represented to be?* Pearson.

Backes, B., Hansen, M., Xu, Z., & Brady, V. (2018). Examining spillover effects from Teach For America corps members in Miami-Dade county public schools. *Journal of Teacher Education, 70*(5), 453–71. https://doi.org/10.1177/0022487117752309

Baker, K., & Stoker, G. (2012). Metagovernance and nuclear power in Europe. *Journal of European Public Policy, 19*(7), 1026–51. https://doi.org/10.1080/13501763.2011.652900

Ball, S. J. (1998). Big policies/small world: An introduction to international perspectives in education policy. *Comparative Education, 34*(2), 119–30. https://doi.org/10.1080/03050069828225

Ball, S. J. (2006). What is policy? Texts, trajectories and toolboxes. In S. J. Ball (Ed.), *Education policy and social class: The selected works of Stephen J. Ball* (pp. 43–54). Routledge. http://public.eblib.com/choice/publicfullrecord.aspx?p=254339

Ball, S. J. (2012). *Global education inc.: New policy networks and the neo-liberal imaginary*. Routledge.

Ball, S. J. (2013). *The education debate* (2nd ed.). Policy Press.

Ball, S. J. (2015). What is policy? 21 years later: reflections on the possibilities of policy research. *Discourse: Studies in the Cultural Politics of Education, 36*(3), 306–13. https://doi.org/10.1080/01596306.2015.1015279

Ball, S. J., & Junemann, C. (2012). *Networks, new governance and education*. Policy Press. http://policypress.universitypressscholarship.com/view/10.1332/policypress/9781847429803.001.0001/upso-9781847429803

Ball, S. J., Junemann, C., & Santori, D. (2017). *Edu.net: Globalisation and education policy mobility*. Routledge.

Ball, S. J., & Thawer, S. (2018). Nodes, pipelines, and policy mobility: The assembling of an education shadow state in India. In K. J. Saltman & A. J. Means (Eds.), *The Wiley handbook of global educational reform* (pp. 71–86). Wiley. http://search.ebscohost.com/login.aspx?direct=true&scope=site&db=nlebk&db=nlabk&AN=1884074

BANBEIS. (2017). *BANBEIS-Educational Database*. http://data.banbeis.gov.bd/

BCB. (2016, 9 October). *Launch of social enterprise policy research baseline study | British Council*. British Council Bangladesh. https://www.britishcouncil.org.bd/en/events/launch-social-enterprise-policy-research-baseline-study

BCG. (2019a). *Reports | British Council*. Reports. https://www.britishcouncil.org/society/social-enterprise/reports

BCG. (2019b). *Social enterprise | British Council*. Social Enterprise. https://www.britishcouncil.hk/en/programmes/society/skills-social-entrepreneurs

Beech, J., & Rizvi, F. (2017). Revisiting Jullien in an era of globalisation. *Compare: A Journal of Comparative and International Education, 47*(3), 374–87. https://doi.org/10.1080/03057925.2016.1277130

Belcher, O., Martin, L., Secor, A., Simon, S., & Wilson, T. (2008). Everywhere and nowhere: The exception and the topological challenge to geography. *Antipode, 40*(4), 499–503. https://doi.org/10.1111/j.1467-8330.2008.00620.x

Berlant, L. G. (2011). *Cruel optimism.* Duke University Press.

BetterStories. (2018a). *About.* BetterStories Foundation. http://www.betterstoriesfoundation.org/about.html

BetterStories. (2018b). *Social enterprise: Market trends.* BetterStories Foundation. http://www.betterstoriesfoundation.org/social-enterprise-market-trends.html

Bhattacharya, D. (2002). *Financial sector reforms in Bangladesh: The next round* (CPD Occasional Paper Series No. 49; pp. 1–17). Centre for Policy Dialogue. https://ideas.repec.org/p/pdb/opaper/22.html

Bhattacharya, D., & Chowdhury, T. A. (2003). *Financial sector reforms in Bangladesh: The next round* (CPD Occasional Paper Series No. 22; pp. 1–17). Centre for Policy Dialogue. https://ideas.repec.org/p/pdb/opaper/22.html

Bigham, J., Karmali, F., & Rundle, J. (2016). *The evolving role of philanthropy in global problem solving* (pp. 1–38). Global Solution Networks.

Bishop, M. (2007, 1 March). What is philanthrocapitalism? *Alliance Magazine.* https://www.alliancemagazine.org/feature/what-is-philanthrocapitalism/

Bishop, M., & Green, M. (2008). *Philanthro-capitalism: How the rich can save the world* (1st US ed.). Bloomsbury Press.

Bishop, M., & Green, M. (2016). How the rich can save the world. In B. Breeze & M. P. Moody (Eds.), *The philanthropy reader* (pp. 441–47). Routledge, Taylor & Francis Group.

Blumenreich, M., & Gupta, A. (2015). The globalization of Teach For America: An analysis of the institutional discourses of Teach For America and Teach For India within local contexts. *Teaching and Teacher Education, 48,* 87–96. https://doi.org/10.1016/j.tate.2015.01.017

Börzel, T. A., & Panke, D. (2008). Network governance: Effective and legitimate? In E. Sørensen & J. Torfing (Eds.), *Theories of democratic network governance* (pp. 130–66). Palgrave Macmillan. http://ezproxy.st-andrews.ac.uk/login?url=http://www.palgraveconnect.com/doifinder/10.1057/9780230625006

Bourdieu, P. (1990). *In other words: Essays towards a reflexive sociology.* Stanford University Press.

Bourdieu, P. (1993). *The field of cultural production: Essays on art and literature* (R. Johnson, Trans.). Columbia University Press.

Bourdieu, P. (2003). *Firing back: Against the tyranny of the market.* New Press.

Bourdieu, P., Sayad, A., Christin, R., Champagne, P., Balazs, G., Wacquant, L., Bougois, P., Lenoir, R., Pialoux, M., Beaud, S., Garcia, S., Pinto, L., Broccolichi, S., Yuvrard, F., Sayad, A., Accardo, A., Soulie, C., Bourdieu, E., Podalydes, D., … Bonvin, F. (1999).

The weight of the world: Social suffering in contemporary society (P. P. Ferguson, Trans.). Stanford University Press.

Bourdieu, P., & Wacquant, L. J. D. (1992). *An invitation to reflexive sociology*. University of Chicago Press.

Bowe, R., Ball, S. J., & Gold, A. (1992). *Reforming education and changing schools: Case studies in policy sociology*. Routledge.

Brenner, N. (2004). *New state spaces: Urban governance and the rescaling of statehood*. Oxford University Press.

Brewer, T. J., & DeMarrais, K. B. (Eds.). (2015). *Teach For America counter-narratives: Alumni speak up and speak out*. Peter Lang.

Brewer, T. J., DeMarrais, K. B., & McFadden, K. L. (Eds.). (2020). *Teach For All counter-narratives: International perspectives on a global reform*. Peter Lang.

Broadfoot, P. (2000). Comparative education for the 21st century: Retrospect and prospect. *Comparative Education, 36*(3), 357–71. https://doi.org/10.1080/03050060050129036

Burawoy, M. (Ed.). (1991). *Ethnography unbound: Power and resistance in the modern metropolis*. University of California Press.

Burawoy, M. (2000). Introduction: Reaching for the global. In M. Burawoy (Ed.), *Global ethnography: Forces, connections, and imaginations in a postmodern world* (pp. 1–40). University of California Press.

Burawoy, M. (2009). *The extended case method: Four countries, four decades, four great transformations, and one theoretical tradition*. University of California Press.

Cagney, P., & Ross, B. (2013). *Global fundraising: How the world is changing the rules of philanthropy*. Wiley.

CAMPE. (2016). *Directory: NGOs with Education Programme, Bangladesh 2016*. Campaign for Popular Education. http://www.campebd.org/Files/25022014040047pmDirectory_of_NGOs_with_Education_Programme___Volume_II.pdf

CAMPE. (2020, 17 January). *Emergence of CAMPE*. https://www.campebd.org/page/Generic/0/3/1

Cann, C. N. (2015). What school movies and TFA teach us about who should teach urban youth: Dominant narratives as public pedagogy. *Urban Education, 50*(3), 288–315. https://doi.org/10.1177/0042085913507458

Carl, N. M. (2014). Reacting to the script: Teach For America teachers' experiences with scripted curricula. *Teacher Education Quarterly, 41*(2), 29–50.

Carney, S. (2009). Negotiating policy in an age of globalization: Exploring educational 'policyscapes' in Denmark, Nepal, and China. *Comparative Education Review, 53*(1), 63–88. https://doi.org/10.1086/593152

Carney, S. (2011). Imagining globalization: Educational policyscapes. In G. Steiner-Khamsi & F. Waldow (Eds.), *Policy borrowing and lending in education* (pp. 339–53). Routledge.

Carney, S. (2019). Writing global education policy research. In M. Parreira do Amaral, G. Steiner-Khamsi & C. Thompson (Eds.), *Researching the global education industry* (pp. 251–72). Springer International Publishing. https://doi.org/10.1007/978-3-030-04236-3_12

Carney, S., & Bista, M. B. (2009). Community schooling in Nepal: A genealogy of education reform since 1990. *Comparative Education Review, 53*(2), 189–211. https://doi.org/10.1086/597394

Carter, H., Amrein-Beardsley, A., & Hansen, C. C. (2017). So NOT amazing! Teach For America corps members' evaluation of the first semester of their teacher preparation program. *Teachers College Record, 113*(5), 861–94.

Castells, M. (2000). *The rise of the network society* (2nd ed.). Blackwell Publishers.

Castells, M. (2016). A sociology of power: My intellectual journey. *Annual Review of Sociology, 42*(1), 1–19. https://doi.org/10.1146/annurev-soc-081715-074158

Chowdhury, R., & Kabir, A. H. (2014). Language wars: English education policy and practice in Bangladesh. *Multilingual Education, 4*(1), 1–16. https://doi.org/10.1186/s13616-014-0021-2

Chowdhury, R., Sarkar, M., Mojumder, F., & Roshid, M. M. (2018). *Engaging in educational research: Revisiting policy and practice in Bangladesh.* http://search.ebscohost.com/login.aspx?direct=true&scope=site&db=nlebk&db=nlabk&AN=1905791

Clarke, J. (2019). Foreword. In N. Papanastasiou (Ed.), *The politics of scale in policy: Scalecraft and education governance* (1st ed., pp. v–xii). Policy Press. https://doi.org/10.2307/j.ctvh9w1zj

Clement, D. (2018). Legitimizing the dilettante: Teach For America and the allure of Ed Cred. *Berkeley Review of Education, 7*(2), 29–75. https://doi.org/10.5070/B8BRE7232956

Cochran-Smith, M., & Zeichner, K. M. (Eds.). (2009). *Studying teacher education: The report of the AERA Panel on Research and Teacher Education.* Lawrence Erlbaum Associates.

Coffman, L. C., Conlon, J. J., Featherstone, C. R., & Kessler, J. B. (2019). Liquidity affects job choice: Evidence from Teach For America. *The Quarterly Journal of Economics, 134*(4), 2203–36. https://doi.org/10.1093/qje/qjz018

Conn, K. M., Lovison, V. S., & Mo, C. H. (2020). How Teach For America affects beliefs about education. *Education Next, Cambridge, 20*(1). https://search-proquest-com.ezproxy.library.uq.edu.au/docview/2319154779?accountid=14723

Connell, R. (2007). *Southern theory: The global dynamics of knowledge in social science* (Reprint). Polity Press.

Cook, B. J., Hite, S. J., & Epstein, E. H. (2004). Discerning trends, contours, and boundaries in comparative education: A survey of comparativists and their literature. *Comparative Education Review, 48*(2), 123–49. https://doi.org/10.1086/382619

Cook, I. R., & Ward, K. (2012). Conferences, informational infrastructures and mobile policies: The process of getting Sweden 'BID ready'. *European Urban and Regional Studies, 19*(2), 137–52. https://doi.org/10.1177/0969776411420029

Covert, L. (2014). *Learning to teach in Teach For America: A case study* [Doctoral thesis]. University of Minnesota.

Cowen, R. (2014). Comparative education: Stones, silences, and siren songs. *Comparative Education, 50*(1), 3–14. https://doi.org/10.1080/03050068.2013.871834

Crawford-Garrett, K. (2013). *Teach For America and the struggle for urban school reform: Searching for agency in an era of standardization.* Peter Lang.

Crawford-Garrett, K. (2017). 'The problem is bigger than us': Grappling with educational inequity in TeachFirst New Zealand. *Teaching and Teacher Education, 68*, 91–8. https://doi.org/10.1016/j.tate.2017.08.010

Crawford-Garrett, K. (2018). Lacking resilience or mounting resistance? Interpreting the actions of indigenous and immigrant youth within TeachFirst New Zealand. *American Educational Research Journal, 55*(5), 1051–75. https://doi.org/10.3102/0002831218769563

Curran, F. C. (2017). Teach For America placement and teacher vacancies: Evidence from the Mississippi Delta. *Teachers College Record, 119*, 1–24.

Darling-Hammond, L., Holtzman, D. J., Gatlin, S. J., & Vasquez Heilig, J. (2005). Does teacher preparation matter? Evidence about teacher certification, Teach For America, and teacher effectiveness. *Education Policy Analysis Archives, 13*(0), 42. https://doi.org/10.14507/epaa.v13n42.2005

Dees, J. G. (1998). Enterprising nonprofits: What do you do when traditional sources of funding fall short? *Harvard Business Review, January/February*, 55–67.

Dehaene, M., & Cauter, L. de. (2008). Heterotopia in a postcivil society. In M. Dehaene & L. de Cauter (Eds.), *Heterotopia and the city: Public space in a postcivil society* (pp. 1–10). Routledge.

Dhaka Tribune. (2016, 10 October). *Social enterprises and how they work in Bangladesh.* https://www.dhakatribune.com/feature/2016/10/10/social-enterprises-work-bangladesh

DiCamillo, L. (2018). Corps members' perspectives of teaching in a new Teach For America region. *Journal of Urban Learning, Teaching, and Research, 14*, 18–26.

Dobbie, W., & Fryer, Jr., R. G. (2015). The impact of voluntary youth service on future outcomes: Evidence from Teach For America. *The B.E. Journal of Economic Analysis & Policy, 15*(3), 1031–65. https://doi.org/10.1515/bejeap-2014-0187

Donaldson, M. (2012). The promise of older novices: Teach For America teachers' age of entry and subsequent retention in teaching and schools. *Teachers College Record, 114*(5), 1–37.

Donaldson, M., & Johnson, S. M. (2010). The price of misassignment: The role of teaching assignments in Teach For America teachers' exit from low-income schools and the teaching profession. *Educational Evaluation and Policy Analysis, 32*(2), 299–323. https://doi.org/10.3102/0162373710367680

Donaldson, M., & Johnson, S. M. (2011). Teach For America teachers: How long do they teach? Why do they leave? *Phi Delta Kappan, 93*(2), 47–51. https://doi.org/10.1177/003172171109300211

Durkheim, E. (1995). *The elementary forms of religious life* (K. E. Fields, Trans.). Free Press.

Dwinal, M. (2012). *Teach For America and rural Southern teacher labour supply: An exploratory case study of Teach For America as a supplement to teacher labour policies in the Mississippi-Arkansas Delta from 2008 to 2010*. University of Oxford Department of Education.

Edwards, M. (2008). 'Philanthrocapitalism' and its limits. *Ethics and Civil Society – IJNL, 10*(2), 22–9.

Eikenberry, A. M., & Kluver, J. D. (2004). The marketization of the nonprofit sector: Civil society at risk? *Public Administration Review, 64*(2), 132–40. https://doi.org/10.1111/j.1540-6210.2004.00355.x

Einstein, A. (1929, 26 October). What life means to Einstein: An interview by George Sylvester Viereck, Start Page 17, Quote Page 117, Column 1 [Interview]. *The Saturday Evening Post*. https://quoteinvestigator.com/2013/01/01/einstein-imagination/

Einstein, A. (2011). *The ultimate quotable Einstein* (A. Calaprice, Ed.). Princeton University Press.

Ellis, V., Maguire, M., Trippestad, T. A., Liu, Y., Yang, X., & Zeichner, K. (2016). Teaching other people's children, elsewhere, for a while: The rhetoric of a travelling educational reform. *Journal of Education Policy, 13*(1), 1–21. https://doi.org/10.1080/02680939.2015.1066871

Elster, J. (2017). The temporal dimension of reflexivity: Linking reflexive orientations to the stock of knowledge. *Distinktion: Journal of Social Theory, 18*(3), 274–93. https://doi.org/10.1080/1600910X.2017.1397527

Emerson, J., & Twersky, F. (Eds.). (1996). *New social entrepreneurs: The success, challenge and lessons of non-profit enterprise creation*. Roberts Foundation, Homeless Economic Development Fund.

Epstein, I. (1995). Comparative education in North America: The search for other through the escape from self? *Compare: A Journal of Comparative and International Education, 25*(1), 5–16. https://doi.org/10.1080/0305792950250102

Escobar, A. (1995). *Encountering development: The making and unmaking of the Third World*. Princeton University Press.

Evans, K., & Robinson-Pant, A. (2007). Windows and mirrors in comparative education. *Compare: A Journal of Comparative and International Education, 37*(1), 1–3. https://doi.org/10.1080/03057920601061620

Fairclough, N. (2000). *New Labour, new language?* Routledge. http://public.eblib.com/choice/publicfullrecord.aspx?p=165902

Fenwick, T., Mangez, E., & Ozga, J. (Eds.). (2014). *Governing knowledge: Comparison, knowledge-based technologies and expertise in the regulation of education* (1. publ). Routledge.

Ferguson, J. (2006). *Global shadows: Africa in the neoliberal world order*. Duke University Press.

Foucault, M. (1975). *Society must be defended: Lectures at the Collège de France, 1975–76* (M. Bertani, A. Fontana, F. Ewald & D. Macey, Trans.; 1st Picador paperback ed.). Picador.

Foucault, M. (1978). *The history of sexuality* (1st Vintage Books ed.). Vintage Books.

Foucault, M. (1982). *The archaeology of knowledge*. Pantheon Books.

Foucault, M. (1986). Of other spaces. *Diacritics*; Ithaca, N.Y., *16*(1), 1–5.

Foucault, M. (1991a). *Discipline and punish: The birth of the prison* (Reprint). Penguin Books.

Foucault, M. (1991b). Governmentality. In G. Burchell, C. Gordon & P. Miller (Eds.), *The Foucault effect: Studies in governmentality: With two lectures by and an interview with Michel Foucault* (pp. 87–104). University of Chicago Press.

Foucault, M., & Senellart, M. (2008). *The birth of biopolitics: Lectures at the Collège de France, 1978–79*. Palgrave Macmillan.

Freireich, J., & Fulton, K. (2009). *Investing for social and environmental impact: A design for catalysing an emerging industry* (No. 33; pp. 1–89). Monitor Institute.

Friedrich, D. (2014). Global microlending in education reform: Enseñá por Argentina and the neoliberalization of the grassroots. *Comparative Education Review*, *58*(2), 296–321. https://doi.org/10.1086/675412

Friedrich, D. (2016). Teach For All, public–private partnerships, and the erosion of the public in education. In A. Verger, C. A. Lubienski & G. Steiner-Khamsi (Eds.), *The global education industry* (pp. 175–91). Routledge, Taylor & Francis Group.

Friedrich, D., Walter, M., & Colmenares, E. (2015). Making all children count: Teach For All and the universalizing appeal of data. *Education Policy Analysis Archives*, *23*(0), 48. https://doi.org/10.14507/epaa.v23.1797

Gabriel, R. (2017). Rubrics and reflection: A discursive analysis of observation debrief conversations between novice Teach For America teachers and mentors. *Action in Teacher Education*, *39*(1), 85–102. https://doi.org/10.1080/01626620.2016.1245636

Gates, B. (2008). A new approach to capitalism: Remarks delivered at the World Economic Forum. In M. E. Kinsley (Ed.), *Creative capitalism: A conversation with Bill Gates, Warren Buffett, and other economic leaders* (pp. 1–16). Simon & Schuster.

Gaventa, J. (2003). *Power after Lukes: A review of the literature*. Institute of Development Studies.

Glazerman, S., Mayer, D., & Decker, P. (2006). Alternative routes to teaching: The impacts of Teach For America on student achievement and other outcomes. *Journal of Policy Analysis and Management*, *25*(1), 75–96.

Gorur, R., Sellar, S., & Steiner-Khamsi, G. (Eds.). (2019). *World Yearbook of Education 2019: Comparative methodology in the era of big data and global networks* (1st ed.). Routledge. https://doi.org/10.4324/9781315147338

Gottfried, M. A., & Straubhaar, R. (2015). The perceived role of the Teach For America program on teachers' long-term career aspirations. *Educational Studies, 41*(5), 481–98. https://doi.org/10.1080/03055698.2015.1044248

Gregory, D. (2004). *The colonial present: Afghanistan, Palestine, and Iraq*. Blackwell Publishers.

Grek, S. (2009). Governing by numbers: The PISA 'effect' in Europe. *Journal of Education Policy, 24*(1), 23–37. https://doi.org/10.1080/02680930802412669

Gulson, K. N., Lewis, S., Lingard, B., Lubienski, C., Takayama, K., & Webb, P. T. (2017). Policy mobilities and methodology: A proposition for inventive methods in education policy studies. *Critical Studies in Education, 58*(2), 224–41. https://doi.org/10.1080/17508487.2017.1288150

Gupta, A., & Ferguson, J. (Eds.). (2001). *Culture, power, place: Explorations in critical anthropology*. Duke University Press.

Gustavsson, S. (1991). *Primary education in Bangladesh: Review, analysis and recommendation*. Swedish International Development Authority.

Hacking, I. (1990). *The taming of chance*. Cambridge University Press.

Hajer, M. A., & Wagenaar, H. (2003). Introduction. In M. A. Hajer & H. Wagenaar (Eds.), *Deliberative policy analysis: Understanding governance in the network society* (pp. 1–32). Cambridge University Press.

Hansen, M., Backes, B., & Brady, V. (2016). Teacher attrition and mobility during the Teach For America clustering strategy in Miami-Dade County public schools. *Educational Evaluation and Policy Analysis, 38*(3), 495–516. https://doi.org/10.3102/0162373716638441

Hardy, I. (2015). 'I'm just a numbers person': The complexity, nature and effects of the quantification of education. *International Studies in Sociology of Education, 25*(1), 20–37. https://doi.org/10.1080/09620214.2014.972971

Hardy, I. (2021). *School reform in an era of standardization: Authentic accountabilities*. Routledge, Taylor & Francis Group.

Hardy, I., & Melville, W. (2018). The activation of epistemological resources in epistemic communities: District educators' professional learning as policy enactment. *Teaching and Teacher Education, 71*, 159–67. https://doi.org/10.1016/j.tate.2017.12.019

Harley, R. (1985, 15 March). Entrepreneurs show India that philanthropy pays. *Christian Science Monitor*. https://www.csmonitor.com/1985/0315/dgan.html

Harvard Business School. (n.d.). *Sir Fazle Hasan Abed – creating emerging markets – business history – Harvard Business School*. http://www.hbs.edu/businesshistory/emerging-markets/pages/profile-detail.aspx?profile=fhabed

Haveri, A., Nyholm, I., Roiseland, A., & Vabo, I. (2009). Governing collaboration: Practices of meta-governance in Finnish and Norwegian local governments. *Local Government Studies*, *35*(5), 539–56. https://doi.org/10.1080/03003930903227360

Heath, S., Fuller, A., & Johnston, B. (2017). How personal networks govern educational decisions. In B. Hollstein, W. Matiaske, & K.-U. Schnapp (Eds.), *Networked governance* (pp. 107–19). Springer International Publishing. https://doi.org/10.1007/978-3-319-50386-8_7

Heineke, A. J., Mazza, B. S., & Tichnor-Wagner, A. (2014). After the two-year commitment: A quantitative and qualitative inquiry of Teach For America teacher retention and attrition. *Urban Education*, *49*(7), 750–82. https://doi.org/10.1177/0042085913488603

Held, D. (1995). *Democracy and the global order: From the modern state to cosmopolitan governance*. Stanford University Press.

Held, D., McGrew, A., Goldblatt, D., & Perraton, J. (1999). Introduction. In *Global transformations: Politics, economics and culture* (pp. 1–31). Stanford University Press.

Hemerijck, A. (Ed.). (2017). *The uses of social investment* (1st ed.). Oxford University Press.

Hennessy, J., & Krishman, C. (2016). *Teach For India: Marketing an idea*. SAGE Publications Ltd. https://doi.org/10.4135/9781473972292

Hepp, A., & Hasebrink, U. (2018). Researching transforming communications in times of deep mediatization: A figurational perspective. In A. Hepp, A. Breiter, & U. Hasebrink (Eds.), *Communicative figurations: Transforming communications in times of deep mediatization* (pp. 15–48). Palgrave Macmillan.

Hepp, A., & Tribe, K. (2013). *Cultures of mediatization*. Polity.

Hoff, D. (2008). From Teach For America to Obama's camp. *Education Week*, *27*(45), 18–19.

Hopkins, M. (2008). Training the next teachers for America: A proposal for reconceptualizing Teach For America. *Phi Delta Kappan*, *89*(10), 721–5. https://doi.org/10.1177/003172170808901006

Howard, P. N. (2002). Network ethnography and the hypermedia organization: New media, new organizations, new methods. *New Media & Society*, *4*(4), 550–74. https://doi.org/10.1177/146144402321466813

Hursh, D. (2016). *The end of public schools: The corporate reform agenda to privatize education*. Routledge, Taylor & Francis Group.

Hursh, D. (2017). The end of public schools? The corporate reform agenda to privatize education. *Policy Futures in Education*, *15*(3), 389–99. https://doi.org/10.1177/1478210317715799

Hurst, P. (1987). Comparative education and its problems. *Compare: A Journal of Comparative and International Education*, *17*(1), 7–16. https://doi.org/10.1080/0305792870170102

Irizarry, J., & Donaldson, M. (2012). Teach For América: The Latinization of US schools and the critical shortage of Latina/o teachers. *American Educational Research Journal*, *49*(1), 155–94. https://doi.org/10.3102/0002831211434764

Islam, S. N. (2016). *Governance for development: Political and administrative reforms in Bangladesh*. Palgrave Macmillan.

Jacobson, D. D. (2016). How and why network governance evolves: Evidence from a public safety network. *Electronic Markets*, *26*(1), 43–54. https://doi.org/10.1007/s12525-015-0203-0

Jacques, K. (2000). *Bangladesh, India and Pakistan: International relations and regional tensions in South Asia*. Palgrave Macmillan.

Jessop, B. (1998). The rise of governance and the risks of failure: The case of economic development. *International Social Science Journal*, *50*(155), 29–45. https://doi.org/10.1111/1468-2451.00107

Jessop, B. (2000). The crisis of the national spatio-temporal fix and the tendential ecological dominance of globalizing capitalism. *International Journal of Urban and Regional Research*, *24*(2), 323–60. https://doi.org/10.1111/1468-2427.00251

Junemann, C., & Olmedo, A. (2019). *In sheep's clothing: Philanthropy and the privatisation of the 'democratic' state*. Education International. https://www.ei-ie.org/en/woe_homepage/woe_detail/16206/%C2%AB-in-sheep%E2%80%99s-clothing-philanthropy-and-the-privatisation-of-the-%E2%80%98democratic%E2%80%99-state-%C2%BB

Kabir, A. H. (2010). Neoliberal policy in the higher education sector in Bangladesh: Autonomy of public universities and the role of the state. *Policy Futures in Education*, *8*(6), 619–31. https://doi.org/10.2304/pfie.2010.8.6.619

Kabir, A. H. (2013). Neoliberalism, policy reforms and higher education in Bangladesh. *Policy Futures in Education*, *11*(2), 154–66. https://doi.org/10.2304/pfie.2013.11.2.154

Kabir, A. H., & Chowdhury, R. (2021). *The privatisation of higher education in postcolonial Bangladesh: The politics of intervention and control* (1st ed.). Routledge Taylor & Francis Group [distributor].

Keen, C. H. (2010). New longitudinal study of Teach For America alumni's civic engagement: What's enough of what kind of engagement? *Journal of College and Character*, *11*(2), 15. https://doi.org/10.2202/1940-1639.1269

Kehl, K., & Then, V. (2012). *Social investment: A sociological outline*. International Conference on 'Democratization, Marketization, and the Third Sector', Siena, Italy. https://www.researchgate.net/publication/285054959_Social_Investment_A_Sociological_Outline

Kelly, A. (2008, 20 February). Critics claim Bangladesh NGO Brac acts as a parallel state. *The Guardian*. https://www.theguardian.com/society/2008/feb/20/internationalaidanddevelopment.bangladesh

Kenis, P., Provan, K., & Kruyen, P. M. (2009). Network-level task and the design of whole networks: Is there a relationship? In A. Bøllingtoft, D. D. Håkonsson, J. F. Nielsen, C. C. Snow & J. Ulhøi (Eds.), *New approaches to organization design* (Vol. 8, pp. 23–40). Springer US. https://doi.org/10.1007/978-1-4419-0627-4_2

Keyes, R. (2004). *The post-truth era: Dishonesty and deception in contemporary life* (1st ed.). St. Martin's Press.

Kickert, W. J. M., Klijn, E.-H., & Koppenjan, J. F. M. (1997). *Managing complex networks: Strategies for the public sector*. SAGE. http://knowledge.sagepub.com/view/managing-complex-networks/SAGE.xml

Kim, T. (2014). The intellect, mobility and epistemic positioning in doing comparisons and comparative education. *Comparative Education*, 50(1), 58–72. https://doi.org/10.1080/03050068.2013.874237

Kim, T. (2020). Diasporic comparative education: An initial tribute to anxiety and hope. *Comparative Education*, 56(1), 111–26. https://doi.org/10.1080/03050068.2020.1714328

Klapka, P., Frantal, B., Halas, M., & Kunc, J. (2010). Spatial organisation: Development, structure and approximation of geographical systems. *Moravian Geographical Reports*, 18(3), 53–66.

Klijn, E.-H., & Edelenbos, J. (2007). Meta-governance as network management. In E. Sørensen & J. Torfing (Eds.), *Theories of Democratic Network Governance* (pp. 199–214). Palgrave Macmillan UK. https://doi.org/10.1057/9780230625006_12

Koo, M.-H. (2013, 30 September). *Interview with Bill Drayton, pioneer of social entrepreneurship*. Forbes. https://www.forbes.com/sites/meehyoekoo/2013/09/30/interview-with-bill-drayton-pioneer-of-social-entrepreneurship/

Kopp, W. (2008). Building the movement to end educational inequity. *Phi Delta Kappan*, 89(10), 734–6. https://doi.org/10.1177/003172170808901009

Kopp, W. (2011). *One day, all children: The unlikely triumph of Teach For America and what I learned along the way*. PublicAffairs.

Kopp, W., & Farr, S. (2012). *A chance to make history: What works and what doesn't in providing an excellent education for all*. PublicAffairs.

Koppenjan, J., & Klijn, E.-H. (2004). *Managing uncertainties in networks: Public private controversies* (1st ed.). Routledge. https://doi.org/10.4324/9780203643457

Koppenjan, J. F. M., Karré, P. M., & Termeer, K. (2019). *Smart hybridity: Potentials and challenges of new governance arrangements*. Eleven International Publishing.

Kretchmar, K. (2014). The revolution will be privatized: Teach For America and charter schools. *Urban Review*, 46(4), 632–53. https://doi.org/10.1007/s11256-014-0271-z

Kretchmar, K., Sondel, B., & Ferrare, J. J. (2018). The power of the network: Teach For America's impact on the deregulation of teacher education. *Educational Policy*, 32(3), 423–53. https://doi.org/10.1177/0895904816637687

Labaree, D. (2010). Teach For America and Teacher Ed: Heads they win, tails we lose. *Journal of Teacher Education*, 61(1–2), 48–55. https://doi.org/10.1177/0022487109347317

Lam, S. (2020). *From 'Teach For America' to 'Teach For China': Global teacher education reform and equity in education*. Routledge.

Lanier, H. K. (2012). *Teaching in the Terrordome: Two years in West Baltimore with Teach For America*. University of Missouri Press.

Larsen, M. A., & Beech, J. (2014). Spatial theorizing in comparative and international education research. *Comparative Education Review*, *58*(2), 191–214. https://doi.org/10.1086/675499

Latour, B. (2005). *Reassembling the social: An introduction to actor-network-theory.* Oxford University Press.

Latour, B. (2018). *Down to earth: Politics in the new climatic regime* (English ed.). Polity Press.

Leadbeater, C. (1997). Who are social entrepreneurs? The qualities, skills and values it takes to be a social entrepreneur. In *The rise of the social entrepreneur* (pp. 53–9). Demos.

Lefebvre, E. E., & Thomas, M. A. M. (2017). 'Shit shows' or 'like-minded schools': Charter schools and the neoliberal logic of Teach For. *Journal of Education Policy*, *32*(3), 357–71. https://doi.org/10.1080/02680939.2017.1280184

Lenhart, V. (2018). Hechtius (1795–1798) – the beginnings of historical-philosophical-idiographic research in comparative education. *Comparative Education*, *54*(1), 26–34. https://doi.org/10.1080/03050068.2017.1396094

Lewis, D. (2011). *Bangladesh: Politics, economics, and civil society.* Cambridge University Press.

Lewis, S., & Hardy, I. (2017). Tracking the topological: The effects of standardised data upon teachers' practice. *British Journal of Educational Studies*, *65*(2), 219–38. https://doi.org/10.1080/00071005.2016.1254157

Lewis, S., Sellar, S., & Lingard, B. (2016). PISA for schools: Topological rationality and new spaces of the OECD's global educational governance. *Comparative Education Review*, *60*(1), 27–57. https://doi.org/10.1086/684458

Lingard, B. (2006). Globalisation, the research imagination and deparochialising the study of education. *Globalisation, Societies and Education*, *4*(2), 287–302. https://doi.org/10.1080/14767720600752734

Lingard, B. (2009). Researching education policy in a globalized world: Theoretical and methodological considerations. *Yearbook of the National Society for the Study of Education*, *108*(2), 226–46. https://doi.org/10.1111/j.1744-7984.2009.01170.x

Lingard, B. (2011). Policy as numbers: Accounting for educational research. *The Australian Educational Researcher*, *38*(4), 355–82. https://doi.org/10.1007/s13384-011-0041-9

Lingard, B. (2014a). It is and it isn't: Vernacular globalization, educational policy, and restructuring. In *Politics, policies and pedagogies in education: The selected works of Bob Lingard* (pp. 86–104). Routledge.

Lingard, B. (2014b). Policy as numbers: Ac/counting for educational research. In *Politics, policies and pedagogies in education: The selected works of Bob Lingard* (pp. 26–50). Routledge.

Lingard, B. (2015). Thinking about theory in educational research: Fieldwork in philosophy. *Educational Philosophy and Theory*, *47*(2), 173–91. https://doi.org/10.1080/00131857.2013.793928

Lingard, B. (2021). Globalisation and education: Theorising and researching changing imbrications in education policy. In B. Lingard (Ed.), *Globalization and education* (pp. 1–27). Routledge, Taylor & Francis Group.

Lingard, B., Martino, W., Rezai-Rashti, G., & Sellar, S. (2016). *Globalizing educational accountabilities*. Routledge.

Lingard, B., & Rawolle, S. (2004). Mediatizing educational policy: The journalistic field, science policy, and cross-field effects. *Journal of Education Policy, 19*(3), 361–80. https://doi.org/10.1080/0268093042000207665

Lingard, B., & Rawolle, S. (2011). New scalar politics: Implications for education policy. *Comparative Education, 47*(4), 489–502. https://doi.org/10.1080/03050068.2011.555941

Lingard, B., & Sellar, S. (2012). A policy sociology reflection on school reform in England: From the 'third way' to the 'big society'. *Journal of Educational Administration and History, 44*(1), 43–63. https://doi.org/10.1080/00220620.2011.634498

Little, A. W. (2010). International and comparative education: What's in a name? *Compare: A Journal of Comparative and International Education, 40*(6), 845–52. https://doi.org/10.1080/03057925.2010.523264

Loughran, K. (2016). Imbricated spaces: The high line, urban parks, and the cultural meaning of city and nature. *Sociological Theory, 34*(4), 311–34. https://doi.org/10.1177/0735275116679192

Low, S. M. (2017). *Spatializing culture: The ethnography of space and place*. Routledge.

Ludwig, A. (2012, 12 March). *Ashoka Chairman Bill Drayton on the power of social entrepreneurship*. Forbes. https://www.forbes.com/sites/techonomy/2012/03/12/ashoka-chairman-bill-drayton-on-the-power-of-social-entrepreneurship/

Luhmann, N. (1990). *Essays on self-reference*. Columbia University Press.

Lury, C., Parisi, L., & Terranova, T. (2012). Introduction: The becoming topological of culture. *Theory, Culture & Society, 29*(4–5), 3–35. https://doi.org/10.1177/0263276412454552

Machranga Television. (2013, 25 July). Interview with Teach For Bangladesh CEO (Part 1 of 2) [YouTube video]. *Ranga Shokal*. https://www.youtube.com/watch?v=jzobx3FVQTE

Maier, A. (2012). Doing good and doing well: Credentialism and Teach For America. *Journal of Teacher Education, 63*(1), 10–22. https://doi.org/10.1177/0022487111422071

Mair, J. (2010). Social entrepreneurship: Taking stock and looking ahead. In A. Fayolle & H. Matlay (Eds.), *Handbook of research on social entrepreneurship* (pp. 15–28). Edward Elgar.

Mannan, M. (2015). *BRAC, global policy language, and women in Bangladesh: Transformation and manipulation*. State University of New York Press.

Manning, E. (2009). *Relationscapes: Movement, art, philosophy*. MIT Press.

Manzon, M. (2018). Comparative education histories: A postscript. *Comparative Education*, *54*(1), 94–107. https://doi.org/10.1080/03050068.2018.1420511

Massey, D. B. (1994a). A global sense of place. In *Space, place, and gender* (pp. 147–55). University of Minnesota Press.

Massey, D. B. (1994b). *Space, place, and gender*. University of Minnesota Press.

Massey, D. B. (2006). *For space*. SAGE.

Massumi, B. (2002). *Parables for the virtual: Movement, affect, sensation*. Duke University Press.

Matsui, S. (2015). *Learning from counternarratives in Teach For America: Moving from idealism towards hope*. Peter Lang.

May, M. A. (2013, 26 May). Want to change the world? Apply to be one of Teach For Bangladesh's first fellows. *BRAC Blog*. http://blog.brac.net/2013/05/want-to-change-the-world-apply-to-be-one-of-teach-for-bangladeshs-first-fellows/

McAdam, D., Tarrow, S. G., & Tilly, C. (2001). *Dynamics of contention*. Cambridge University Press.

McKenzie, M. (2017). Affect theory and policy mobility: Challenges and possibilities for critical policy research. *Critical Studies in Education*, *58*(2), 187–204. https://doi.org/10.1080/17508487.2017.1308875

McMahon, S., & Harwood, V. (2016). Foucauldian archaeological analyses. In George Ritzer (Ed.), *The Blackwell Encyclopedia of Sociology* (pp. 1–4). American Cancer Society. https://doi.org/10.1002/9781405165518.wbeosf062.pub2

McNeill, D., & Sandberg, K. I. (2014). Trust in global health governance: The GAVI experience. *Global Governance*, *20*(2), 325–43. JSTOR.

McNess, E., Arthur, L., & Crossley, M. (2015). 'Ethnographic dazzle' and the construction of the 'Other': Revisiting dimensions of insider and outsider research for international and comparative education. *Compare: A Journal of Comparative and International Education*, *45*(2), 295–316. https://doi.org/10.1080/03057925.2013.854616

McNew-Birren, J., Hildebrand, T., & Belknap, G. (2018). Strange bedfellows in science teacher preparation: Conflicting perspectives on social justice presented in a Teach For America-university partnership. *Cultural Studies of Science Education*, *13*(2), 437–62. https://doi.org/10.1007/s11422-016-9791-z

Milward, H. B., Provan, K., Fish, A., Isett, K. R., & Huang, K. (2010). Governance and collaboration: An evolutionary study of two mental health networks. *Journal of Public Administration Research and Theory*, *20*(Supplement 1), i125–i141. https://doi.org/10.1093/jopart/mup038

Molin, M. D., & Masella, C. (2016). From fragmentation to comprehensiveness in network governance. *Public Organization Review*, *16*(4), 493–508. https://doi.org/10.1007/s11115-015-0320-4

MoPME. (2015). *Third Primary Education Development Programme (PEDP-3) – Revised*. Program Division, Directorate of Primary Education, Ministry of Primary and Mass Education. http://dpe.portal.gov.bd/sites/default/files/files/dpe.portal.gov.

bd/page/093c72ab_a76a_4b67_bb19_df382677bebe/PEDP-3%20Brief%20(Revised).pdf

Morrill, R. L. (1974). *The spatial organization of society* (2nd ed.). Duxbury Press.

Morris, P. (2015). Comparative education, PISA, politics and educational reform: A cautionary note. *Compare: A Journal of Comparative and International Education, 45*(3), 470–4. https://doi.org/10.1080/03057925.2015.1027510

Morvaridi, B. (2015). *New philanthropy and social justice: Debating the conceptual and policy discourse*. Policy Press.

Mozena, D. (2014, 29 September). *US ambassador Dan Mozena on Teach For Bangladesh* [Organizational video posting]. YouTube. https://www.youtube.com/watch?v=WDnK641nodU

Mueller, M. (2010). *Networks and states: The global politics of Internet governance*. MIT Press.

Mundy, K., & Menashy, F. (2014). The World Bank and private provision of schooling: A look through the lens of sociological theories of organizational hypocrisy. *Comparative Education Review, 58*(3), 401–27. https://doi.org/10.1086/676329

Muñoz, S. M., Vasquez Heilig, J., & Del Real, M. (2019). Property functions of whiteness: Counter-narrative analysis of Teach For America and their partnership with black and Latinx fraternities and sororities: Property functions of whiteness: Counter-narrative analysis. *New Directions for Student Services, 2019*(165), 61–71. https://doi.org/10.1002/ss.20294

Nesje, K. (2016). Teach First Norway – who joins and what are their initial motivations for teaching? *Acta Didactica Norge, 10*(2), 150–78. https://doi.org/10.5617/adno.2512

Ness, M. (2013). *Lessons to learn voices from the front lines of Teach For America*. Routledge.

NGOAB. (2017). *List of all NGOs*. NGO Affairs Bureau, The Prime Minister's Office of Bangladesh. http://ngoab.portal.gov.bd/sites/default/files/files/ngoab.portal.gov.bd/page/a86a0782_47b2_4756_b226_58e2fd6a97b4/List%20of%20Total%20NGOs%20(1).pdf

NGOAB Document. (2014). *July 22 letter of Porticus Global's regional director Asia Philip Booth to NGOAB*. NGO Affairs Bureau, the Prime Minister's Office of Bangladesh.

NGOAB Document. (2015). *Teach For Bangladesh: Leadership development – Phase-2 project proposal (approved version)*. NGO Affairs Bureau, the Prime Minister's Office of Bangladesh.

Nguyen, C. V., & Ali, M. M. (2013). Washington Consensus development hypothesis: The case of Bangladesh. *ELK Asia Pacific Journal of Finance and Risk Management, 4*(4), 1–9.

Nielsen, W. A. (1996). *Inside American philanthropy: The dramas of donorship*. University of Oklahoma Press.

Ninnes, P., & Burnett, G. (2003). Comparative education research: Poststructuralist possibilities. *Comparative Education*, *39*(3), 279–97. https://doi.org/10.1080/0305006032000134355

No'Voa, A., & Yariv-Mashal, T. (2003). Comparative research in education: A mode of governance or a historical journey? *Comparative Education*, *39*(4), 423–38. https://doi.org/10.1080/0305006032000162002

Nuruzzaman, M. (2004). Neoliberal economic reforms, the rich and the poor in Bangladesh. *Journal of Contemporary Asia*, *34*(1), 33–54. https://doi.org/10.1080/00472330480000291

Nye, J. S. (1990). Soft power. *Foreign Policy*, *80*, 153. https://doi.org/10.2307/1148580

ODI. (2018, April). *About ODI*. ODI. https://www.odi.org/about-odi

Offe, C. (1984). *Contradictions of the welfare state* (J. Keane, Ed.). Hutchinson.

Olmedo, A. (2016). Philanthropic governance: Charitable companies, the commercialization of education and that thing called 'democracy'. In A. Verger, C. A. Lubienski & G. Steiner-Khamsi (Eds.), *The global education industry* (pp. 72–91). Routledge, Taylor & Francis Group.

Olmedo, A. (2017). Something old, not much new, and a lot borrowed: Philanthropy, business, and the changing roles of government in global education policy networks. *Oxford Review of Education*, *43*(1), 69–87. https://doi.org/10.1080/03054985.2016.1259104

Olmedo, A., Bailey, P. L. J., & Ball, S. J. (2013). To infinity and beyond ...: Heterarchical governance, the Teach For All network in Europe and the making of profits and minds. *European Educational Research Journal*, *12*(4), 492–512. https://doi.org/10.2304/eerj.2013.12.4.492

Ozga, J. (1987). Studying education policy through the lives of policy makers. In S. Walker & L. Barton (Eds.), *Changing policies, changing teachers: New directions for schooling?*, (pp. 138–50). Open University Press.

Ozga, J. (2000). *Policy research in educational settings: Contested terrain*. Open University Press.

Ozga, J. (2009). Governing education through data in England: From regulation to self-evaluation. *Journal of Education Policy*, *24*(2), 149–62. https://doi.org/10.1080/02680930902733121

Ozga, J. (2019). Problematising policy: The development of (critical) policy sociology. *Critical Studies in Education*, 1–16. https://doi.org/10.1080/17508487.2019.1697718

Papanastasiou, N. (2019). *The politics of scale in policy: Scalecraft and education governance*. Policy Press.

Parisi, L. (2012). Digital design and topological control. *Theory, Culture & Society*, *29*(4–5), 165–92. https://doi.org/10.1177/0263276412443568

Peck, J. (2011). Geographies of policy: From transfer-diffusion to mobility-mutation. *Progress in Human Geography*, *35*(6), 773–97. https://doi.org/10.1177/0309132510394010

Peck, J., & Theodore, N. (2015). *Fast policy: Experimental statecraft at the thresholds of neoliberalism*. University of Minnesota Press.

Penner, E. K. (2014). *Teaching For All? Variation in the effects of Teach For America* [Doctoral thesis]. University of California.

Penner, E. K. (2016). Teaching for all? Teach For America's effects across the distribution of student achievement. *Journal of Research on Educational Effectiveness*, 9(3), 259–82. https://doi.org/10.1080/19345747.2016.1164779

Penner, E. K. (2019). Teach For America and teacher quality: Increasing achievement over time. *Educational Policy*, 31, 1–38. https://doi.org/10.1177/0895904819843595

Phillips, D., & Schweisfurth, M. (2014). *Comparative and international education: An introduction to theory, method, and practice* (2nd ed.). Bloomsbury Academic.

Piattoeva, N. (2019). How can transnational connection hold? An actor-network theory inspired approach to the materiality of transnational education governance. In A. Wilkins & A. Olmedo (Eds.), *Education governance and social theory: Interdisciplinary approaches to research* (pp. 103–19). Bloomsbury Academic.

Popkewitz, T. S. (1998). *Struggling for the soul: The politics of schooling and the construction of the teacher*. Teachers College Press.

Powell, J. J. W. (2020). Comparative education in an age of competition and collaboration. *Comparative Education*, 56(1), 57–78. https://doi.org/10.1080/03050068.2019.1701248

Prime Minister's Office. (2017). *Public Private Partnership Authority Bangladesh*. https://www.pppo.gov.bd/government_policy.php

Provan, K., Beagles, J. E., & Leischow, S. J. (2011). Network formation, governance, and evolution in public health: The North American Quitline Consortium case. *Health Care Management Review*, 36(4), 315–26. https://doi.org/10.1097/HMR.0b013e31820e1124

Provan, K., & Kenis, P. (2007). Modes of network governance: Structure, management, and effectiveness. *Journal of Public Administration Research and Theory*, 18(2), 229–52. https://doi.org/10.1093/jopart/mum015

Quadir, F. (2000). The political economy of pro-market reforms in Bangladesh: Regime consolidation through economic liberalization? *Contemporary South Asia*, 9(2), 197–212. https://doi.org/10.1080/713658731

Quibria, M. G., & Ahmad, S. (2007, December). Aid effectiveness in Bangladesh. *Munich Personal RePEc Archive*. BIDS Golden Jubilee Conference, Dhaka, Bangladesh. http://mpra.ub.uni-muenchen.de/10299/

Radnor, Z., Osborne, S. P., & Glennon, R. (2016). Public management theory. In C. Ansell & J. Torfing (Eds.), *Handbook on theories of governance* (pp. 46–60). Edward Elgar Publishing. https://doi.org/10.4337/9781782548508

Rafferty, J. P. (2009, 23 February). *Anthropocene epoch | Definition & evidence*. Encyclopedia Britannica. https://www.britannica.com/science/Anthropocene-Epoch

Rappleye, J. (2012). Comparative education: The construction of a field. *Comparative Education*, 48(3), 403–6. https://doi.org/10.1080/03050068.2012.692180

Rappleye, J. (2019). Comparative education as cultural critique. *Comparative Education*, 56(1), 39–56. https://doi.org/10.1080/03050068.2019.1701247

Rappleye, J., & Komatsu, H. (2020). Towards (comparative) educational research for a finite future. *Comparative Education*, 56(2), 190–217. https://doi.org/10.1080/03050 068.2020.1741197

Rawolle, S. (2005). Cross-field effects and temporary social fields: A case study of the mediatization of recent Australian knowledge economy policies. *Journal of Education Policy*, 20(6), 705–24. https://doi.org/10.1080/02680930500238622

Rhodes, R. A. W. (1997). *Understanding governance: Policy networks, governance, reflexivity, and accountability*. Open University Press.

Rhodes, R. A. W. (2017a). *Network governance and the differentiated polity: Selected essays. Volume I* (1st ed.). Oxford University Press.

Rhodes, R. A. W. (2017b). *Analysing networks as narratives of beliefs and practices* (Vol. 1). Oxford University Press. https://doi.org/10.1093/oso/9780198786108.003.0007

Rhodes, R. A. W. (2017c). *Policy networks* (Vol. 1). Oxford University Press. https://doi.org/10.1093/oso/9780198786108.003.0003

Rizvi, F., & Lingard, B. (2010). *Globalizing education policy*. Routledge.

Robertson, R. (1994). Globalisation or glocalisation? *Journal of International Communication*, 1(1), 33–52. https://doi.org/10.1080/13216597.1994.9751780

Robertson, S. (2005). Re-imagining and rescripting the future of education: Global knowledge economy discourses and the challenge to education systems. *Comparative Education*, 41(2), 151–70. https://doi.org/10.1080/03050060500150922

Robertson, S., & Dale, R. (2008). 'Making Europe': State, space, strategy and subjectivities. *Globalisation, Societies and Education*, 6(3), 203–6. https://doi.org/10.1080/14767720802343290

Rosenau, J. N. (1997). *Along the domestic-foreign frontier: Exploring governance in a turbulent world*. Cambridge University Press.

Sahlberg, P. (2016). The global education reform movement and its impact on schooling. In K. E. Mundy, A. Green, B. Lingard & A. Verger (Eds.), *The handbook of global education policy* (pp. 128–44). Wiley.

Salamon, L. M. (Ed.). (2014). *New frontiers of philanthropy: A guide to the new tools and actors reshaping global philanthropy and social investing*. Oxford University Press.

Santori, D., Ball, S. J., & Junemann, C. (2016). Financial markets and investment in education. In A. Verger, C. A. Lubienski & G. Steiner-Khamsi (Eds.), *The global education industry* (pp. 235–54). Routledge, Taylor & Francis Group.

Santos, B. de S. (2002). The processes of globalisation (S. Caldmell, Trans.). *Eurozine: Revista Crítica de Ciências Sociais and Eurozine*, August, 1–48.

Sassen, S. (2001). Global cities and developmentalist states: How to derail what could be an interesting debate: A response to Hill and Kim. *Urban Studies*, 38(13), 2537–40. https://doi.org/10.1080/00420980120094650

Sassen, S. (2002). Introduction: Locating cities on global circuits. In S. Sassen (Ed.), *Global networks, linked cities* (pp. 1–38). Routledge.

Sassen, S. (2003). Globalization or denationalization? *Review of International Political Economy, 10*(1), 1–22. https://doi.org/10.1080/0969229032000048853

Sassen, S. (2007). *Sociology of globalization* (1st ed.). W.W. Norton.

Sassen, S. (2013). When the global arises inside the national. In T. Seddon & J. Levin (Eds.), *Educators, professionalism and politics: Global transitions, national spaces and professional projects* (pp. 27–41). Routledge.

Savage, G. C. (2018). Policy assemblages and human devices: A reflection on 'assembling policy'. *Discourse: Studies in the Cultural Politics of Education, 39*(2), 309–21. https://doi.org/10.1080/01596306.2017.1389431

Savage, M. (2007, 13 December). *The big question: What is the British Council, and does it still serve.* The Independent. http://www.independent.co.uk/news/world/europe/the-big-question-what-is-the-british-council-and-does-it-still-serve-a-useful-purpose-764836.html

Sawchuk, S. (2013). Grant will expand Teach For America. *Education Week, 32*(37), 5–6.

Schneider, J. (2014). Rhetoric and practice in pre-service teacher education: The case of Teach For America. *Journal of Education Policy, 29*(4), 425–42. https://doi.org/10.1080/02680939.2013.825329

Schriewer, J. (1988). The method of comparison and the need for comparison: Methodological criteria and sociological concept. In J. Schriewer & B. Holmes (Eds.), *Theories and methods in comparative education* (pp. 25–83). P. Lang.

Schriewer, J. (1990). The method of comparison and the need for externalization: Methodological criteria and sociological concepts. In J. Schriewer & B. Holmes (Eds.), *Theories and methods in comparative education* (3rd ed., pp. 25–83). P. Lang.

Schriewer, J., & Martinez, C. (2004). Constructions of internationality in education. In G. Steiner-Khamsi (Ed.), *The global politics of educational borrowing and lending* (pp. 29–53). Teachers College Press.

Sellar, S., & Lingard, B. (2013). Looking East: Shanghai, PISA 2009 and the reconstitution of reference societies in the global education policy field. *Comparative Education, 49*(4), 464–85. https://doi.org/10.1080/03050068.2013.770943

SEUK. (2018). *Who we are.* Social Enterprise UK. https://www.socialenterprise.org.uk/about-us

Shahjahan, R. A. (2016). International organizations (IOs), epistemic tools of influence, and the colonial geopolitics of knowledge production in higher education policy. *Journal of Education Policy, 31*(6), 694–710. https://doi.org/10.1080/02680939.2016.1206623

Shamir, R. (2008). The age of responsibilization: On market-embedded morality. *Economy and Society, 37*(1), 1–19. https://doi.org/10.1080/03085140701760833

Shore, C., & Wright, S. (2011). Conceptualising policy: Technologies of governance and the politics of visibility. In C. Shore, S. Wright, & D. Però (Eds.), *Policy* worlds: Anthropology and the analysis of contemporary power (pp. 1–26). Berghahn Books.

Silova, I. (2019). Toward a Wonderland of comparative education. *Comparative Education, 55*(4), 444–72. https://doi.org/10.1080/03050068.2019.1657699

Silova, I., Rappleye, J., & Auld, E. (2020). Chapter 1 beyond the Western horizon: Rethinking education, values, and policy transfer. In G. Fan & T. S. Popkewitz (Eds.), *Handbook of education policy studies: Values, governance, globalization, and methodology, Volume 1* (pp. 3–30). https://doi.org/10.1007/978-981-13-8347-2

Sismondo, S. (2017). Post-truth? *Social Studies of Science, 47*(1), 3–6. https://doi.org/10.1177/0306312717692076

Sobe, N. W. (2017). Travelling researchers, colonial difference: Comparative education in an age of exploration. *Compare: A Journal of Comparative and International Education, 47*(3), 332–43. https://doi.org/10.1080/03057925.2016.1273760

Sondel, B. (2015). Raising citizens or raising test scores? Teach For America, 'No Excuses' charters, and the development of the neoliberal citizen. *Theory & Research in Social Education, 43*(3), 289–313. https://doi.org/10.1080/00933104.2015.1064505

Söpper, K. (2014). Governance and culture – a new approach to understanding structures of collaboration. *European Spatial Research and Policy, 21*(1), 53–64. https://doi.org/10.2478/esrp-2014-0005

Sørensen, E., & Torfing, J. (2008). Introduction governance network research: Towards a second generation. In E. Sørensen & J. Torfing (Eds.), *Theories of democratic network governance* (1st paperback ed., pp. 1–21). Palgrave Macmillan.

Spivak, G. C. (2012). *An aesthetic education in the era of globalization* (1st Harvard University Press paperback ed.). Harvard University Press.

Srećković, M., & Windsperger, J. (2013). The impact of trust on the choice of knowledge transfer mechanisms in clusters. In T. Ehrmann, J. Windsperger, G. Cliquet & G. Hendrikse (Eds.), *Network governance* (pp. 73–85). Springer Berlin Heidelberg. https://doi.org/10.1007/978-3-7908-2867-2_5

Steiner-Khamsi, G. (2002). Reterritorializing educational import. In A. Nóvoa & M. Lawn (Eds.), *Fabricating Europe* (pp. 69–86). Kluwer Academic Publishers. https://doi.org/10.1007/0-306-47561-8_7

Steiner-Khamsi, G. (2004). Blazing a trail for policy theory and practice. In G. Steiner-Khamsi (Ed.), *The global politics of educational borrowing and lending* (pp. 201–20). Teachers College Press.

Steiner-Khamsi, G. (2006). The economics of policy borrowing and lending: A study of late adopters. *Oxford Review of Education, 32*(5), 665–78. https://doi.org/10.1080/03054980600976353

Stoneburner, J. (2018). *Understanding teacher stress and wellbeing at Teach For America's summer institute* [Doctoral thesis]. University of California.

Straubhaar, R. (2019). Teaching For America across two hemispheres: Comparing the ideological appeal of the Teach For All teacher education model in the United States and Brazil. *Journal of Teacher Education.* https://doi.org/10.1177/0022487119845635

Straubhaar, R., & Friedrich, D. (2015). Theorizing and documenting the spread of Teach For All and its impact on global education reform. *Education Policy Analysis Archives, 23*(44), 1–11. https://doi.org/10.14507/epaa.v23.2055

Straubhaar, R., & Gottfried, M. (2016). Who joins Teach For America and why? Insights into the 'typical' recruit in an urban school district. *Education and Urban Society, 48*(7), 627–49. https://doi.org/10.1177/0013124514541463

Suiter, J. (2016). Post-truth politics. *Political Insight, 7*(3), 25–7. https://doi.org/10.1177/2041905816680417

Takayama, K. (2011). A comparativist's predicaments of writing about 'other' education: A self-reflective, critical review of studies of Japanese education. *Comparative Education, 47*(4), 449–70. https://doi.org/10.1080/03050068.2011.561542

Takayama, K. (2018). The constitution of East Asia as a counter reference society through PISA: A postcolonial/de-colonial intervention. *Globalisation, Societies and Education, 16*(5), 609–23. https://doi.org/10.1080/14767724.2018.1532282

Takayama, K. (2019). An invitation to 'negative' comparative education. *Comparative Education, 56*(1), 79–95. https://doi.org/10.1080/03050068.2019.1701250

Takayama, K. (2020a). Engaging with the more-than-human and decolonial turns in the land of Shinto cosmologies: 'Negative' comparative education in practice. *ECNU Review of Education, 3*(1), 46–65. https://doi.org/10.1177/2096531120906298

Takayama, K. (2020b). Towards a new articulation of comparative educations: Cross-culturalising research imaginations. In M. Manzon (Ed.), *Origins and traditions in comparative education* (1st ed., pp. 77–93). Routledge. https://doi.org/10.4324/9780429287381-6

Takayama, K., Sriprakash, A., & Connell, R. (2017). Toward a postcolonial comparative and international education. *Comparative Education Review, 61*(S1), S1–S24. https://doi.org/10.1086/690455

Taylor, C. (2004). *Modern social imaginaries.* Duke University Press.

Taylor, R. H. (2017). *From the classroom to the principal's office: How the Teach For America experience influences school leadership* [Doctor of education thesis]. University of Pennsylvania.

Teach For All. (2020, 3 September). *About.* Teach For All. https://teachforall.org/about

Teach For All, FAQ. (2015). *Frequently asked questions* [Text]. Teach For All. http://teachforall.org/en/about/faq

TFB Official Tweet. (2015, 12 May). https://www.facebook.com/tfbangladesh/posts/974607219268103

TFB Official Tweet. (2015, 21 October). https://www.facebook.com/tfbangladesh/posts/1051994771529347

TFB Official Tweet. (2015, 22 October). https://www.facebook.com/tfbangladesh/photos/a.451461924915971/1053278491400975

TFB Official Tweet. (2015, 28 October). https://www.facebook.com/tfbangladesh/posts/2149195361809277
TFB Official Tweet. (2015, 18 November). https://www.facebook.com/tfbangladesh/photos/a.451461924915971/1064719946923496
Then, V., Schober, C., Rauscher, O., & Kehl, K. (2017). *Social return on investment analysis: Measuring the impact of social investment* (1st ed.). Palgrave Macmillan.
Thomas, M. A. M. (2018a). 'Policy embodiment': Alternative certification and Teach For America teachers in traditional public schools. *Teaching and Teacher Education*, 70, 186–95. https://doi.org/10.1016/j.tate.2017.11.011
Thomas, M. A. M. (2018b). 'Good intentions can only get you so far': Critical reflections from Teach For America corps members placed in special education. *Education and Urban Society*, 50(5), 435–60. https://doi.org/10.1177/0013124517713604
Thomas, M. A. M., & Lefebvre, E. E. (2018). The dangers of relentless pursuit: Teaching, personal health, and the symbolic/real violence of Teach For America. *Discourse: Studies in the Cultural Politics of Education*, 39(6), 856–67. https://doi.org/10.1080/01596306.2017.1311298
Thomas, M. A. M., & Lefebvre, E. E. (2020). Teaching synchronous-service teachers: Traditional teacher education at a crossroads. *Teachers College Record*, 122(7), 1–34.
Thomas, M. A. M., Rauschenberger, E., & Crawford-Garrett, K. (Eds.). (2020). *Examining Teach For All: International perspectives on a growing global network* (1st ed.). Routledge. https://doi.org/10.4324/9780429331695
Thompson, G., & Cook, I. (2015). Becoming-topologies of education: Deformations, networks and the database effect. *Discourse: Studies in the Cultural Politics of Education*, 36(5), 732–48. https://doi.org/10.1080/01596306.2014.890411
Thomson, P., Hall, C., & Jones, K. (2013). Towards educational change leadership as a discursive practice – or should all school leaders read Foucault? *International Journal of Leadership in Education*, 16(2), 155–72. https://doi.org/10.1080/13603124.2012.693204
Thrift, N. (1999). 15: Steps to an ecology of place. In D. B. Massey, J. Allen, & P. Sarre (Eds.), *Human geography today* (pp. 295–322). Polity Press; Blackwell Publishers.
Thrift, N. (2005). *Knowing capitalism*. SAGE Publications.
Tompkins-Stange, M. E. (2016). *Policy patrons: Philanthropy, education reform, and the politics of influence*. Harvard Education Press.
Torfing, J. (2007). Introduction: Democratic network governance. In M. Marcussen & J. Torfing (Eds.), *Democratic network governance in Europe* (pp. 1–20). Palgrave Macmillan UK. https://doi.org/10.1057/9780230596283
Trujillo, T., & Scott, J. (2014). Superheroes and transformers: Rethinking Teach For America's leadership models. *Phi Delta Kappan*, 95(8), 57–61. https://doi.org/10.1177/003172171409500813
Trujillo, T., Scott, J., & Rivera, M. (2017). Follow the yellow brick road: Teach For America and the making of educational leaders. *American Journal of Education*, 123(3), 353–91. https://doi.org/10.1086/691232

Turner, H., Ncube, M., Turner, A., Boruch, R., & Ibekwe, N. (2018). What are the effects of Teach For America on math, English language arts, and science outcomes of K-12 students in the USA? *Campbell Systematic Reviews, 14*(1), 1–60. https://doi.org/10.4073/csr.2018.7

UnLtd. (2018). UnLtd. Wikipedia. https://en.wikipedia.org/w/index.php?title=UnLtd&oldid=834160865

Vavrus, F. (2021). *Schooling as uncertainty: An ethnographic memoir in comparative education*. Bloomsbury Academic.

Veltri, B. T. (2008). Teaching or service? The site-based realities of Teach For America teachers in poor, urban schools. *Education and Urban Society, 40*(5), 511–42. https://doi.org/10.1177/0013124508319281

Veltri, B. T., & Brewer, T. J. (2019). Comply, embrace, cope, counterсrusade, subvert: Teach For America corps members respond to (internal) and external mandates. *Education and Urban Society, 52*(5), 675–703. https://doi.org/10.1177/0013124519883628

Vertovec, S. (2009). *Transnationalism*. Routledge.

VoA, B. (2014, 2 November). শিক্ষাদানে নতুন মাইলফলক. ভিডিও. http://www.voabangla.com/content/drrc-report-75/2503891.html

Waldow, F. (2012). Standardisation and legitimacy: Two central concepts in research on educational borrowing and lending. In G. Steiner-Khamsi & F. Waldow (Eds.), *Policy borrowing and lending in education* (pp. 411–27). Routledge.

Walker, J. (2017). Solving the world's biggest problems: Better philanthropy through systems change (SSIR). *Stanford Social Innovation Review*, 5 April. https://ssir.org/articles/entry/better_philanthropy_through_systems_change

Warren, M. (1992). Democratic theory and self-transformation. *American Political Science Review, 86*(1), 8–23. https://doi.org/10.2307/1964012

Webb, P. T. (2014). Policy problematization. *International Journal of Qualitative Studies in Education, 27*(3), 364–76. https://doi.org/10.1080/09518398.2012.762480

Wells, D. (2010). *Ashoka fellows change the world* [Development outreach, pp. 36–37]. World Bank. http://siteresources.worldbank.org/WBI/Resources/213798-1278955272198/Ashoka_Fellows_Change_the_World.pdf

Whitty, G., & Wisby, E. (2016). Education in England – a testbed for network governance? *Oxford Review of Education, 42*(3), 316–29. https://doi.org/10.1080/03054985.2016.1184873

Wiepking, P., & Handy, F. (Eds.). (2017). *The Palgrave handbook of global philanthropy*. Palgrave. http://www.credoreference.com/book/macp

Wilkins, A., & Olmedo, A. (2019). *Education governance and social theory: Interdisciplinary approaches to research*. Bloomsbury Academic.

Williams, R. (1977). *Marxism and literature* (Reprint). Oxford University Press.

Williams, R. (2005). *Culture and materialism: Selected essays*. Verso.

Williamson, B. (2019). Digitizing education governance: Pearson, real-time data analytics, visualization and machine intelligence. In A. Wilkins & A. Olmedo (Eds.),

Education governance and social theory: Interdisciplinary approaches to research (pp. 21–41). Bloomsbury Academic.

Wright, S. (2011). Studying policy: Methods, paradigms, perspectives. In C. Shore, S. Wright, & D. Però (Eds.), *Policy worlds: Anthropology and the analysis of contemporary power* (pp. 27–31). Berghahn Books.

Wuyts, S., & Bulte, C. V. den. (2012). Network governance. In G. Lilien & R. Grewal (Eds.), *Handbook of business-to-business marketing* (pp. 73–89). Edward Elgar Publishing. https://doi.org/10.4337/9781781002445

Xu, Z., Hannaway, J., & Taylor, C. (2011). Making a difference? The effects of Teach For America in high school: *Journal of Policy Analysis and Management, 30*(3), 447–69. https://doi.org/10.1002/pam.20585

Zafarullah, H. (2015). Network governance and policy making: Developments and directions in Asia. In I. Jamil, S. M. Aminuzzaman & Sk. T. M. Haque (Eds.), *Governance in South, Southeast, and East Asia* (pp. 45–63). Springer International Publishing. https://doi.org/10.1007/978-3-319-15218-9_4

Zakaria, F. (2020). *Ten lessons for a post-pandemic world* (1st ed.). W. W. Norton & Company.

Zappetti, L. (2019). *Teach for America corps members' perceptions of classroom self-efficacy*. The Graduate School of Education and Human Development of the George Washington University.

Zeichner, K., & Peña-Sandoval, C. (2015). Venture philanthropy and teacher education policy in the US: The role of the new schools venture fund. *Teachers College Record, 117*, 1–44.

Zeleny, M. (Ed.). (1981). *Autopoiesis, a theory of living organization*. North Holland.

Zuboff, S. (2019). *The age of surveillance capitalism: The fight for a human future at the new frontier of power* (1st trade paperback ed.). PublicAffairs.

Index

Abed, Sir Fazle Hasan 132, 137–8, 139, 143, 172, 177 n.5(ch 4)
Ace, Tristan 99, 100, 102–3, 104, 107, 110
active networks 41, 53, 56, 99, 122
Adhikary, Rino Wiseman 22, 23
Ahmann, C. 143
Allen, J. 41, 46, 47
Allman, K. A. 158
Alvord, S. H. 158
Amin, A. 40, 42
Anderson, B. R. O. 49, 103, 115
Anheier, H. K. 158
Anthropocene 19, 153, 154, 155
anti-multilateralism 51, 153
Anwar, Minhaz 98, 99, 103, 104–5, 107
Appadurai, A. 3, 4, 20, 21, 91, 105, 173
  on collective aspirations 50
  on dimensions of cultural flows of globalization 35, 36, 95, 169
  distinction between culture and cultural 171–2
  on imagination 49–51, 85, 88, 144
  on imagined community 103
  on imagined worlds 35, 114
  on nation and state in globalization context 116
  'play of pastiche' theory 102, 125
Arranz, N. 65
Ashoka Fellows 133, 177 n.7
Ashoka: Innovators for the Public 98, 139, 177 n.7
aspirational imagination 88–9, 103
  and governmentality 121
  of policy 160
aspirations 35–6, 88, 137–9, 154, 161
  career aspirations 11
  and collaborations 168
  collective aspirations 41, 50, 88–9, 103, 117, 119, 162, 171–2
  and funding 148
  global aspirations 91

  of global-local actors and organizations 31, 59, 137
  and imagination 125
  and networks 29
  policy mobility 151
  of TFB founder 126, 127–8
  work-making capacity 51
associology 155, 170
AVPN (Asian Venture Philanthropy Network) conference 113

Ball, S. J. 4, 20, 117, 157
Bangladesh 62, *see also* Teach For Bangladesh (TFB)
  cultural rootedness of SEs in 132
  definition of SE in 107–8
  education policies 5–6
  education system 6
  education system, symbiosis between TFB and authority 137
  endorsement of EFA movement 64
  exogenous influences 6
  government structures 108, 116, 164
  history of 5
  I/NGOs in 6–7
  localization of social entrepreneurial policy 116
  macroeconomic policy reforms 5
  NGOs in 6–7, 94, 119
  open market economy 5
  political and economical transformations 5
  poverty and inequality 6
  pre-PEDP III roles of government 70
  Primary Education Development Programmes 6
  reimagination of education policy in 166–7
  SE-sector policy in/for (*see* social entrepreneurial sector policy (SE-sector policy))

social investment market in 110
taxation 86
women and youth in social entrepreneurial activities in 102
Beech, J. 21, 52, 83, 154
Belcher, O. 45
best practice 16, 71, 74, 88, 106, 131–2, 137, 141, 169
BetterStories 98, 100, 103, 104, 108
bi-/multilateral donors 63, 70
biopower 45, 77
Bista, M. B. 61–2
bounded territories 46
Bourdieu, P. 5, 21, 22, 36
Bowe, R. 117
BRAC Institute of Educational Development, master's programme 8
Brenninkmeijer family entrepreneurs 139, 178 n.4
British Council 91, 94, 98, 108, 118, 150
  Bangladesh NGOs and their activities reconstitution by 119
  baseline research on social enterprise 97
  efforts to constitute the UK as a reference society 112
  policy and structural reforms 102
  policy manoeuvres 101–2
  research authority role 101
British Council Bangladesh (BCB) 31–2, 85–6, 93, 106, 149, 164, 165
  attempt to convince the government to reimagine NGOs as SEs 118–19
  DfID funding for 90
  emergence of 89–90, 117
  global reach responsibility 116
  imagined world of social entrepreneurial policy, and administrative/political state 116
  organizing capacity and network coordination 89
  'play of pastiche' activation 102–3
  policy making world 86
  policy steering 90
  presentation of SE as a policy panacea 165
  progress 91
  pursuing social entrepreneurial policies and structures 86–7
  as SE 90
  self-referential research of 101–2, 106
  and SEs in Bangladesh 89–96
British Council Global (BCG) 86, 90–1, 117
broad-based partnerships, in teacher education 147
budget funding 76–7
Building Resources Across Communities (BRAC) 6, 92, 134, 138, 140, 172, 178 n.5, 178 n.8
  challenges from government 95–6
  projection as SE 93
Bulte, C. V. den 65
business entrepreneurs and social entrepreneurs, difference between 158

Campaign for Popular Education (CAMPE) 73, 81, 147, 164
  advocacy role 74
  authority 76
  civil society representation 64, 75
  and EFA's special funding 73–4
  nature of involvement of 75
  participation in PESoB governance 74
capitalist power, centralization of 45
Carney, S. 4, 22, 61–2
Castells, Manuel 45, 46, 115
catalytic capital 159
certification 101, 105, 106, 146, 147
change (reform) 38–9
  and culture 43
  in the local education policy landscape in Bangladesh 163–4
  system-level change 177 n.7
Changemakers 98
civil society (CS) 3, 64, 81
  CAMPE as 64, 75
  global-national imbrications 82–3
  leaders 63
  network 68, 72
  NGOs as 72, 76
  organizations 102, 157
  and philanthropic partnerships 157
  World Bank official's view on the role of 75
climate emergency 19, 154–5
collective actions 115
collective aspirations, see aspirations
collective representations 50, 176 n.9
Comic Relief 98

Community Action Network 98
comparative education 4, 14–20, 61, 83, 170–1, 173
  and Anthropocene 19
  and climate emergency 19–20
  and coloniality of power 19
  danger in 22
  enabling of reforms 17
  focus of 15
  as a form of cultural critique 17–18
  as mode of governance 15
  multiplicity 18
  phases 14–15
  policy 4–5
  and policymaking 16
  policy research 155
  problem-solution terms 15
  reference societies 15
  reforms 16
connectivities 40, 43, 56, 57
contemporary politics, global rescaling of 39
context generative 20, 111–14, 172
context productive 20, 96, 111–14, 172
corporate social responsibilities (CSR) 157
COVID-19 pandemic 34–5, 155, 173
creational, being 115
creative capitalism 50
cultural dimensions 30, 36, 57, 149, 151, 160, 162, 167, 171
cultural disjunctures 137
cultural flows of globalization 4, 35, 36, 63, 122, 168, 169
cultural imagination 89–96
cultural imbrications 49–51
cultural logics 99–102
cultural phenomena, localization of 36
cultural production, as a form of power 45
cultural programmes 168
cultural respatializations 37
cultural topology 43–4
culture 30, 33, 34, 35, 42–4, 44
  and change 43
  connectivity logic of 43
  as continuous change 44
  definition of 150
  as a globally relational field of co-emergence 35
  and imbrication 34
  relationality 43
cyber spaces 39

data
  data-driven perspectives 113
  first-hand data (data of presence) 55
  flow of data 162–3
data steering policy 99–102
de Arroyabe, J. C. 65
decentralization 5, 76
deep mediatization of life 51
democracy 28, 83
diasporic imagination 172
direct for-profit impact investors 159
Directorate of Primary Education (DPE) 7, 59–60, 63, 64, 69, 121
director general (DG) of NGOAB 97, 111–13
Disbursement Linked to Indicators (DLIs) 77–8, 82, 145–6
disciplinary power 45
discourses 54, 176 n.12
DLIs, *see* Disbursement Linked to Indicators (DLIs)
Donor Consortium (DC) 64, 70–2, 81, 146, 163–4
  assessment of government work 78
  evolution of 72
  teacher education prioritization 146
  and World Bank 71–2, 82
Drayton, Bill 133
Durkheim, Emile 176 n.9

Education for All (EFA) 15, 60, 68–9, 82, 176 n.3(ch 2)
  Commitment 11, national implementation of 74
  mobilization of special funding of 73
  and PESoB 68
  as programme of/for globalization of education 69
  youth and women in 102
education governance, *see also* governance
  and BRAC 161
  changes in 3
Education Local Consultative Group (ELCG) 72–3, 74, 82
education policy 20, *see also* policies
  analysis 19
  government actors of 155

mobility and mutation 35
mobility-fixity binary 4
sociology of 169–70
education sector budget 63–4
eduplayers 159–60
Einstein, Albert 114
Ellis, V. 2, 12–13, 171
employment practices 142
empowerment of heterarchies 39
epistemic community 86, 97–9, 101–3, 106–7, 112, 114–15, 117, 119, 165
epistemic diaspora 142
epistemological reflexivity 17, 18, 22, 62, 124
essential legislation 88
ethical beliefs 95
ethnographic approach 18, 30, 51, 53, 136
ethnographic networks 23, 30, 53–7, 97–9, 135–7
ethnography 18, 57, 151
ethnography spatialized 56
ethnonationalisms 16, 18, 21, 50, 51, 153, 155, 173
Euclidian place-space dichotomy 39
evidence-based approaches 16, 88, 118, 159
expansive democracy 83
experts 87, 91, 99, 117
expert visits 141–2
externalization 15, 92–3, 101, 106, 112

family foundations 50
fast mobility 154
fast-policy conditions 165–6, 169
fast policymaking 4, 17
fast policy sociology 87
Fast Track Initiative (FTI) 64, 73–4, 81
fellow teachers 8–9
  leadership capacities of 2
  social-mediatization 143
financescape 77, 159
fixities 53, *see also* mobility-fixity binary
for-profit impact investors 159
Foucault, Michel 60, 175–6 n.2
founder of TFB 149, 161
  and Abed 138
  description of government's support for TFB 133–4
  emphasis on organizational best practice 131–2

entrepreneurial imagination 127–8
  and Gowher 143
  gradual steps in forming TFB 127–8
  imagination about her social entrepreneurial development 123–8
  on key ideas related to SE 129
  on leadership 130–1
  network of grit to localize TFB 150
  on quality organizations and exemplary institutional practices 131
  on scarcity of funding 134
  seeking government approvals 140, 161
  social entrepreneurial imagination, productive dimension of 128–9
  support for 140–1
  understanding of SE 129
  view of NGO-SE nexus 132–3
free trade zones 20, 40
Friedrich, Daniel 13, 171
funding 73, 139
  and aspirations 148
  DfID funding for British Council Bangladesh 90
  EFA's special funding, and Campaign for Popular Education 73–4
  PEDP III 76–7
  pooled funding 76–7
  from Porticus Global 128
  professionalization of fundraising activities 157
  scarcity of 134
  social impact funding 158–9
  for Teach For All 3
  for TFB 134, 139

genealogical approach 61–2
generative imagination 123, 128–30
GIZ (German Federal Enterprise for International Cooperation) 89–90
global
  and local, relationship between 98
  local roots of 36, 46, 92, 151
  ontologization of 36
global conferences 142
global corporations 50
global education policy field 4, 15, 20, 105, 170
global entrepreneurial subjectivities 128
global ethnography 18, 55–6, 57
global governmentality 49, 114, 125

globalization 18, 30–1, 33, 114, 153, 154
  in active/verb sense 38
  alternative forms of spatial
    manifestations 39–40
  creational power drive 114
  cultural flows of 4, 35, 36, 63, 122,
    168, 169
  of economy 20
  flows of 4, 40
  as governance globalized 69
  multiple spatialities of 19
  ontology of 40, 54–7
  and policy mobilities 37
  power properties of 39
  as a process of governance 39
  as process of reorganized governance
    37–8, 44
  as respatialization of governance
    30, 33, 34
  and spatialities 34
  speed, intensity and spatial extensions 37
  topological environment 34, 35, 49
  topological impact on policy cycles 117
  as transformation of power 37
  as a transformative process of
    respatialization 39
globalized localism 92, 172
global-local imbrications 18, 20, 38, 52–3,
  54, 57, 74
  at cultural level 92
  at imagination level 69
  and imagination of governmentality
    123
globally defined fields of possibilities
  50, 91
globally mobile policy models 151–2,
  166, 170
global-national imbrications 82–3
global-national-local imbrication 20–1,
  22, 166, 167, 172, 173
global networks 39, 54, 86, 110, 165
Global North 3–4, 23, 26–7, 28, 172, 173
global pandemic 40
Global Partnership for Education (GPE)
  64, 73, 76, 81, 164
global philanthropies 19, 113, 117, 118,
  119, 148, 161, 163, 164
global policy mobilities 13, 17, 166, 171
Global South 23, 46, 170, 173
  impact of UN agendas 15

schooling policy in 4
glocal/glocalisms 41
  collaborators 119
  glocal imagination of partnerships 163
  networks, convincing government to
    reimagine NGOs as SEs 118–19
  NGOs 119
GO-NGO collaborations 163
Gorur, R. 17
governance 37–8, 51, 83
  and cultural flows 168
  mechanisms 66
  of networks 80
  under rationalities of development
    economics 77
  respatialized and globally imagined 38
governance networks 31, 32, 75, 79, 83,
  121, 155
  as policy networks 60
  in the sense of heterarchies 65
governance relationships symbiosis 82
governing policy 79
Grameen 92–3
group identities 18
Gulson, K. N. 17, 167

hand network 53, 118, 119
Hardy, Ian 27–8
head network 53, 118, 119
Held, D. 37, 38, 43
heterarchic governance 3, 36, 65–6, 72, 75,
  78, 154, 163, 165
heterarchies 34, 39, 42, 82
  constructed through certification and
    self-referencing 106
  in education policy 49
  empowerment of 39
  of global governance 106
  imbricative role of 37
  'net' and 'work' 44
  as power topologies 48
  of transnational politics 105–6
heterarchization 105, 117
heterotopias 40–1, 42, 72, 118, 149, 162,
  165, 175–6 n.2
hierarchies 3, 100, 105–6, 160, 166
high-range impact investors 159
human capital 5
Huq, M. Azizul 143
hybrid forms 32, 55

imaginaire 50, 89, 103, 121, 139, 161, 172
imagination 50, 53, 85, 114–18, 122, 127, 172
  Andersonian and Appaduraian sense, comparison between 49
  Appadurai on 114–15
  and cultural frames of reasoning 125
  Einstein on 114
  globalizing role of 115
  and its cultural properties, as central to global-local imbrications 96
  and life's work 115
  and mobility/fixity 148–50
  policy mobilities understanding 169
  and social life 149
  spatial de-formations and re-formations 38
  SWAP (*see* System Wide Approach to Programming (SWAP))
  underpinning TFB 122–3
  value of 51
imagination productive 123–8, 130, 148
imagined communities 20, 35, 89, 103, 115, 116, 135, 161
imagined gaps, in training 147
imagined lives 121–2
imagined worlds 35, 49–50, 114–15, 116, 149, 169
imbrications 33–4, 41, 47, 54, 56, 149–50, 171
  cultural imbrications 34, 49–51
  and cultural progression 116
  global-local imbrications (*see* global-local imbrications)
  global-national imbrications 82–3
  global-national-local imbrication 20–1, 22, 166, 167, 172, 173
  and heterarchies 37
  imbricative co-imagination 96
  play of pastiche 136
IMF 5, 20
impact imagination
  and the government 133–5
  and national sectors 130–3
impact investment 129, 156–7, 158–9
indigenization of policy reforms 95, 106
influence 44, 53, 161–2
  context of 117
  of data-driven perspectives 113
  exogenous influences 6

numbers and imagination 102–7
personal network influence 80
I/NGOs 6–7, 147
innovative SEs 133, 157–8, 169
in-person exchange of digital resources 142
intensity 37, 160, 167, 168, 169
Internal Revenue Service (IRS) 127
International Finance Corporation (IFC) 179 n.3
internationalization 21, 106, 106
International Large Scale Assessments (ILSAs) 15, 16
international learning trips 142
interregional flows 38
investments 110, 129
Islam, Md. Ashadul 99, 103, 105

Jacobson, D. D. 66
Joint Annual Review Missions (JARMs) 76, 82, 145
Joint Consultative Meetings (JCMs) 76, 82, 145
Junemann, C. 157

Kelly, Annie 92
Kenis, P. 66
Khan, Muhaimin 98
Klijn, E.-H. 3
Komatsu, H. 19, 155
Kopp, Wendy 138, 141
Koppenjan, J. F. M. 3

Lam, S. 171
Larsen, M. A. 21, 52, 83, 154
Latour, Bruno 155, 169–70, 173
leadership
  capacity building 2, 13, 139
  entrepreneurial leadership 130–1
  training 64, 130–1
  women leadership 100, 103
lead organizations 66, 71, 81, 82, 89
Lefebvre, E. E. 132
Lingard, Bob 16, 25–7, 77, 105–6, 154
localized globalism 29, 92
locational situatedness 34
Loughran, K. 33–4
Low, S. M. 57
Luhmann, N. 101–2
Lury, C. 43

Mannan, M. 134
Masella, C. 66
Massey, D. B. 41, 42
mass literacy 20
McNess, E. 18
media 143–4, 161–2
mediatization 51, 143–4
meta-governance 65–6, 67, 72, 77, 80, 82
meta tools 67, 75–8, 82
methodological decisions 57
methodological globalism 15, 19, 20–1, 153, 170, 173
methodological innovation 56
methodological nationalism 15, 19, 20–1, 22, 153, 170, 173
middle-range impact investors 159
Ministry of Finance (MoF) 77, 78
Ministry of Primary and Mass Education (MoPME) 64
Misbah, Munawar 143
mobilities 51, 53
mobility-fixity binary 4, 33–4, 51
  and imagination 148–50
  Teach For Bangladesh 150–1
Möbius strip 83
modernity 49, 59
modernity trap 153, 168
Molin, M. D. 66
Mozena, Dan 143
multilevel governance 80
multinational corporations, corporate social responsibilities (CSR) 157
multiple spatialities 19
multiple worlds 52

National Board of Revenue (NBR) 113
national identifiers 19
nationalized government primary schools 63
nation-states 37, 38, 55, 69, 136, 151, 153, 173
  boundaries of 115–16
  power of authority and sovereignty 45
neoliberal aspirations 37
neoliberal capitalism 5
neoliberal economic globalization 36
neoliberal free trade regime 20
neoliberal globalization 5–6, 14
neoliberal social entrepreneurship 2

network administrative organizations (NAOs) 66
network-centric transformations 31, 59, 62, 79
networked civil society (CS) 76
networked epistemic community 115
networked flows 46
networked global cities 36
networked heterarchies, and cultural topology 43–4
networked power 47, 48, *see also* power
networked spaces 47, 165, *see also* space(s)
network effects 65, 79, 81
network ethnography 18, 23, 29, 52, 55–6, 57
network governance 3, 4, 13, 18, 61, 62, 66–7, 79, 80
network governance effects 65–6, 67, 72, 75, 79, 80, 82
  DLIs (disbursement-linked indicators) 77–8
  Joint Annual Review Missions 76
  Joint Consultative Meeting (JCM) 76
  pooled funding 76–7
  results-based framework 77–8
  working groups 76
networking
  as governance 80
  with right kinds of relationships 42
networks 34, 61, 79
  in action 56
  construction of 47–8
  designing and implementation of 80
  of global cities 45–6
  and governance 79
  governed for and by policies 60
  management of 72
  meta-governance 82
  'net + work' 41, 44, 47, 48, 161, 162
  network of grit 135, 149, 150, 161, 165
  and power 46–9
  shadow network 53
  and space 40–1
networks imagined, donor consortium 70–2
new nationalism 16, 21, 153
new philanthropy (NP) 50, 87, 90, 156–8, 164, 165

NGO Affairs Bureau of Bangladesh (NGOAB) 32, 85–6, 88, 91, 110, 116, 121, 164
  director general (DG) of 97, 111–13
  funding documentation 128
  and Teach For Bangladesh (TFB) 7, 8, 31
Nogales, X. E. de 158
non-governmental organizations (NGOs) 2, 6, 85, 147
  network 73–5
  NGO+1 133
  NGO-turned-SEs 97
  stages of evolution 134–5
  unsettling or anachronistic with 134
non-state actors 3
No'Voa, A. 14, 15, 18, 171

OECD 14, 20
Offe, C. 119
Overseas Development Institute (ODI) 98

panel discussion 96–7, 118
  central dilemma of 109
  on data steering policy 99–102
  'draft a policy' proposal 113–14
  on ethnographic network 97–8
  on government hierarchy 106
  participants on 98–9
  on youth and women's leadership 103–4
Parisi, L. 44
partnerships 116
  broad-based partnerships 147
  glocal imagination of 163
  philanthropic and CS partnerships 157
  public-private partnerships 163
Peck, J. 17, 29, 33, 114, 135, 165, 166, 169, 171, 172
PEDP (Primary Education Development Programme) 6, 31, 59–60, 68, 80, 118, 145, 147, 164
  heterarchic governance 65
  influenced choices underpinning 69
  initial conditions 69
  institutionalization of networks as 67
  and PESoB 60
  principal entity responsible for 60
  reforms 64
  SWAP arrangements 81, 86
  topological analytics 67

PEDP I 70, 146
PEDP II 70, 72, 74, 146
PEDP III 64
  areas of improvements 78
  funding 76–7
  and transformation of ELCG into a DC 72
PEDP IV 164
performative cultural engagement spheres 57
philanthrocapitalism 50, 129, 155, 159, 166
philanthropic actors, 'net' of 161
philanthropists 156–8, 176 n.11
Piattoeva, N. 154
placeless power 45, 115, 150
placement of SE practice 42, 48, 52, 96–7
  consolidation 111–14
  data steering policy 99–102
  ethnographic network 97–9
  issues and debates 107–10
  numbers influencing imagination 102–7
place(s) 39, 42, 63, 67, 150
  authority of 150
  construction of 'here' and 'now' 42
  hybrids 42
  as moments of encounter 42
  place making 150
  and space, interconnection between 41
play of pastiche 50, 88, 102, 125, 136
policies
  analysis of 52
  deparliamentarization of 119
  documents 154
  influence of data-driven perspectives 113
  manifestation of 169
  narrative storylines 154
  as numbers 105
  policy dialogue event 42, 96–7
  policy events 42
  under rationalities of development economics 77
  reform policy 35, 42, 160, 167
  vernacularized enactment 20
policy imaginations/imaginaries 20, 88
  de-bordered nature of 4, 20, 60, 83, 93, 135
  differences in 94–5
  market-oriented 104

policymaking 16
policymaking imaginaries 4
policymaking worlds 30, 80, 160, 166, 169, *see also* PEDP (Primary Education Development Programme)
policy mediatization 144
policy message system 144
policy mobilities 55, 122, 151, 167, 168–9
policy networks 17, 31, 60, 80, 86, 155
policyscapes 4, 26, 91, 101, 133
policy steering 54, 90, 91, 118
pooled funding 76–7, 82
Porticus Asia Limited (PAL) 139
Porticus Global 129, 130, 148, 164, 178 n.4
positionality of researchers 21–2
    Adhikary, Rino 22, 23, 24–5
    Hardy, Ian 27–8
    Lingard, Bob 25–7
post-truth 144, 162
post-Westphalian politics 4, 14, 20
power 11, 30, 33, 34, 35, 37, 39, 44–6, 168
    axes of spatialities 46
    of connection 48
    and connectivities 44
    cultural production as form of 45
    exercise of 37, 38
    of naming and categorizing 106
    and networks 46–9
    new networked forms of 47
    placeless power 45
    placement of practice 46
    of reach 48
    reach and presence 35
    and relationalities 44–5
    territorial and scalar formulations 46–7
    of 'work' involved in networking 48
powerful imaginations/imaginaries 63, 67, 70, 115, 135
power networks 47
power relations 35, 47, 60, 173
practice 112, *see also* placement of SE practice
    best practice 16, 71, 74, 88, 106, 131–2, 137, 141, 169
    context of 117
    employment practices 142
    of encompassment 75
primary education sector/system of Bangladesh (PESoB) 7, 31, 59, 63, 79, 82, 163, 164
    emergence of heterarchic governance within 61
    governance network arrangement 60
    and PEDP (Primary Education Development Programme) 60
problem imaginations 125, 126–7, 130, 144, 162
productive imagination 123, 128–9
proximity 35, 46, 48, 75, 80, 96, 168
public-private partnerships 163

Rahman-Islam, Anita Ghazi 99, 103, 104, 107–8, 109, 113–14
Raihan, Ananya 99, 103, 104, 107, 108, 109
Rana, Quasim 139
Rappleye, J. 17, 19, 155
reach 39, 48, 53
realism 135
reconstituted fast-policy worlds 169
reference societies positionality 15, 88, 100, 112
reimagination 93–4, 104–5
    of local NGO activities as globally followed SE models 92
    of SEs development 93–4
relationality 39, 44
relationships 39, 40, 138, 139–41
religio-moral assumptions 95
research
    for policy 16
    of policy 16
researcher, *see* positionality of researchers
results-based frameworks 77–8, 82
Rizvi, F. 16
Rizvi, Gowher 143
Runyan-Gless, Katelyn 142

Said, Edward 23
Santori, Diego 159
Santos, Boaventura de Sousa 36, 46, 92, 150
Sassen, S. 21, 45–6
Scarman Trust, The 98
School for Social Entrepreneurs, The 98
sector development 88, 94
sector leaders 91, 98, 105, 117
self-referential autopoietic system 105
self-referential societies 101–2
SENSCOT 98

sentiments 115
service-governance 50–1
shared governance 66, 71
Silicon Valley Consensus (SVC) 157
Silova, I. 20
social enterprises (SEs) 2, 50, 53, 56, 87, 129, 156–7
  as an historically evolved form of NGOs 108
  and bureaucratic national 121
  categories of 158
  constituted as an overriding policy in Bangladesh 164–5
  definition from a legal perspective 107
  definition of 108
  ecosystem 103, 104, 105
  emergence as an all-sector panacea 60
  global-local imbrication 92
  government's redundancy concern 112
  impact 131
  innovative SEs 133, 157–8, 169
  leaders 105
  leadership training 130–1
  movement 85
  organizational thinking 108
  practices 112
  as social investment utilizers 110
  subjectivities 13, 126
  taxation 109–10
  tension 93–4
  TFB as 7, 14, 31–2
  and TFB's work and future 164–5
  TF organizations as 13
  in UK 112
  women leadership in 100
Social Enterprise UK (SEUK) 98
social entrepreneurial sector policy (SE-sector policy) 90, 112, 116–17, 118
  and collective aspirations of actors and organizations 117
  construction through commissioned survey 117
  context-productive and context-generative mediation 111
  embeddedness 165
  essential *problématique* underlying movement of 88
  imagination 90, 93

social entrepreneurs
  and business entrepreneurs, difference between 158
  emergence of 89–90
social imaginary 162
social impact funding 158–9
social investments 50, 158–9
social-mediatization 143–4, 161–2
social networks 40
soft power 118–19
Söpper, K. 168
space-place-time relationships 40
space(s)
  as immanent forces 34, 40
  and place 41
  and time 34
spatial de-formations and re-formations 38
spatialities 15, 18, 30, 33, 34, 35, 39–42, 41, 150
  of culture and power 34
  of globalization 42
  multiple spatialities 19
spatialization of power 40
spatial organization 37–8
spatio-cultural formulations 34, 52, 63, 96–7
speed 51, 167
Spivak, G. C. 141
start-ups 158
state, *see also* nation-states
  restructuring of 39
  scalar understanding of 40
  support in the local institutionalization of TFB 163
Steiner-Khamsi, G. 106
strategic philanthropy 157
support systems 104–5, 106, 115, 118
system-level networks 81
System Wide Approach to Programming (SWAP) 32, 61, 70, 73, 121
  importance of 71
  and World Bank 70

Takayama, K. 14, 19
taxation 88, 109, 110, 119, 128
teacher education
  broad-based partnerships 147
  identification of gaps in 147

pre-service and refresher teacher
training 146–8
transformations 146
Teacher Education in Bangladesh 144–8
Teach First 2
Teach First alumnae 142
Teach For All (TFAll) 1–2, 127, 129–30,
148, 158
applicability to all nations' educational
problems 141–2
founding of 2
functions of 2–3
funding sources 3
goal of 2
imagination productive 130
as a multilateral agency 13
online partner learning portal 141
partners 2
as policyscapes 4
and SEs 133
and social entrepreneurs 2
Teach For America (TFA) 2, 123, 125–6
Teach For America (TFA) curriculum
experts 142
Teach For Argentina 13
Teach For Bangladesh (TFB) 1, 29, 33, 88,
118, 121, 127, 154, 156
activities 7
alternative programme 136–7
aspirations for 137–9
as de facto SE 85, 128–35, 171
emergence of 119
and epistemic diaspora 142
establishment in the United States 128
Facebook activities 144, 161–2
fellow teachers 8–9
foundation of 128
and funding 134, 139
future plan 9
generative imagination 128–35
and global-local imbrications 148–50
global policy DNA 52
goal 145
hybrid identity 87
as a hybrid organizational conduit 163
impact for 129–30
impact investments 129–30
independency 130
JCM and JARM meetings 145

as a localized extension of a global
policy network 121
and local NGOs, difference between
148
mandate for systemic change 134
market embeddedness and
philanthrocapitalist nature of 128
media, TFAll/America's globalized
teacher education reform model
through 161–2
media work 131
mobility and fixity 150–1
and NGO Affairs Bureau of Bangladesh
(NGOAB) 7, 8, 31
NGO-social enterprises hybridization
32
past and future 160–6
and philanthrocapitalism 168
policy labour 161
as policyscapes 4
programme rationale 7–8
and relationships 139–41
as social enterprise 2, 7, 30
and social-mediatization 143–4
and stakeholder groups 8
and teacher education 144–8
and technologies 141–2
TFAll/America's global teacher
education reform policy 160–1
TFB-USA, funding of 139
three-year plan of action 8
transformative vision 133
work and future 164–5
world of policy (*see* world of policy)
Teach-For centrism 141–2
Teach For movement 29
Teach For networks and organizations 1
focus of 1
goal of 1–2
literature on 9–14
as social enterprise 13
as social entrepreneurial vehicles of
transformation of public governance
171
Teach For phenomenon 3, 122
Teach-For reliance 142
technologies 141–2
territorial and scalar formulations
36, 46–7

text production 3, 117
Theodore, N. 17, 29, 33, 114, 135, 165, 166, 169, 171, 172
third liminal space 18
Thomas, M. A. M. 132, 171
Thrift, N. 42
time 34, 40, 42
topological culture 40, 44
topological environment 34, 35, 49
topological policy environment of globalization 36–9
   culture 42–4
   power 44–6
   spatialities 39–42
topological power 40, 44, 45, 83, 162
topological rationalities 34, 40, 43–4, 48–9, 71, *see also* culture; power; spatialities
topologies 4, 19, 33, 44, 175 n.1(ch 2)
Torfing, J. 62, 65–6
training
   cultural training 142
   of fellows 8, 142
   leadership training 64, 130–1
   refresher training 146–7
   teacher training 70, 146–7
transcontinental 38
transcultural mixing 19
transformatory SEs 158
transnational and postnational solidarities 115
transnational flows 39
trust, in global framing and governance 62

United Nations 7, 15, 20, 69
   MDGs 7, 15, 64, 82, 102
   SDGs 7, 15, 64, 82, 102, 154, 170
   UNESCO 3
universe-like map 135–6
UnLtd 98

Untied Kingdom, SE taxation model 110

venture philanthropy 50, 129, 176 n.11
vernacularization 35, 135, 144, 162
Vertovec, S. 177 n.8
Voice of America 143

Waldow, Florian 15
web-based articulations, differences in 12–13
Western epistemologies 21–2, 23
Wigdortz, Brett 141
Williams, Raymond 36
Winter Academy 8, 142, 143
women leadership in social enterprises 100
Wood, Richard 142
working groups 76, 82
World Bank 64, 150, 160, 165
   and creation of DC 71–2
   role in ELCG and DC 82
   and SWAP initiatives 70
   and teacher education transformation 146
world-making 35–6, 149
world of policy 121–2, 135–7
   aspirations 137–9
   epistemic diaspora 142
   funding 139
   relationships 139–41
   social-mediatization 143–4
   technologies 141–2
WTO 20
Wuyts, S. 65

Yariv-Mashal, T. 14, 15, 18, 171
Yunus, Muhammad 132, 177 n.6

Zeleny, Milan 101
Zuboff, S. 51

www.ingramcontent.com/pod-product-compliance
Lightning Source LLC
Chambersburg PA
CBHW062219300426
44115CB00012BA/2129